THE STRETCHER BEARERS

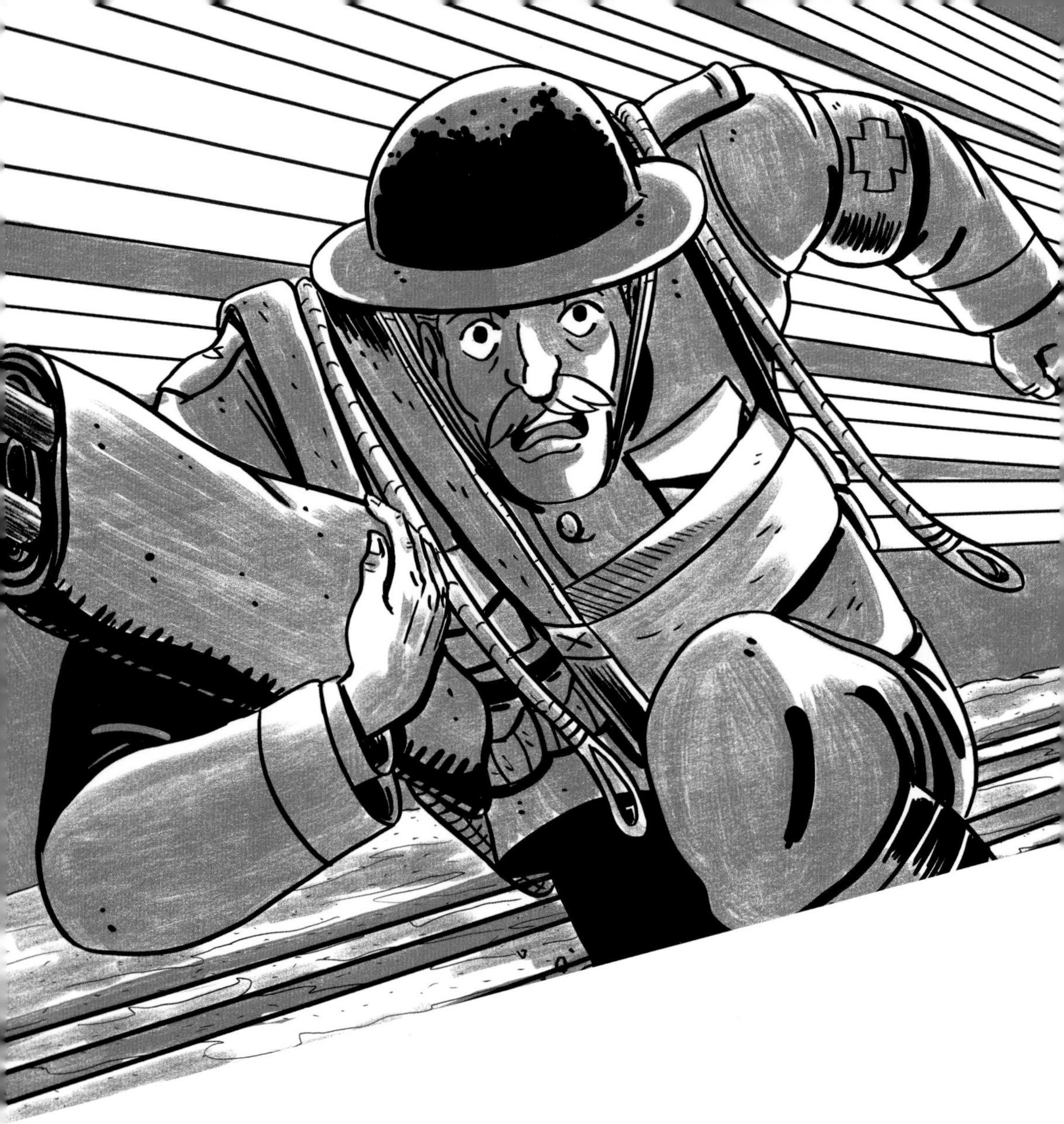

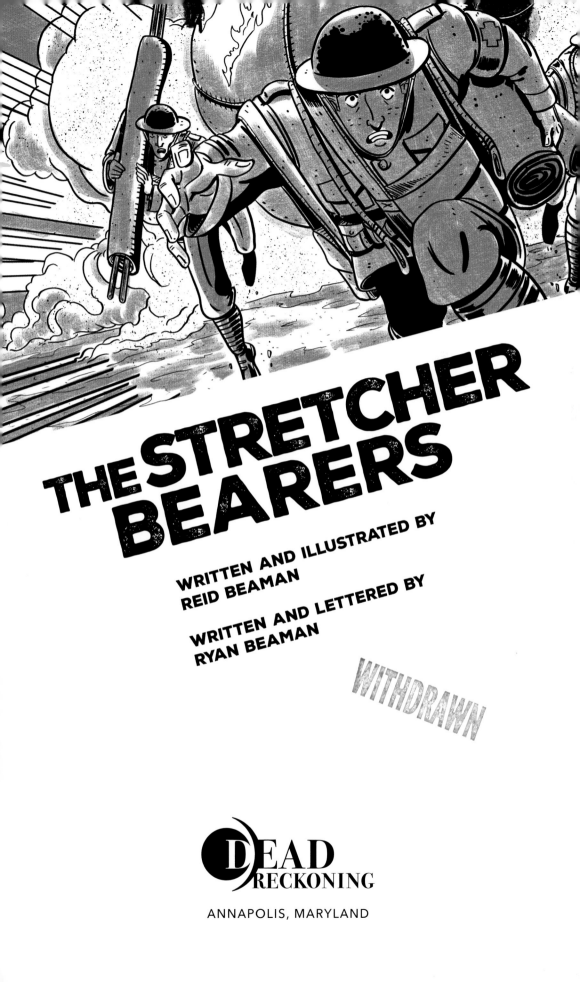

THE STRETCHER BEARERS

**WRITTEN AND ILLUSTRATED BY
REID BEAMAN**

**WRITTEN AND LETTERED BY
RYAN BEAMAN**

DEAD RECKONING

ANNAPOLIS, MARYLAND

Published by Dead Reckoning
291 Wood Road
Annapolis, MD 21402

Library of Congress Cataloging-in-Publication Data

Names: Beaman, Reid, writer, illustrator. | Beaman, Ryan, writer, letterer.

Title: The stretcher bearers / written and illustrated by Reid Beaman ;
   written and lettered Ryan Beaman.
Description: Annapolis, MD : Dead Reckoning, [2022]
Identifiers: LCCN 2021053106 (print) | LCCN 2021053107 (ebook) | ISBN
   9781682476192 (paperback) | ISBN 9781682477915 (epub)
Subjects: LCSH: United States. Army. Infantry Division, 4th--Comic books,
   strips, etc. | World War, 1914-1918--Medical care--Comic books, strips,
   etc. | LCGFT: Historical comics. | Graphic novels.
Classification: LCC PN6727.B37556 S77 2022 (print) | LCC PN6727.B37556
   (ebook) | DDC 741.5/973--dc23/eng/20211103
LC record available at https://lccn.loc.gov/2021053106
LC ebook record available at https://lccn.loc.gov/2021053107

♾ Print editions meet the requirements of ANSI/NISO z39.48-1992 (Permanence of Paper).
Printed in the United States of America.

30 29 28 27 26 25 24 23 22   9 8 7 6 5 4 3 2 1
First printing

To my family and my wonderful wife, Kylie. My dear, without your support and love this comic would've never gotten made. Thank you for believing in me and my dreams.

—REID BEAMAN

To our Dad and Grandad, who both proudly served our country and taught us that freedom isn't free. Thank you both for all the love, support, and stories. They will forever be memories that will stay with us.

—RYAN BEAMAN

This book is also dedicated to all veterans and those who are currently on active duty. You have our appreciation and our prayers for all that you do and the sacrifices that it entails.

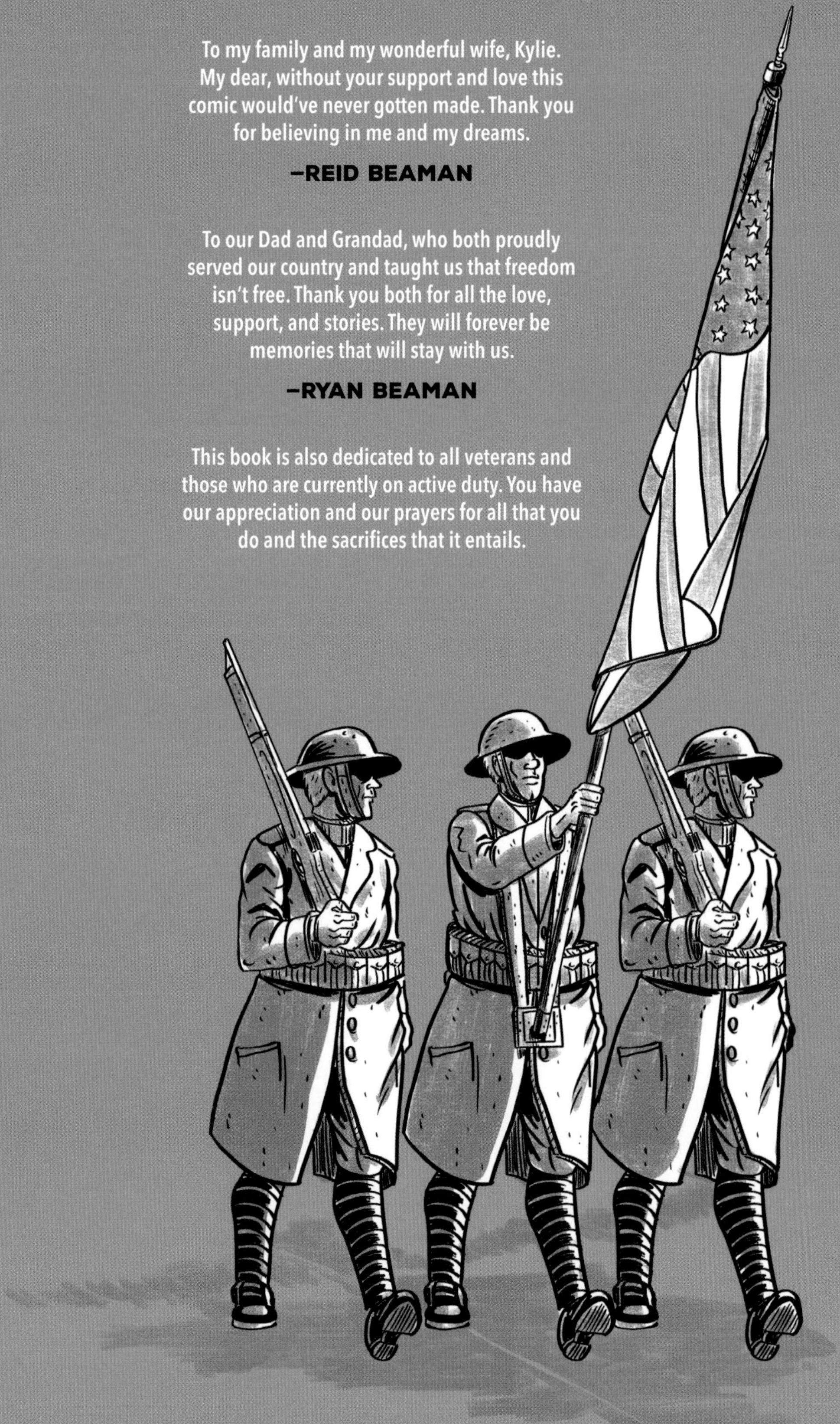

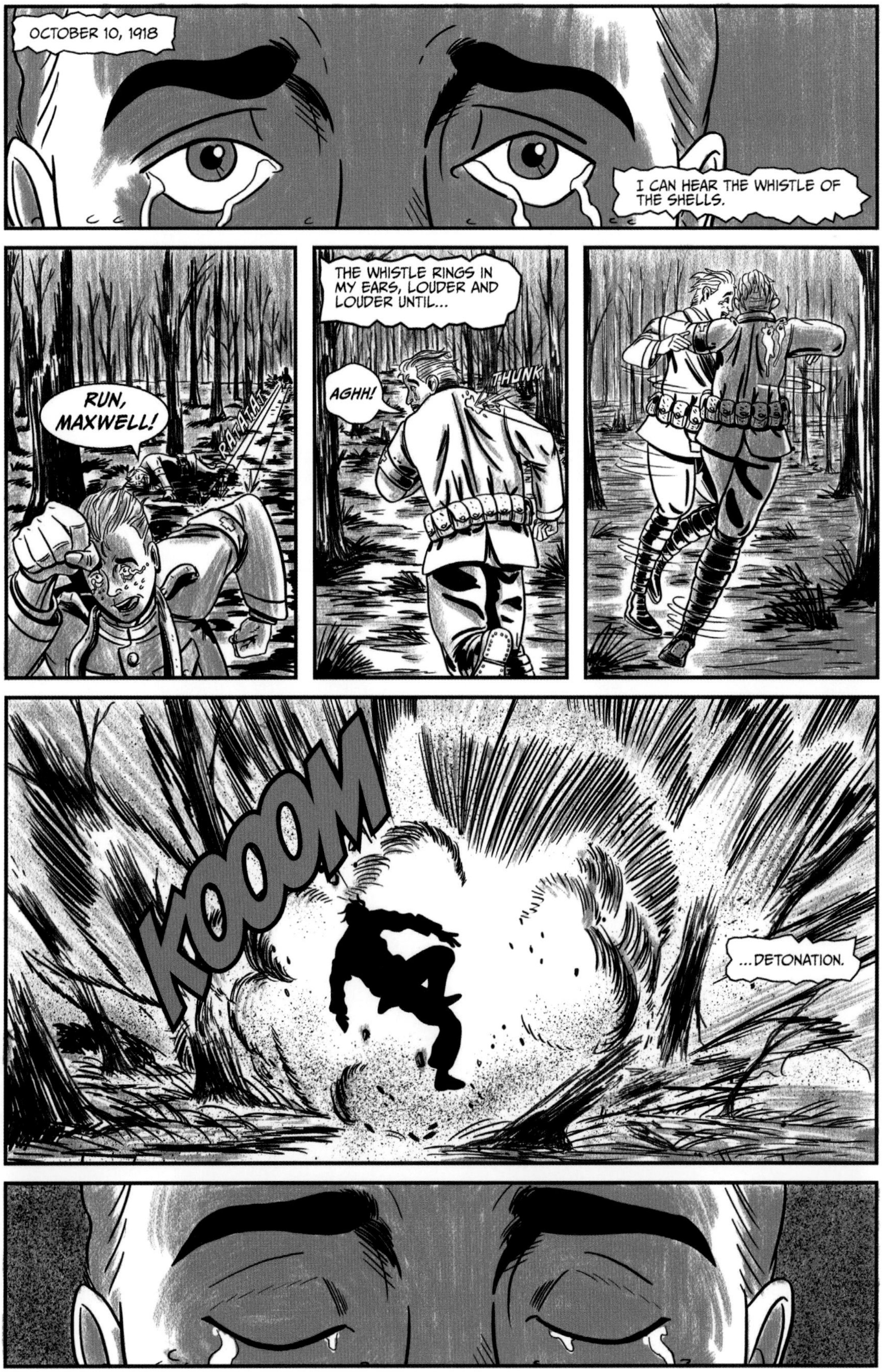
OCTOBER 10, 1918
I CAN HEAR THE WHISTLE OF THE SHELLS.
RUN, MAXWELL!
RATATAT
THE WHISTLE RINGS IN MY EARS, LOUDER AND LOUDER UNTIL...
AGHH!
THUNK
KOOOM
...DETONATION.

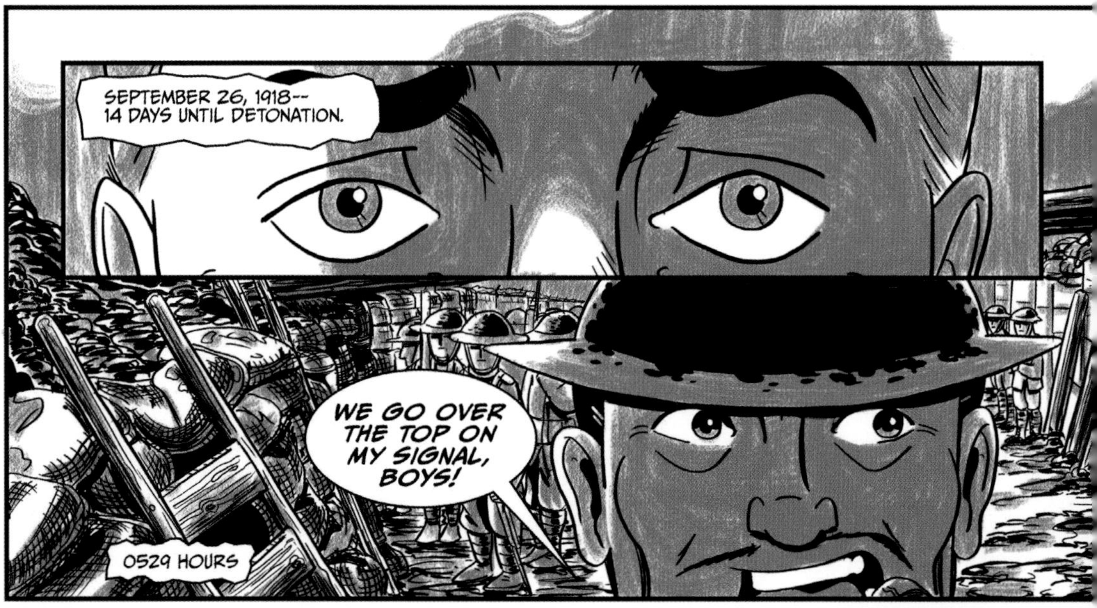
SEPTEMBER 26, 1918--
14 DAYS UNTIL DETONATION.
WE GO OVER THE TOP ON MY SIGNAL, BOYS!
0529 HOURS

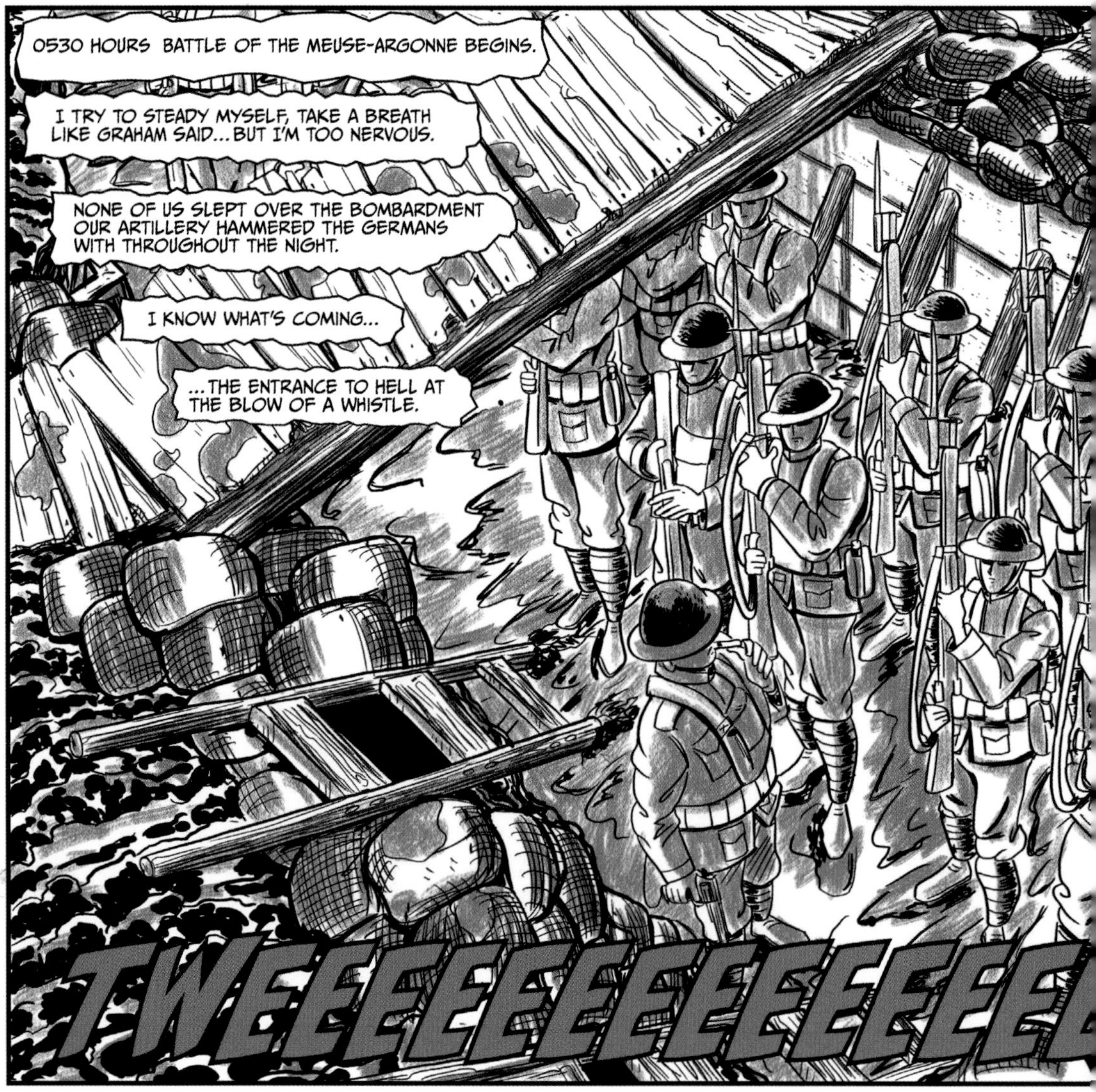
0530 HOURS BATTLE OF THE MEUSE-ARGONNE BEGINS.
I TRY TO STEADY MYSELF, TAKE A BREATH LIKE GRAHAM SAID... BUT I'M TOO NERVOUS.
NONE OF US SLEPT OVER THE BOMBARDMENT OUR ARTILLERY HAMMERED THE GERMANS WITH THROUGHOUT THE NIGHT.
I KNOW WHAT'S COMING...
...THE ENTRANCE TO HELL AT THE BLOW OF A WHISTLE.
TWEEEEEEEEEEEEEEE

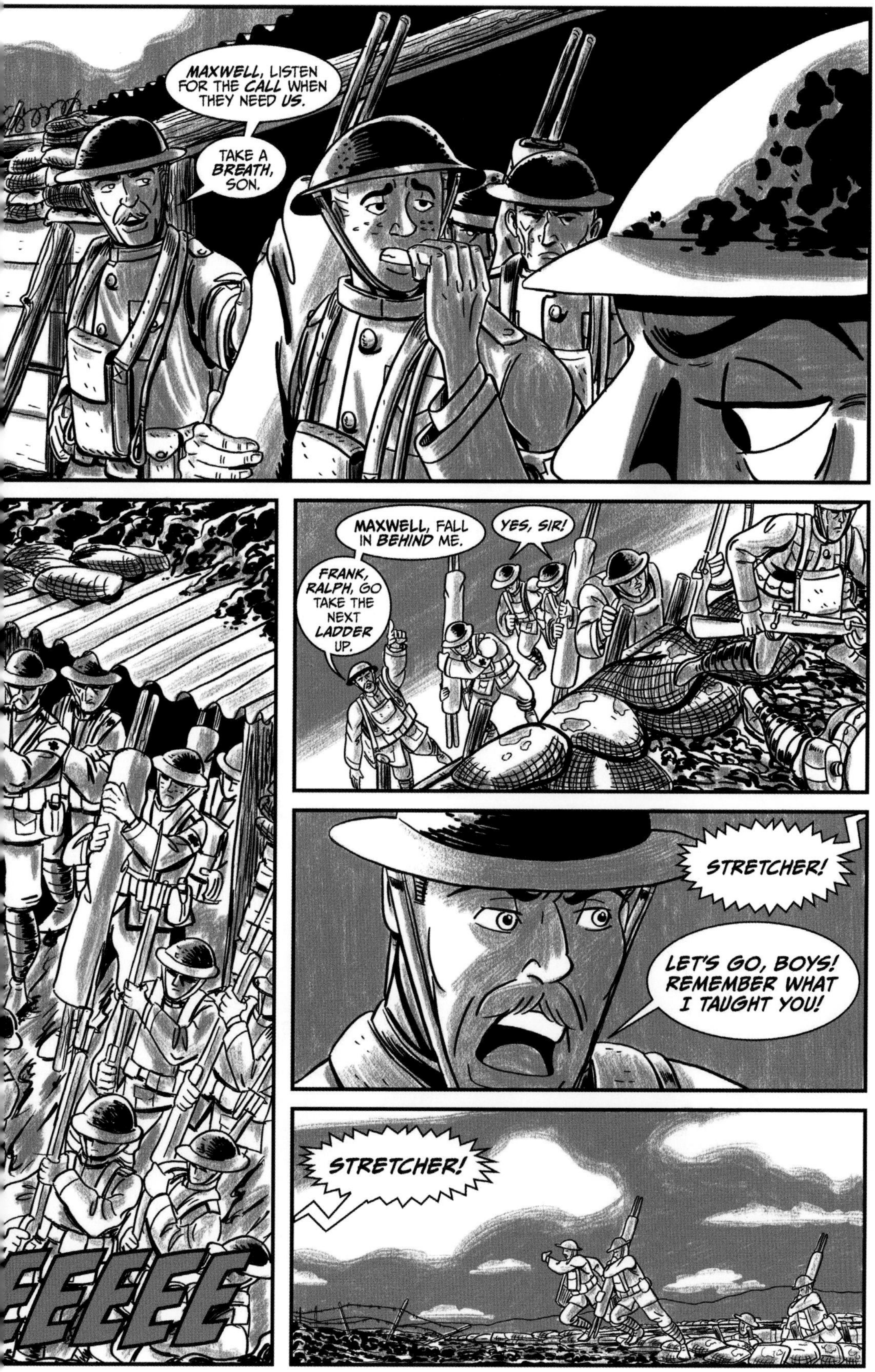
MAXWELL, LISTEN FOR THE CALL WHEN THEY NEED US.
TAKE A BREATH, SON.
EEEEE
MAXWELL, FALL IN BEHIND ME.
FRANK, RALPH, GO TAKE THE NEXT LADDER UP.
YES, SIR!
STRETCHER!
LET'S GO, BOYS! REMEMBER WHAT I TAUGHT YOU!
STRETCHER!

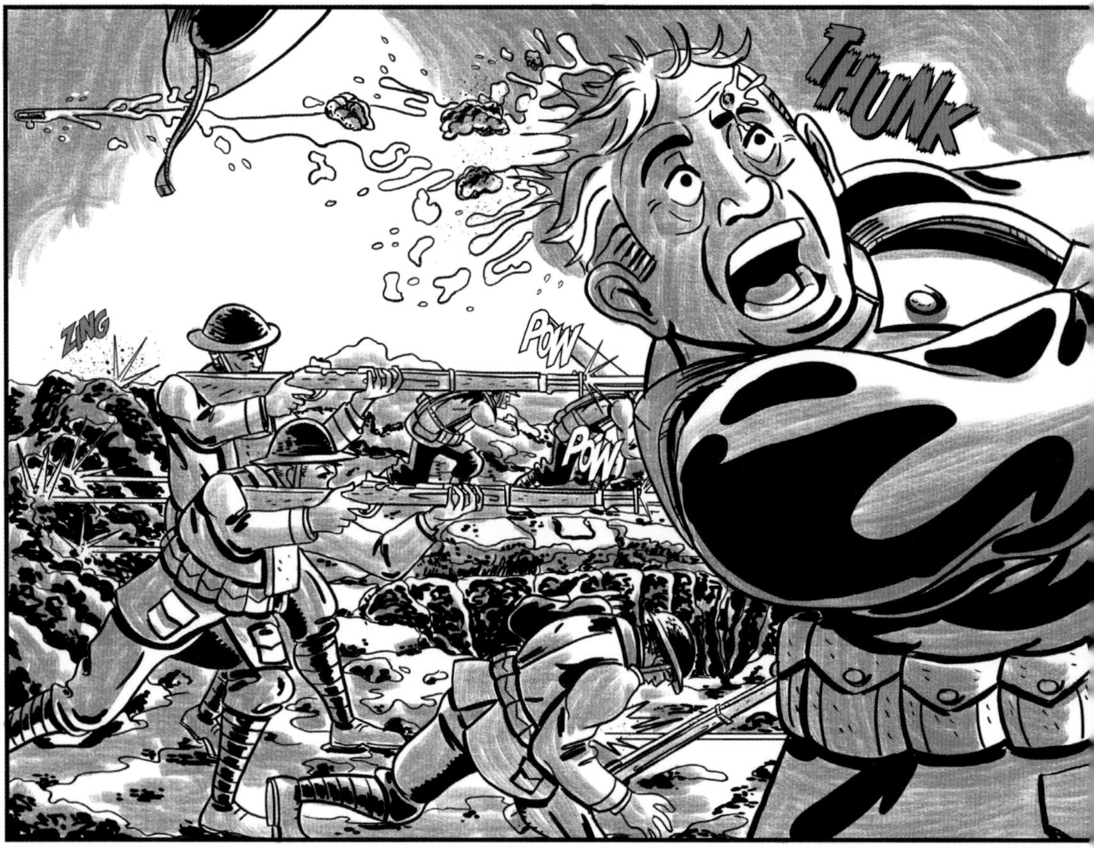
THUNK
ZING
POW
POW

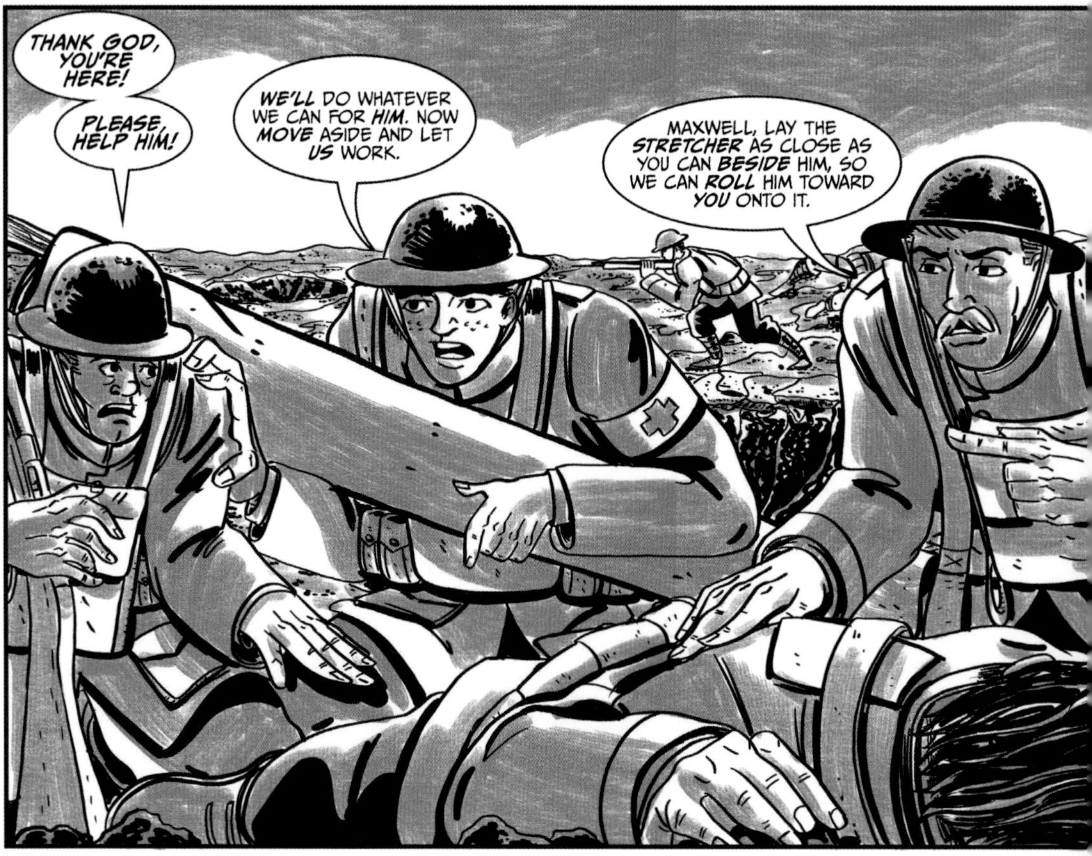
THANK GOD, YOU'RE HERE!
PLEASE, HELP HIM!
WE'LL DO WHATEVER WE CAN FOR HIM. NOW MOVE ASIDE AND LET US WORK.
MAXWELL, LAY THE STRETCHER AS CLOSE AS YOU CAN BESIDE HIM, SO WE CAN ROLL HIM TOWARD YOU ONTO IT.

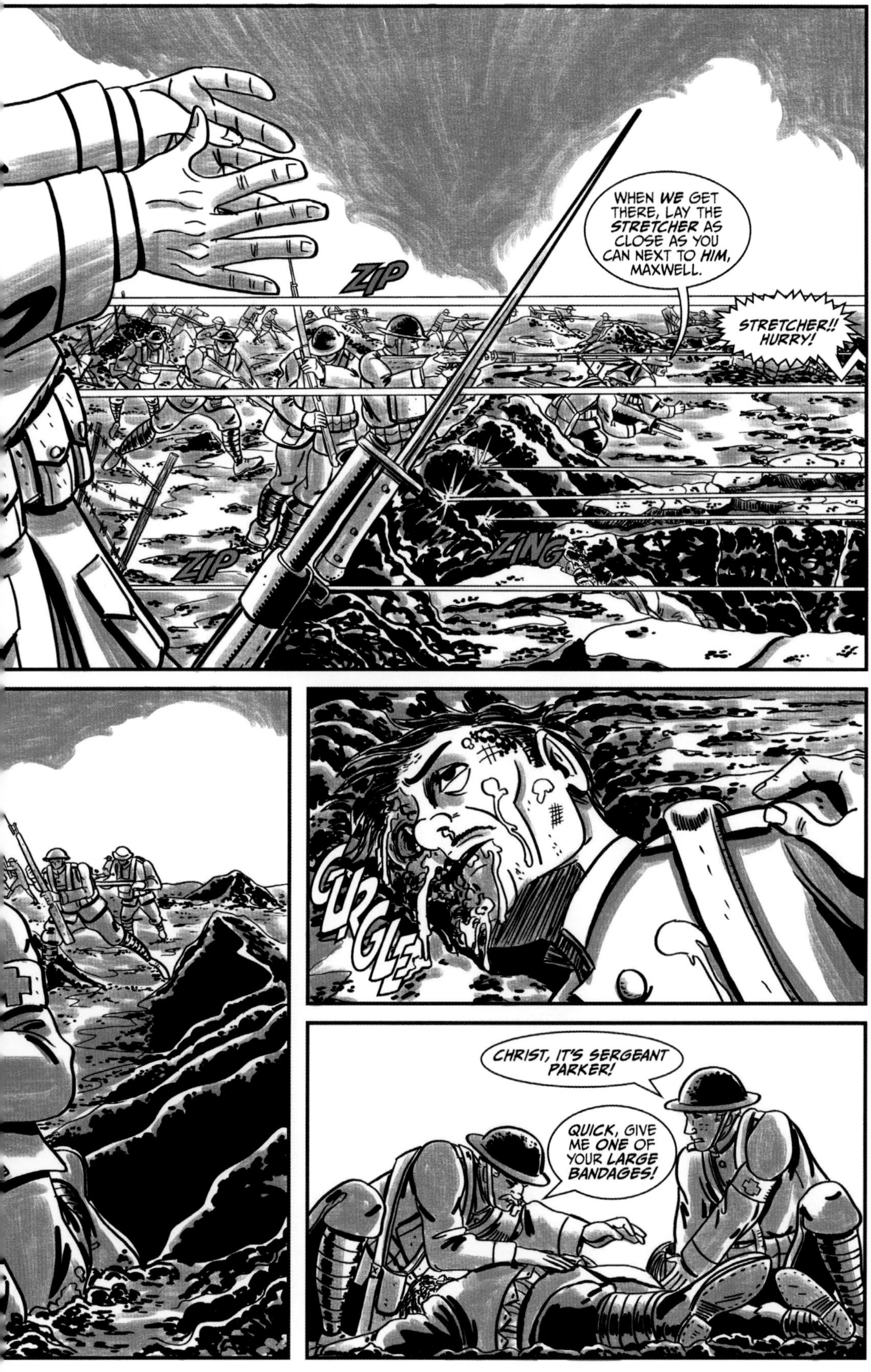
WHEN WE GET THERE, LAY THE STRETCHER AS CLOSE AS YOU CAN NEXT TO HIM, MAXWELL.
STRETCHER!! HURRY!
ZIP
ZING
ZIP
GURGLE
CHRIST, IT'S SERGEANT PARKER!
QUICK, GIVE ME ONE OF YOUR LARGE BANDAGES!

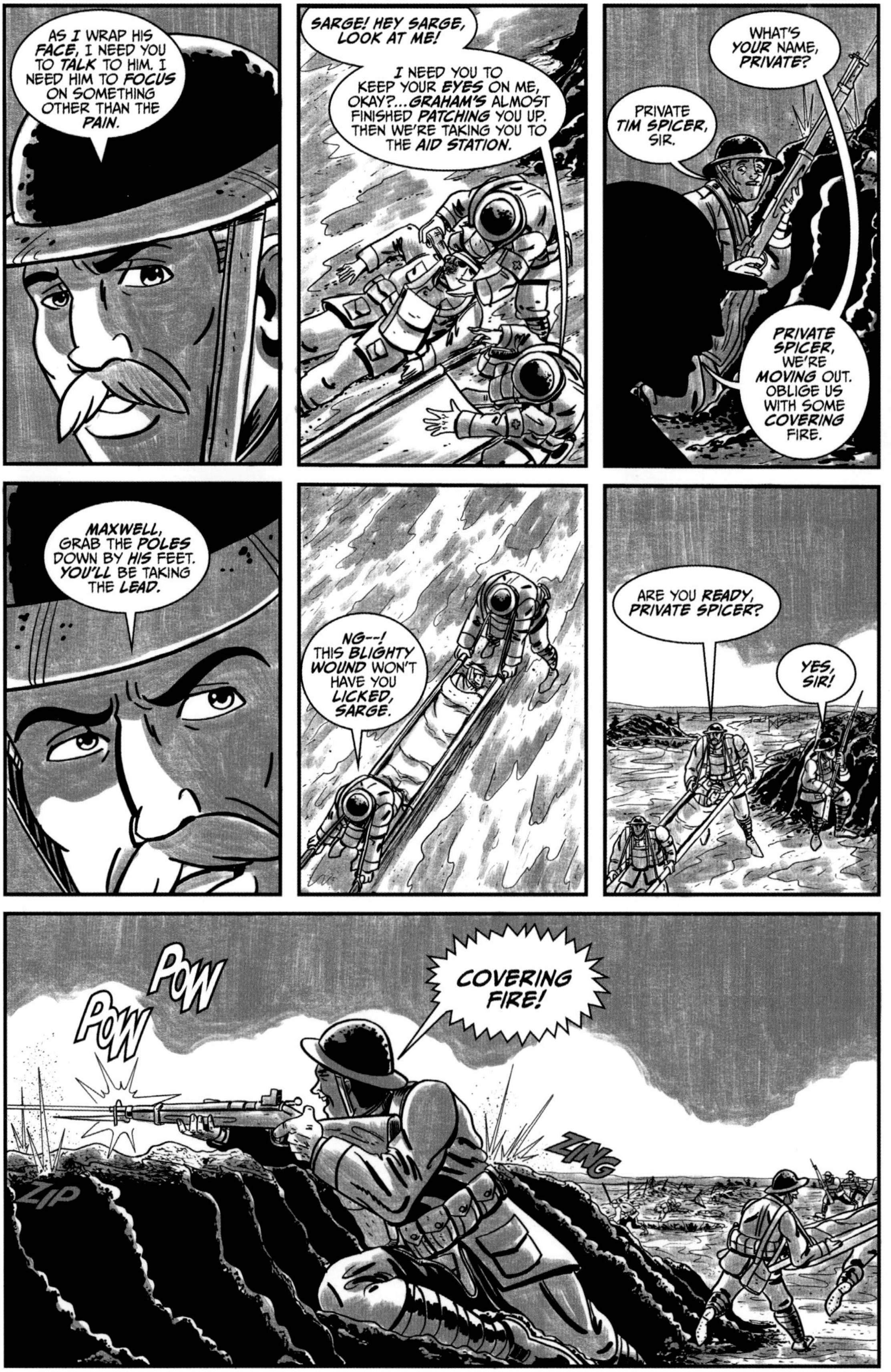
AS I WRAP HIS FACE, I NEED YOU TO TALK TO HIM. I NEED HIM TO FOCUS ON SOMETHING OTHER THAN THE PAIN.
SARGE! HEY SARGE, LOOK AT ME!
I NEED YOU TO KEEP YOUR EYES ON ME, OKAY?...GRAHAM'S ALMOST FINISHED PATCHING YOU UP. THEN WE'RE TAKING YOU TO THE AID STATION.
WHAT'S YOUR NAME, PRIVATE?
PRIVATE TIM SPICER, SIR.
PRIVATE SPICER, WE'RE MOVING OUT. OBLIGE US WITH SOME COVERING FIRE.
MAXWELL, GRAB THE POLES DOWN BY HIS FEET. YOU'LL BE TAKING THE LEAD.
NG--! THIS BLIGHTY WOUND WON'T HAVE YOU LICKED, SARGE.
ARE YOU READY, PRIVATE SPICER?
YES, SIR!
POW
POW
COVERING FIRE!
ZING
ZIP

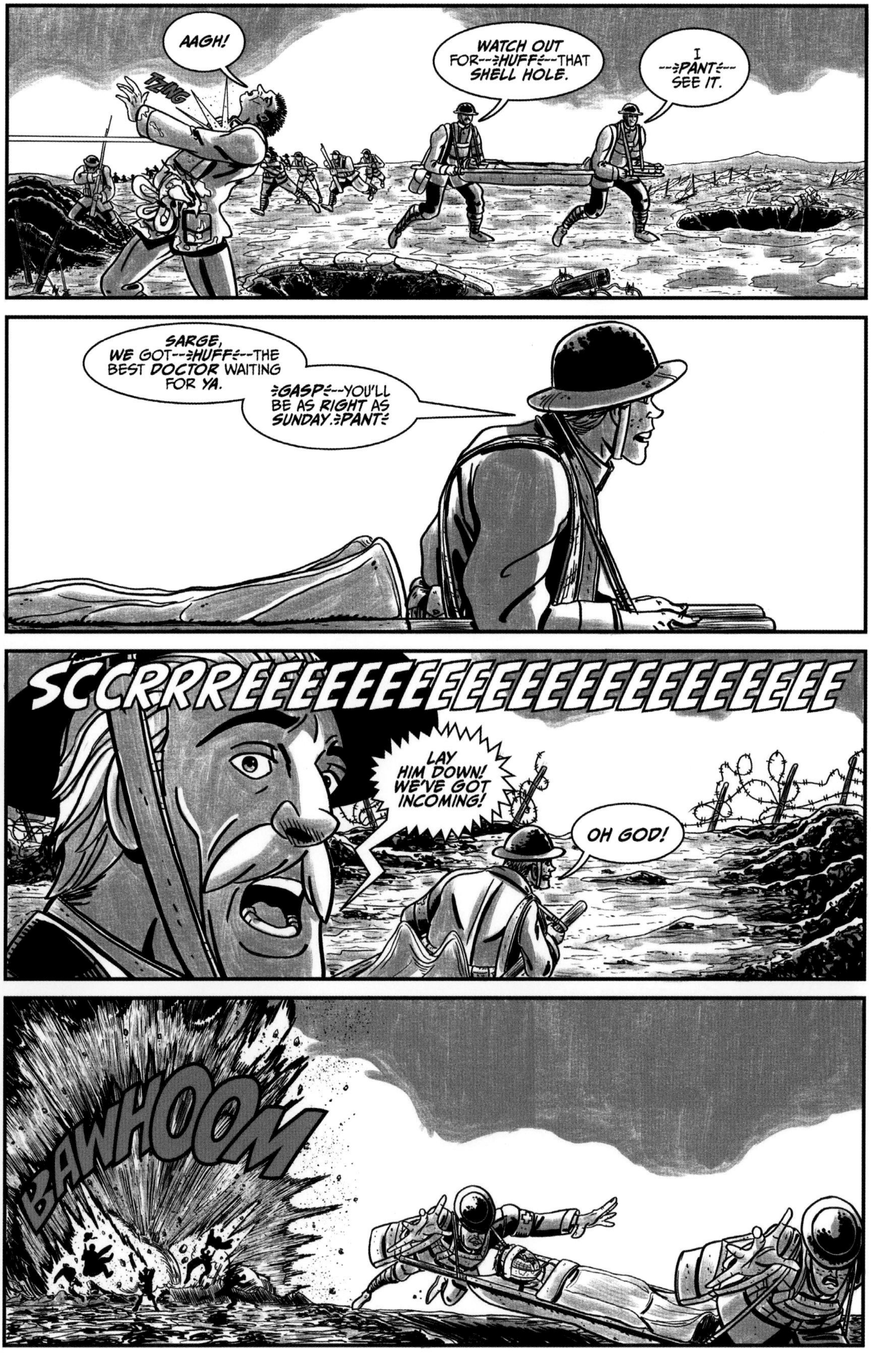
AAGH!
TZING
WATCH OUT FOR--⸗HUFF⸗--THAT SHELL HOLE.
I --⸗PANT⸗-- SEE IT.
SARGE, WE GOT--⸗HUFF⸗--THE BEST DOCTOR WAITING FOR YA.
⸗GASP⸗--YOU'LL BE AS RIGHT AS SUNDAY.⸗PANT⸗
SCCRRRREEEEEEEEEEEEEEEEEEEEEEEE
LAY HIM DOWN! WE'VE GOT INCOMING!
OH GOD!
BAWHOOM

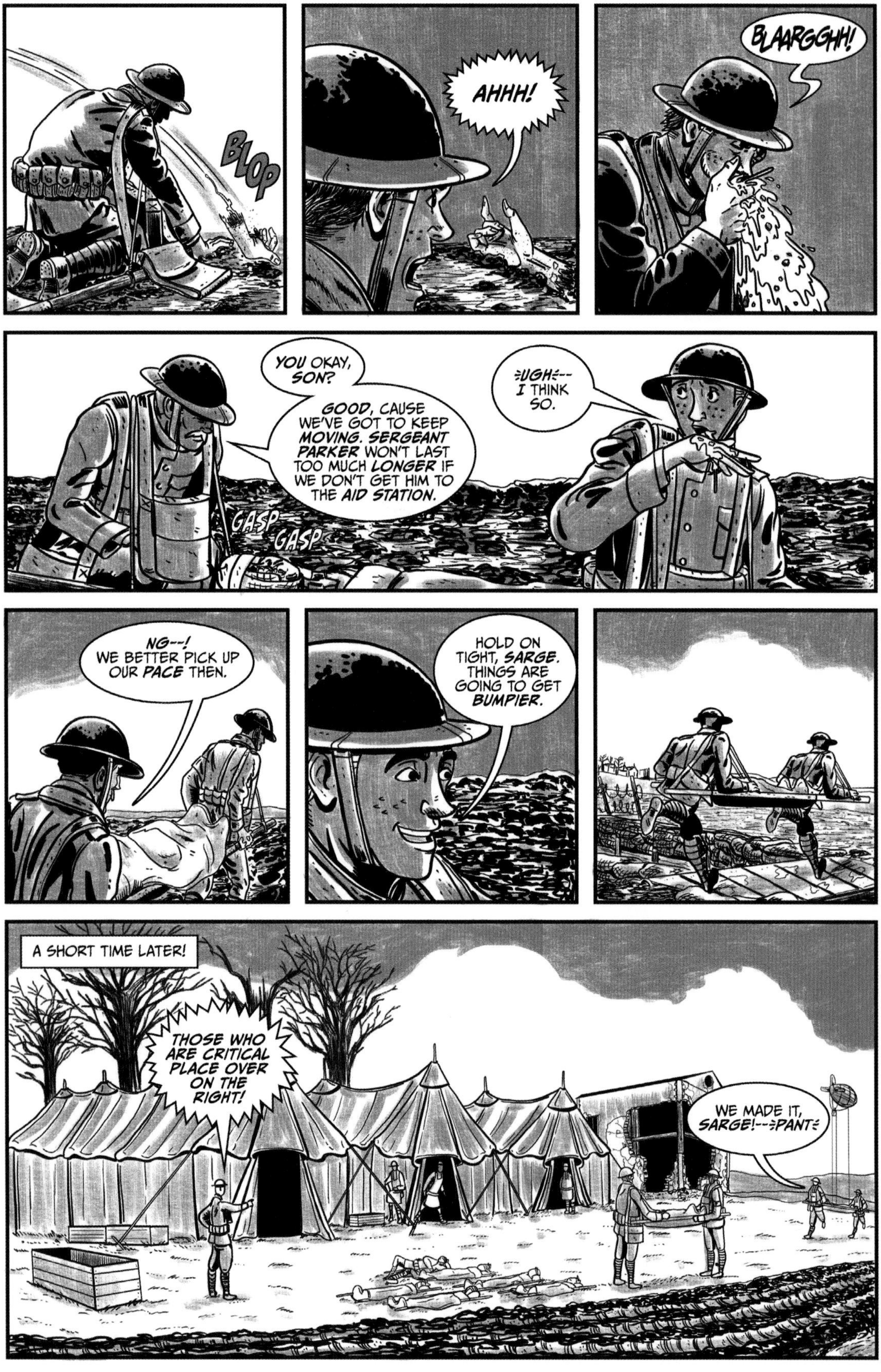
BLOP
AHHH!
BLAARGGHH!
YOU OKAY, SON?
=UGH=-- I THINK SO.
GOOD, CAUSE WE'VE GOT TO KEEP MOVING. SERGEANT PARKER WON'T LAST TOO MUCH LONGER IF WE DON'T GET HIM TO THE AID STATION.
GASP GASP
NG--! WE BETTER PICK UP OUR PACE THEN.
HOLD ON TIGHT, SARGE. THINGS ARE GOING TO GET BUMPIER.
A SHORT TIME LATER!
THOSE WHO ARE CRITICAL PLACE OVER ON THE RIGHT!
WE MADE IT, SARGE!--=PANT=

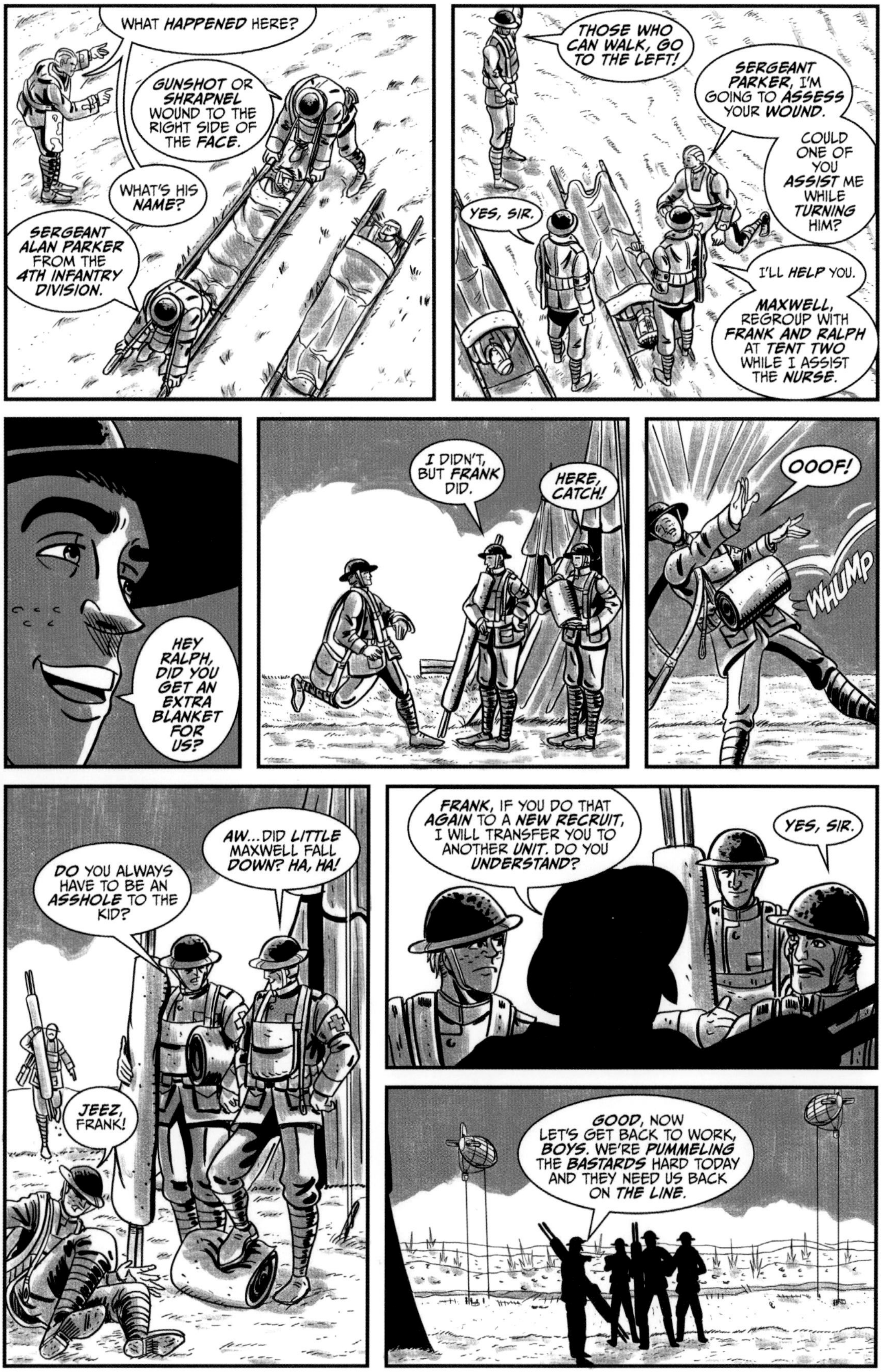
WHAT HAPPENED HERE?
GUNSHOT OR SHRAPNEL WOUND TO THE RIGHT SIDE OF THE FACE.
WHAT'S HIS NAME?
SERGEANT ALAN PARKER FROM THE 4TH INFANTRY DIVISION.
THOSE WHO CAN WALK, GO TO THE LEFT!
SERGEANT PARKER, I'M GOING TO ASSESS YOUR WOUND.
COULD ONE OF YOU ASSIST ME WHILE TURNING HIM?
YES, SIR.
I'LL HELP YOU.
MAXWELL, REGROUP WITH FRANK AND RALPH AT TENT TWO WHILE I ASSIST THE NURSE.
HEY RALPH, DID YOU GET AN EXTRA BLANKET FOR US?
I DIDN'T, BUT FRANK DID.
HERE, CATCH!
OOOF!
WHUMP
DO YOU ALWAYS HAVE TO BE AN ASSHOLE TO THE KID?
AW...DID LITTLE MAXWELL FALL DOWN? HA, HA!
JEEZ, FRANK!
FRANK, IF YOU DO THAT AGAIN TO A NEW RECRUIT, I WILL TRANSFER YOU TO ANOTHER UNIT. DO YOU UNDERSTAND?
YES, SIR.
GOOD, NOW LET'S GET BACK TO WORK, BOYS. WE'RE PUMMELING THE BASTARDS HARD TODAY AND THEY NEED US BACK ON THE LINE.

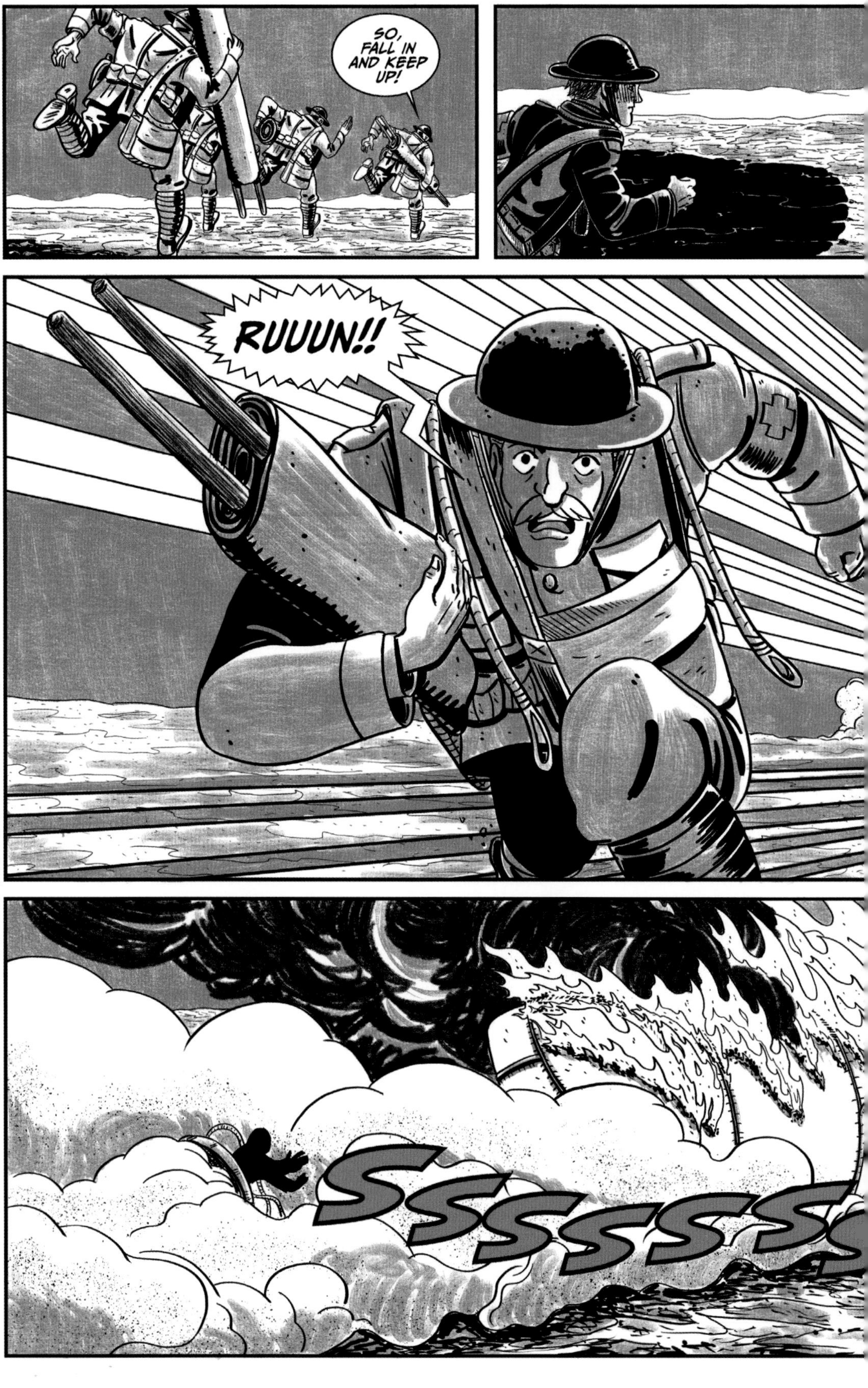
SO, FALL IN AND KEEP UP!
RUUUN!!
SSSSSSS

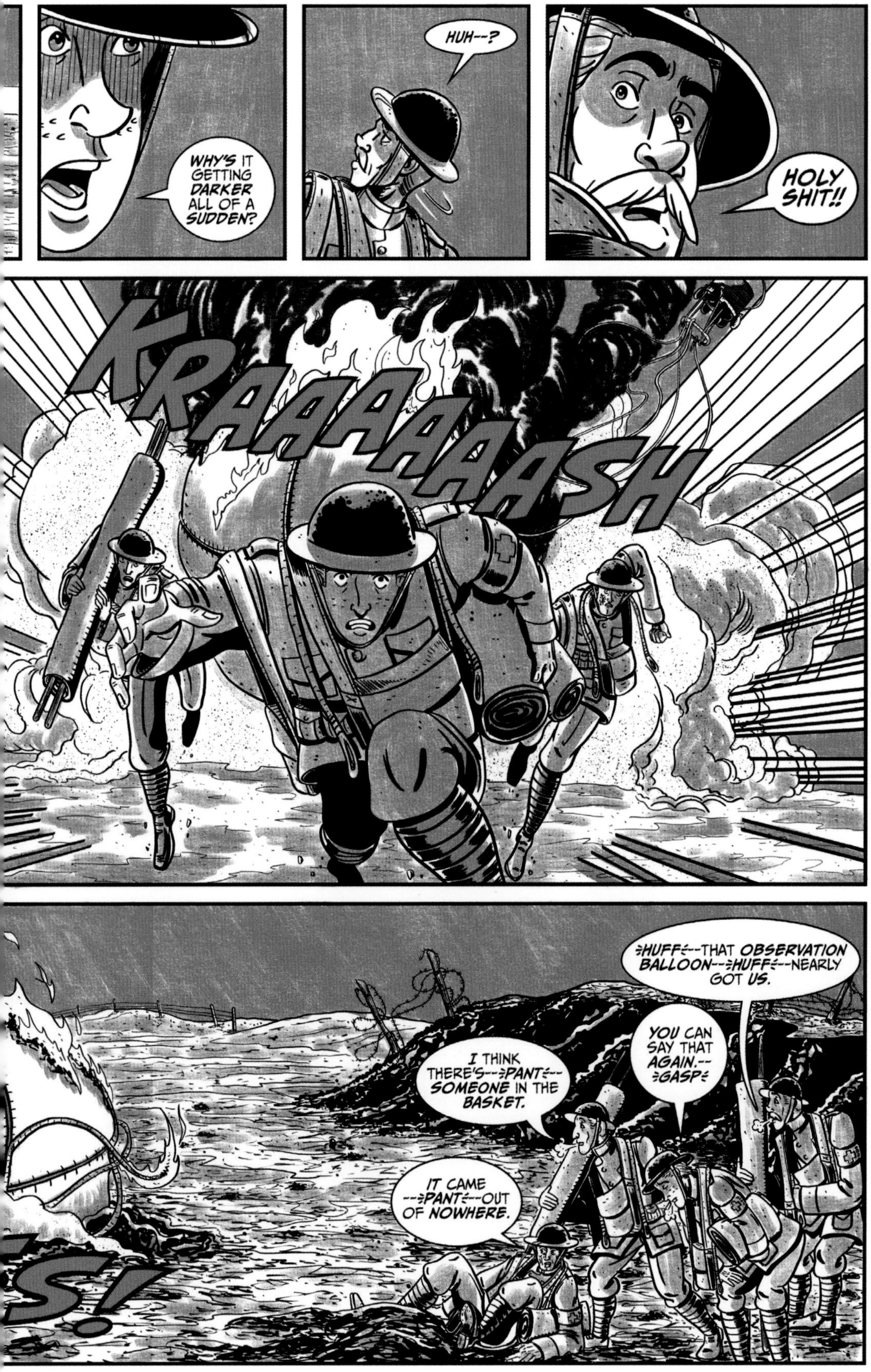
WHY'S IT GETTING DARKER ALL OF A SUDDEN?
HUH--?
HOLY SHIT!!
KRAAAAAAAASH
⋟HUFF⋞--THAT OBSERVATION BALLOON--⋟HUFF⋞--NEARLY GOT US.
YOU CAN SAY THAT AGAIN.-- ⋟GASP⋞
I THINK THERE'S--⋟PANT⋞--SOMEONE IN THE BASKET.
IT CAME --⋟PANT⋞--OUT OF NOWHERE.

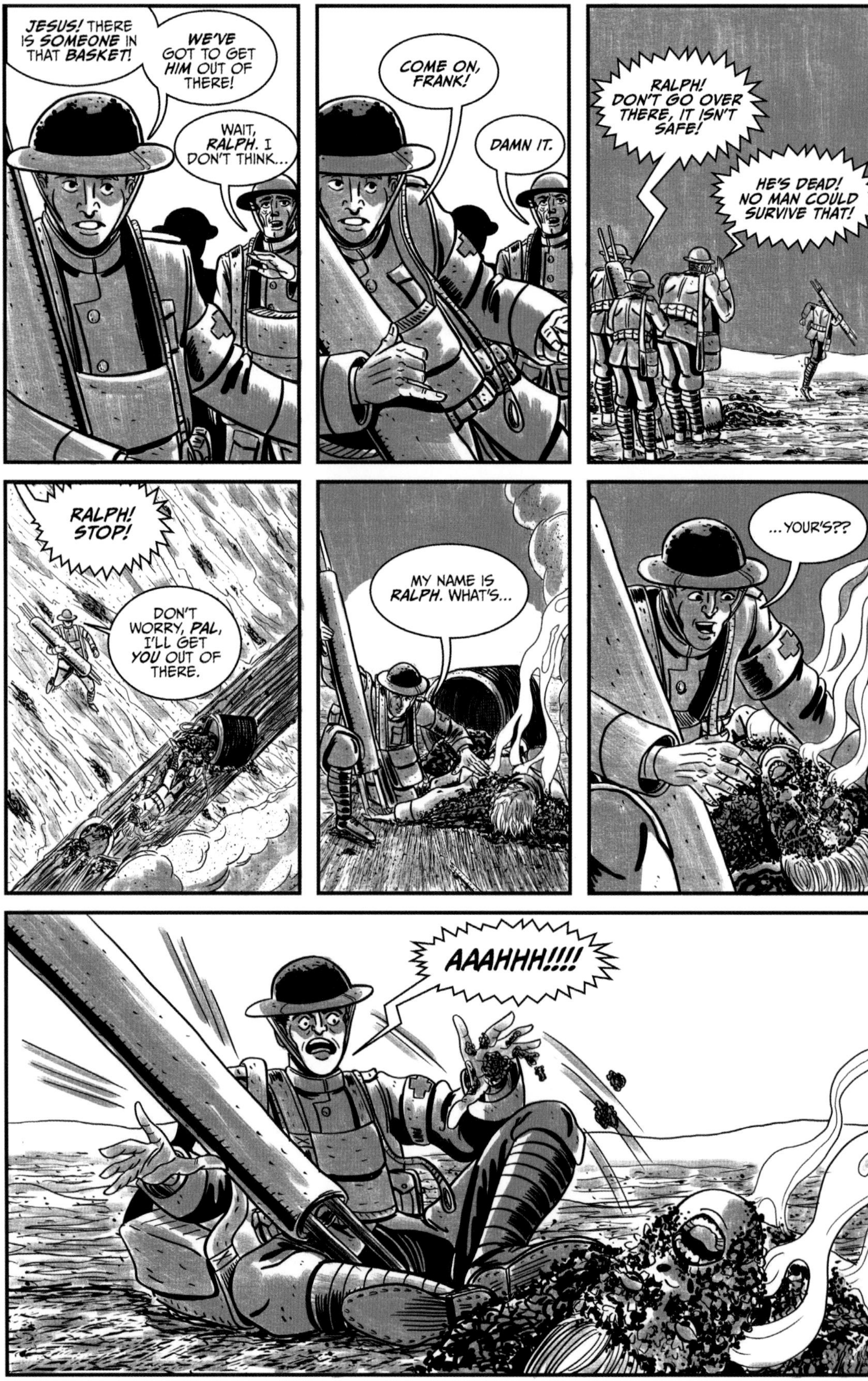
JESUS! THERE IS SOMEONE IN THAT BASKET!
WE'VE GOT TO GET HIM OUT OF THERE!
WAIT, RALPH. I DON'T THINK...
COME ON, FRANK!
DAMN IT.
RALPH! DON'T GO OVER THERE, IT ISN'T SAFE!
HE'S DEAD! NO MAN COULD SURVIVE THAT!
RALPH! STOP!
DON'T WORRY, PAL, I'LL GET YOU OUT OF THERE.
MY NAME IS RALPH. WHAT'S...
...YOUR'S??
AAAHHH!!!!

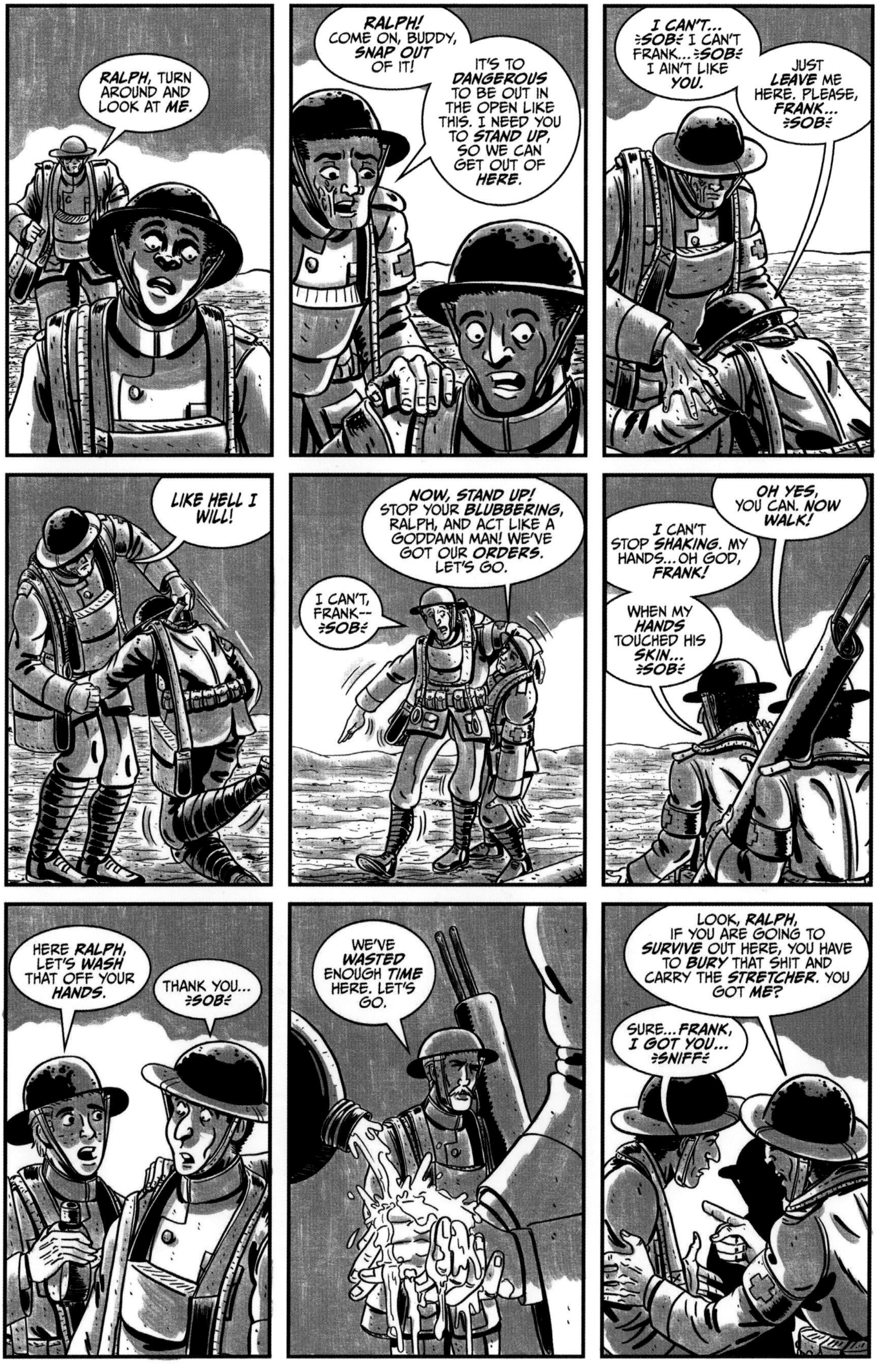
RALPH, TURN AROUND AND LOOK AT ME.
RALPH! COME ON, BUDDY, SNAP OUT OF IT!
IT'S TO DANGEROUS TO BE OUT IN THE OPEN LIKE THIS. I NEED YOU TO STAND UP, SO WE CAN GET OUT OF HERE.
I CAN'T... SOB I CAN'T FRANK... SOB I AIN'T LIKE YOU.
JUST LEAVE ME HERE. PLEASE, FRANK... SOB
LIKE HELL I WILL!
NOW, STAND UP! STOP YOUR BLUBBERING, RALPH, AND ACT LIKE A GODDAMN MAN! WE'VE GOT OUR ORDERS. LET'S GO.
I CAN'T, FRANK-- SOB
I CAN'T STOP SHAKING. MY HANDS...OH GOD, FRANK!
OH YES, YOU CAN. NOW WALK!
WHEN MY HANDS TOUCHED HIS SKIN... SOB
HERE RALPH, LET'S WASH THAT OFF YOUR HANDS.
THANK YOU... SOB
WE'VE WASTED ENOUGH TIME HERE. LET'S GO.
LOOK, RALPH, IF YOU ARE GOING TO SURVIVE OUT HERE, YOU HAVE TO BURY THAT SHIT AND CARRY THE STRETCHER. YOU GOT ME?
SURE...FRANK, I GOT YOU... SNIFF

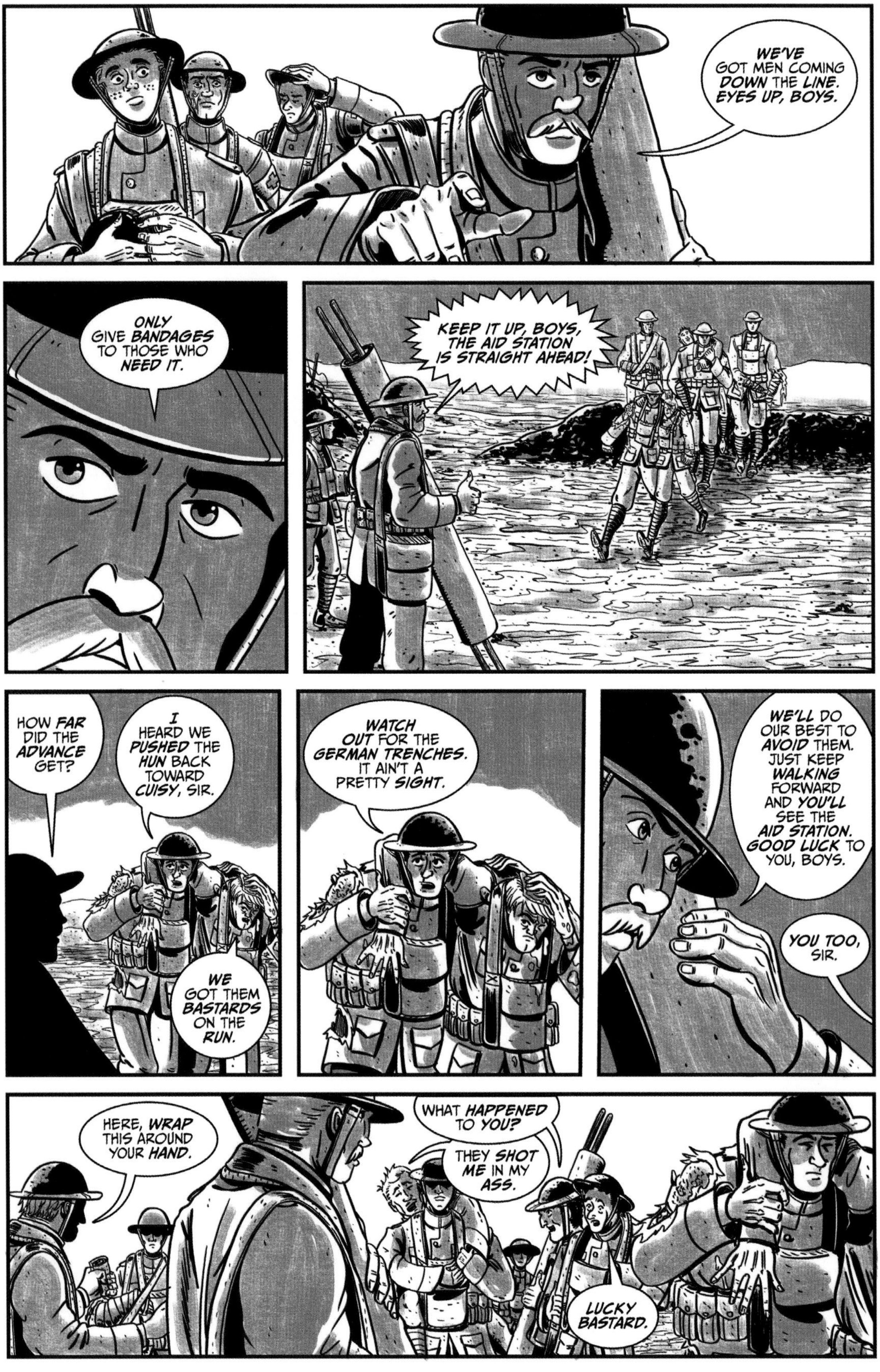
WE'VE GOT MEN COMING DOWN THE LINE. EYES UP, BOYS.
ONLY GIVE BANDAGES TO THOSE WHO NEED IT.
KEEP IT UP, BOYS, THE AID STATION IS STRAIGHT AHEAD!
HOW FAR DID THE ADVANCE GET?
I HEARD WE PUSHED THE HUN BACK TOWARD CUISY, SIR.
WE GOT THEM BASTARDS ON THE RUN.
WATCH OUT FOR THE GERMAN TRENCHES. IT AIN'T A PRETTY SIGHT.
WE'LL DO OUR BEST TO AVOID THEM. JUST KEEP WALKING FORWARD AND YOU'LL SEE THE AID STATION. GOOD LUCK TO YOU, BOYS.
YOU TOO, SIR.
HERE, WRAP THIS AROUND YOUR HAND.
WHAT HAPPENED TO YOU?
THEY SHOT ME IN MY ASS.
LUCKY BASTARD.

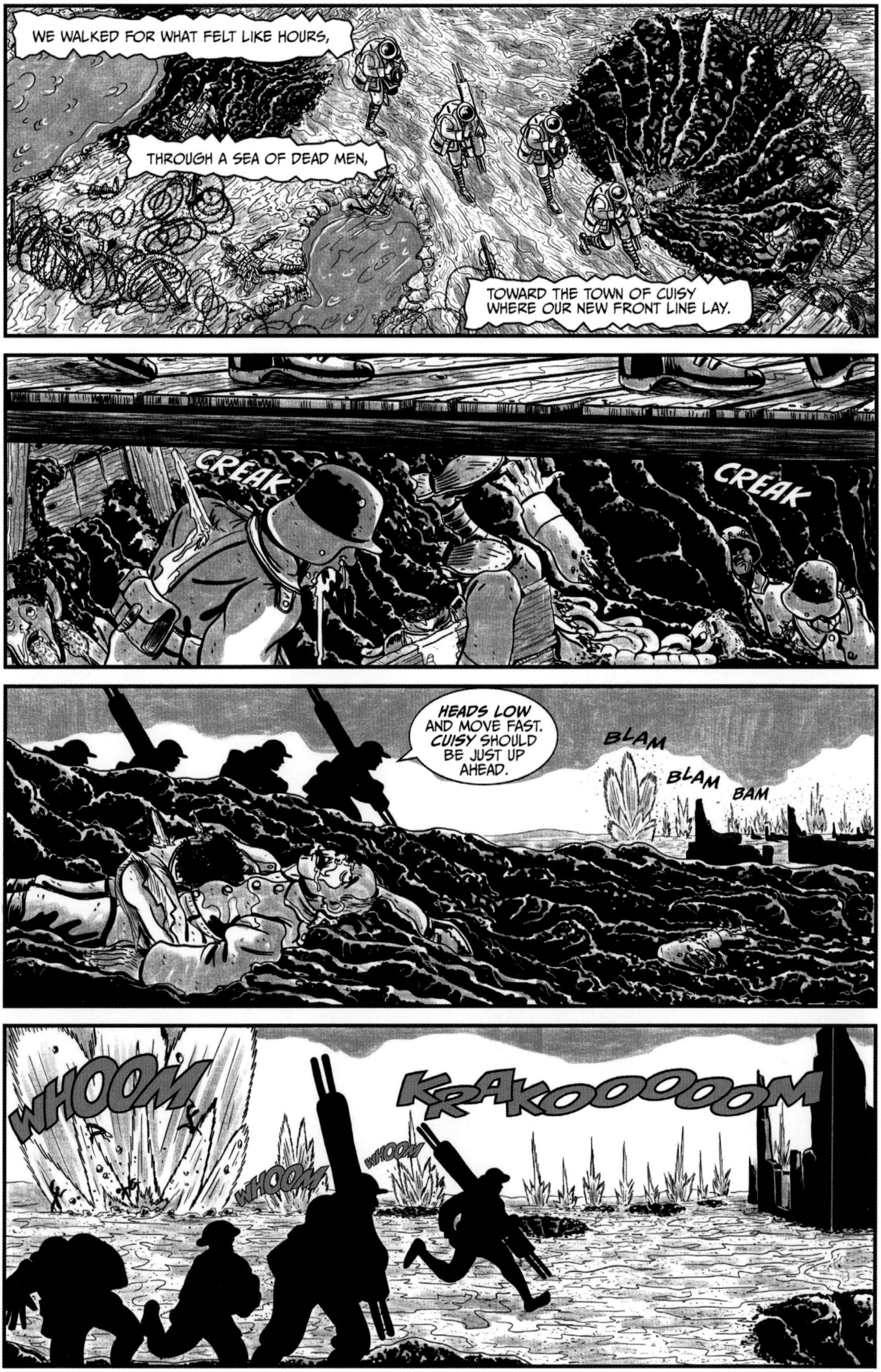
WE WALKED FOR WHAT FELT LIKE HOURS,
THROUGH A SEA OF DEAD MEN,
TOWARD THE TOWN OF CUISY WHERE OUR NEW FRONT LINE LAY.
CREAK
CREAK
HEADS LOW AND MOVE FAST. CUISY SHOULD BE JUST UP AHEAD.
BLAM
BLAM
BAM
WHOOM
KRAKOOOOOOM
WHOOM
WHOOM

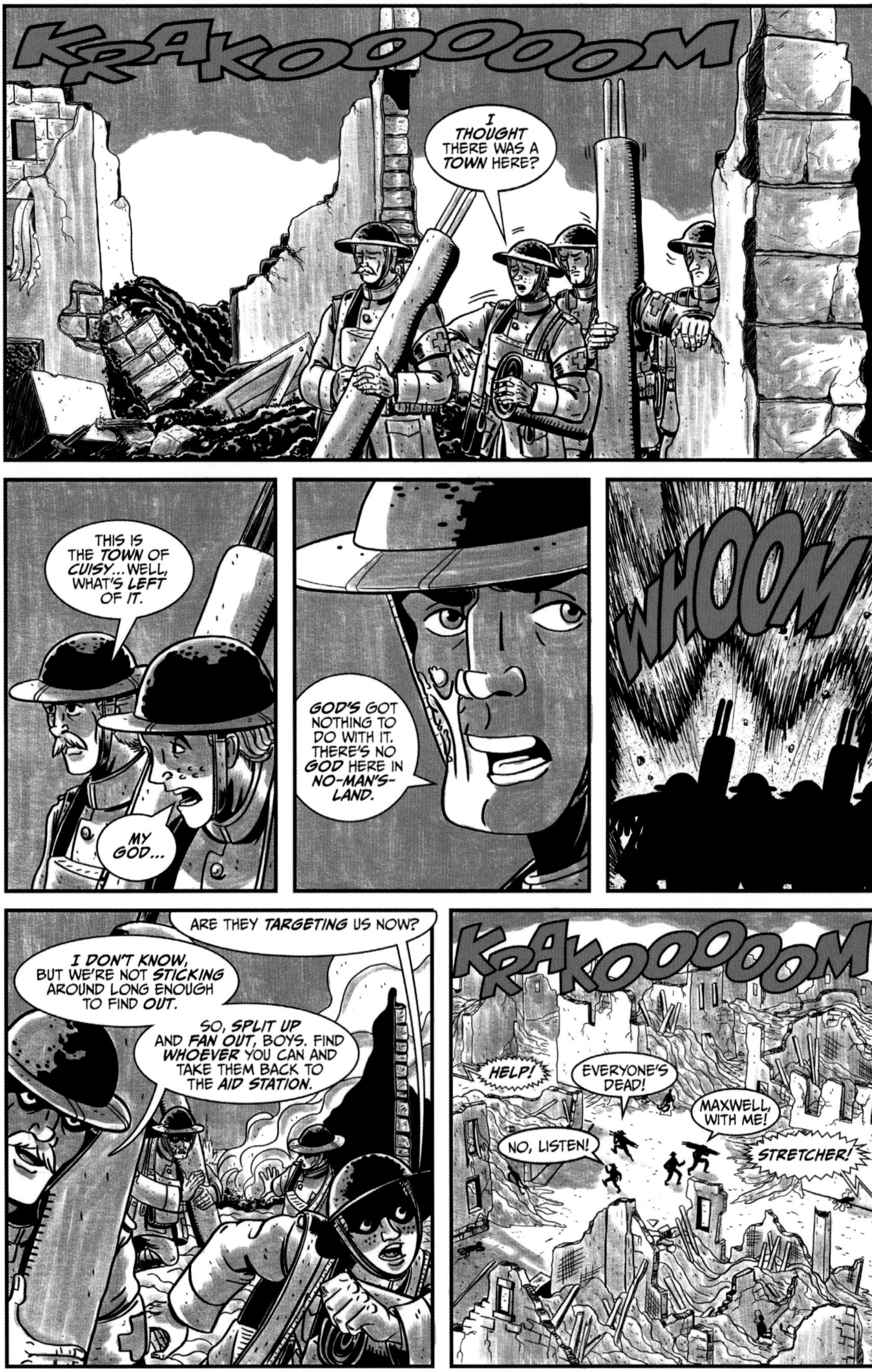
KRAKOOOOOOM
I THOUGHT THERE WAS A TOWN HERE?
THIS IS THE TOWN OF CUISY...WELL, WHAT'S LEFT OF IT.
MY GOD...
GOD'S GOT NOTHING TO DO WITH IT. THERE'S NO GOD HERE IN NO-MAN'S-LAND.
WHOOM
ARE THEY TARGETING US NOW?
I DON'T KNOW, BUT WE'RE NOT STICKING AROUND LONG ENOUGH TO FIND OUT.
SO, SPLIT UP AND FAN OUT, BOYS. FIND WHOEVER YOU CAN AND TAKE THEM BACK TO THE AID STATION.
KRAKOOOOOM
HELP!
EVERYONE'S DEAD!
MAXWELL, WITH ME!
NO, LISTEN!
STRETCHER!

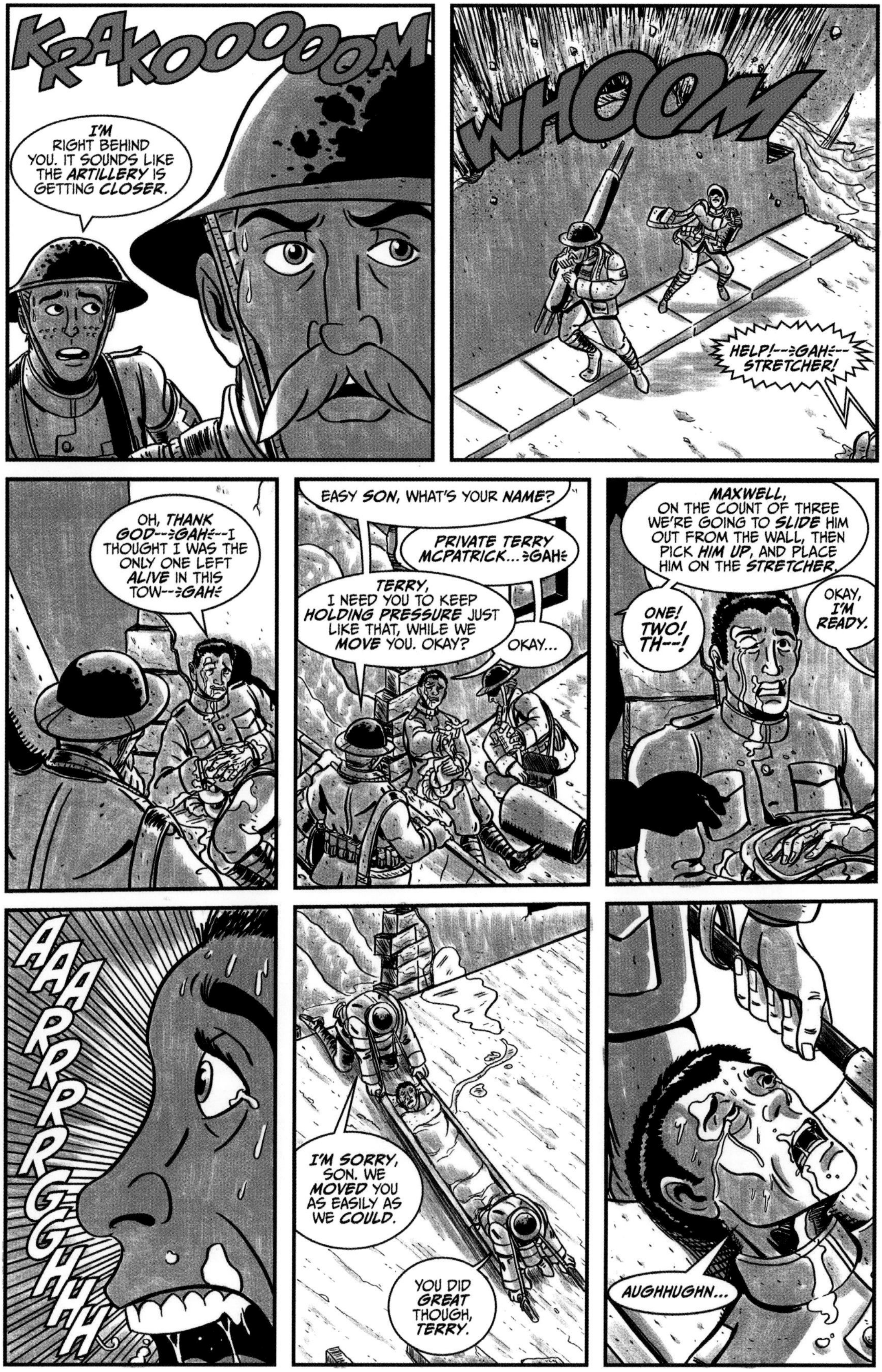
KRAKOOOOOOM
I'M RIGHT BEHIND YOU. IT SOUNDS LIKE THE ARTILLERY IS GETTING CLOSER.
WHOOM
HELP!--GAH--STRETCHER!
OH, THANK GOD--GAH--I THOUGHT I WAS THE ONLY ONE LEFT ALIVE IN THIS TOW--GAH
EASY SON, WHAT'S YOUR NAME?
PRIVATE TERRY MCPATRICK...GAH
TERRY, I NEED YOU TO KEEP HOLDING PRESSURE JUST LIKE THAT, WHILE WE MOVE YOU. OKAY?
OKAY...
MAXWELL, ON THE COUNT OF THREE WE'RE GOING TO SLIDE HIM OUT FROM THE WALL, THEN PICK HIM UP, AND PLACE HIM ON THE STRETCHER.
OKAY, I'M READY.
ONE! TWO! TH--!
AAARRRRGGHHH
I'M SORRY, SON. WE MOVED YOU AS EASILY AS WE COULD.
YOU DID GREAT THOUGH, TERRY.
AUGHHUGHN...

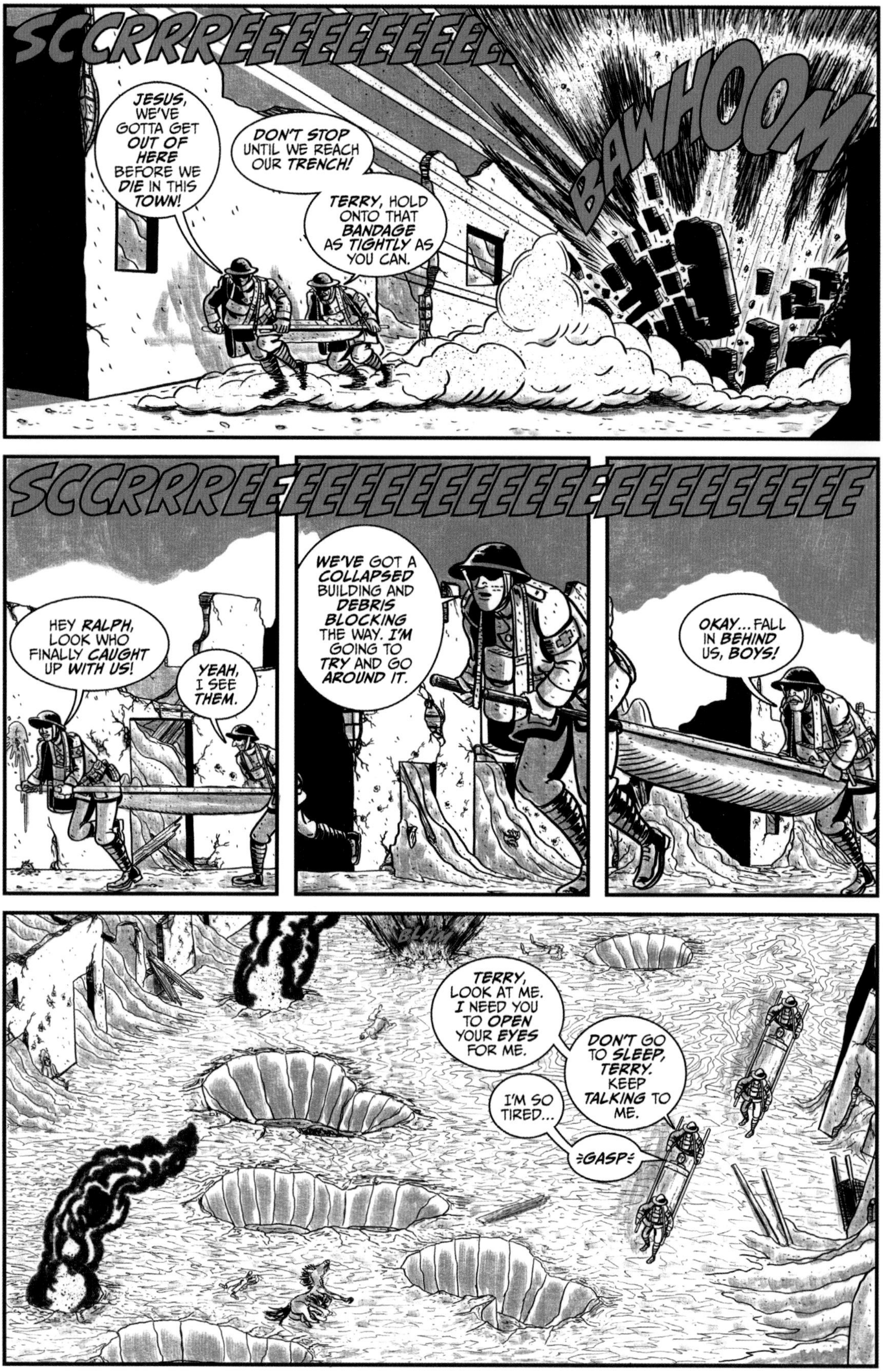
SCCRRREEEEEEEEEEEE
JESUS, WE'VE GOTTA GET OUT OF HERE BEFORE WE DIE IN THIS TOWN!
DON'T STOP UNTIL WE REACH OUR TRENCH!
TERRY, HOLD ONTO THAT BANDAGE AS TIGHTLY AS YOU CAN.
BAWHOOM
SCCRRREEEEEEEEEEEEEEEEEEEEEEEE
HEY RALPH, LOOK WHO FINALLY CAUGHT UP WITH US!
YEAH, I SEE THEM.
WE'VE GOT A COLLAPSED BUILDING AND DEBRIS BLOCKING THE WAY. I'M GOING TO TRY AND GO AROUND IT.
OKAY... FALL IN BEHIND US, BOYS!
TERRY, LOOK AT ME. I NEED YOU TO OPEN YOUR EYES FOR ME.
DON'T GO TO SLEEP, TERRY. KEEP TALKING TO ME.
I'M SO TIRED...
GASP

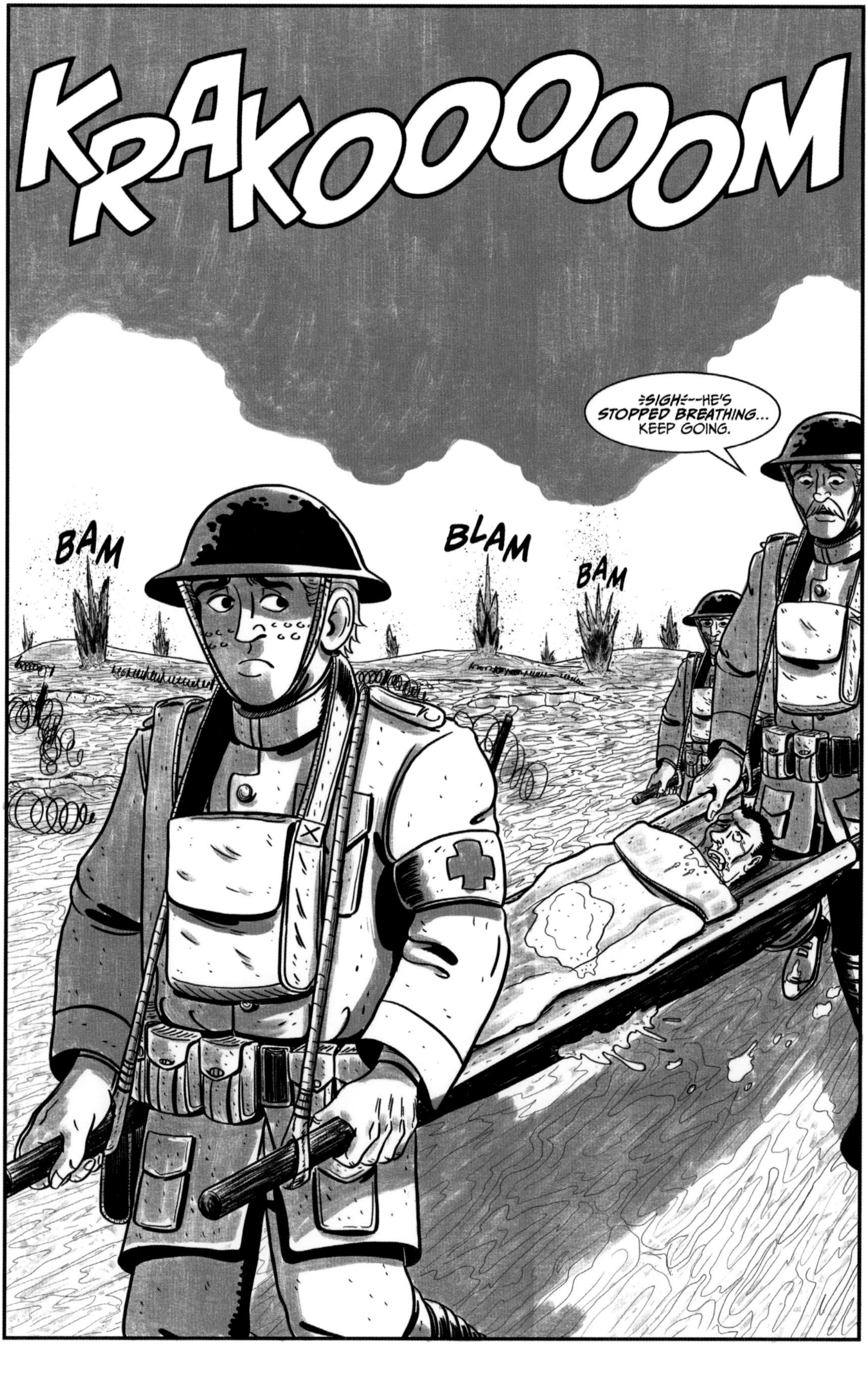
KRAKOOOOOM
≠SIGH≠--HE'S STOPPED BREATHING... KEEP GOING.
BAM
BLAM
BAM

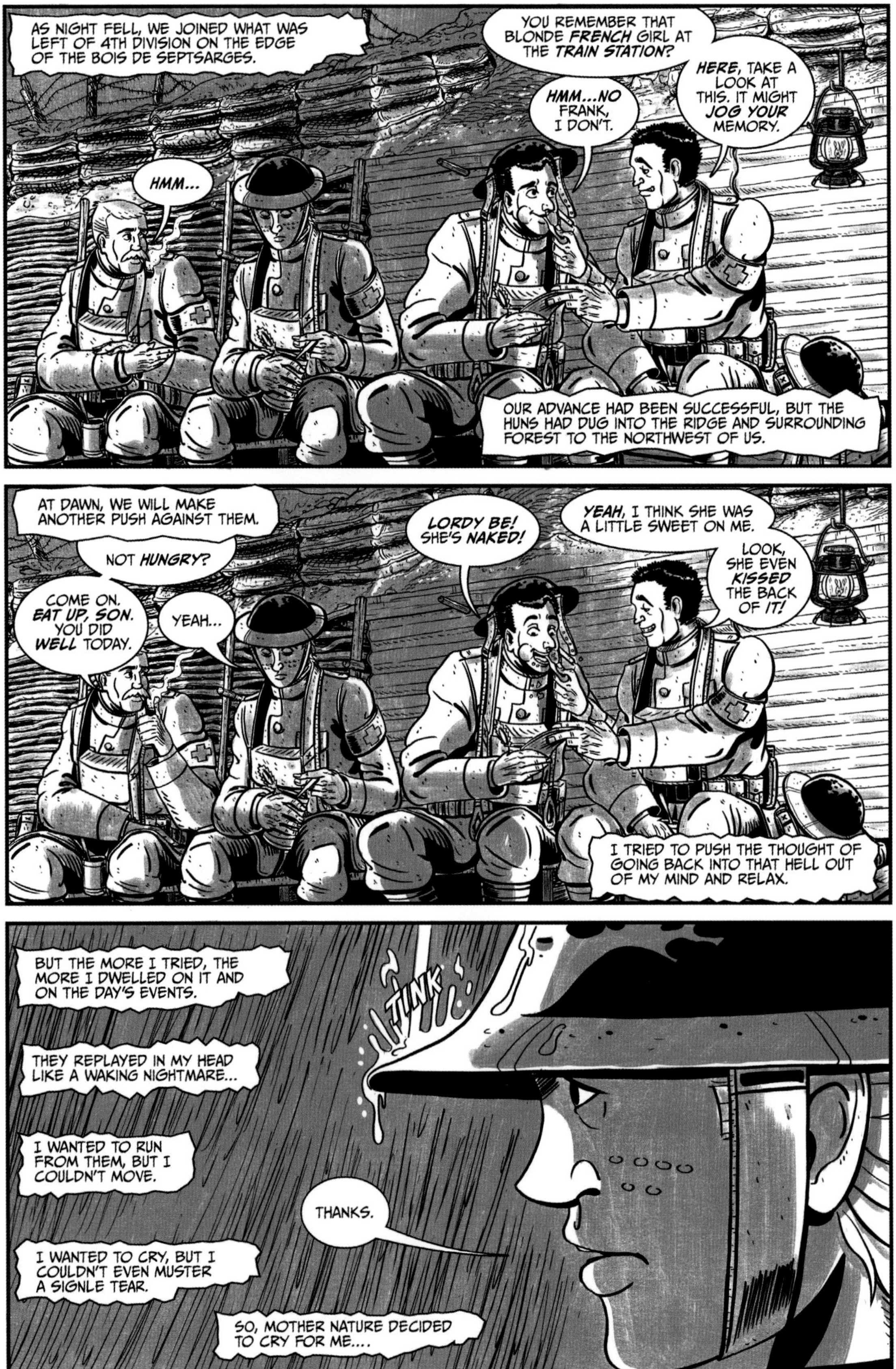
AS NIGHT FELL, WE JOINED WHAT WAS LEFT OF 4TH DIVISION ON THE EDGE OF THE BOIS DE SEPTSARGES.
YOU REMEMBER THAT BLONDE FRENCH GIRL AT THE TRAIN STATION?
HMM...NO FRANK, I DON'T.
HERE, TAKE A LOOK AT THIS. IT MIGHT JOG YOUR MEMORY.
HMM...
OUR ADVANCE HAD BEEN SUCCESSFUL, BUT THE HUNS HAD DUG INTO THE RIDGE AND SURROUNDING FOREST TO THE NORTHWEST OF US.
AT DAWN, WE WILL MAKE ANOTHER PUSH AGAINST THEM.
NOT HUNGRY?
COME ON. EAT UP, SON. YOU DID WELL TODAY.
YEAH...
LORDY BE! SHE'S NAKED!
YEAH, I THINK SHE WAS A LITTLE SWEET ON ME.
LOOK, SHE EVEN KISSED THE BACK OF IT!
I TRIED TO PUSH THE THOUGHT OF GOING BACK INTO THAT HELL OUT OF MY MIND AND RELAX.
BUT THE MORE I TRIED, THE MORE I DWELLED ON IT AND ON THE DAY'S EVENTS.
TINK
THEY REPLAYED IN MY HEAD LIKE A WAKING NIGHTMARE...
I WANTED TO RUN FROM THEM, BUT I COULDN'T MOVE.
THANKS.
I WANTED TO CRY, BUT I COULDN'T EVEN MUSTER A SIGNLE TEAR.
SO, MOTHER NATURE DECIDED TO CRY FOR ME....

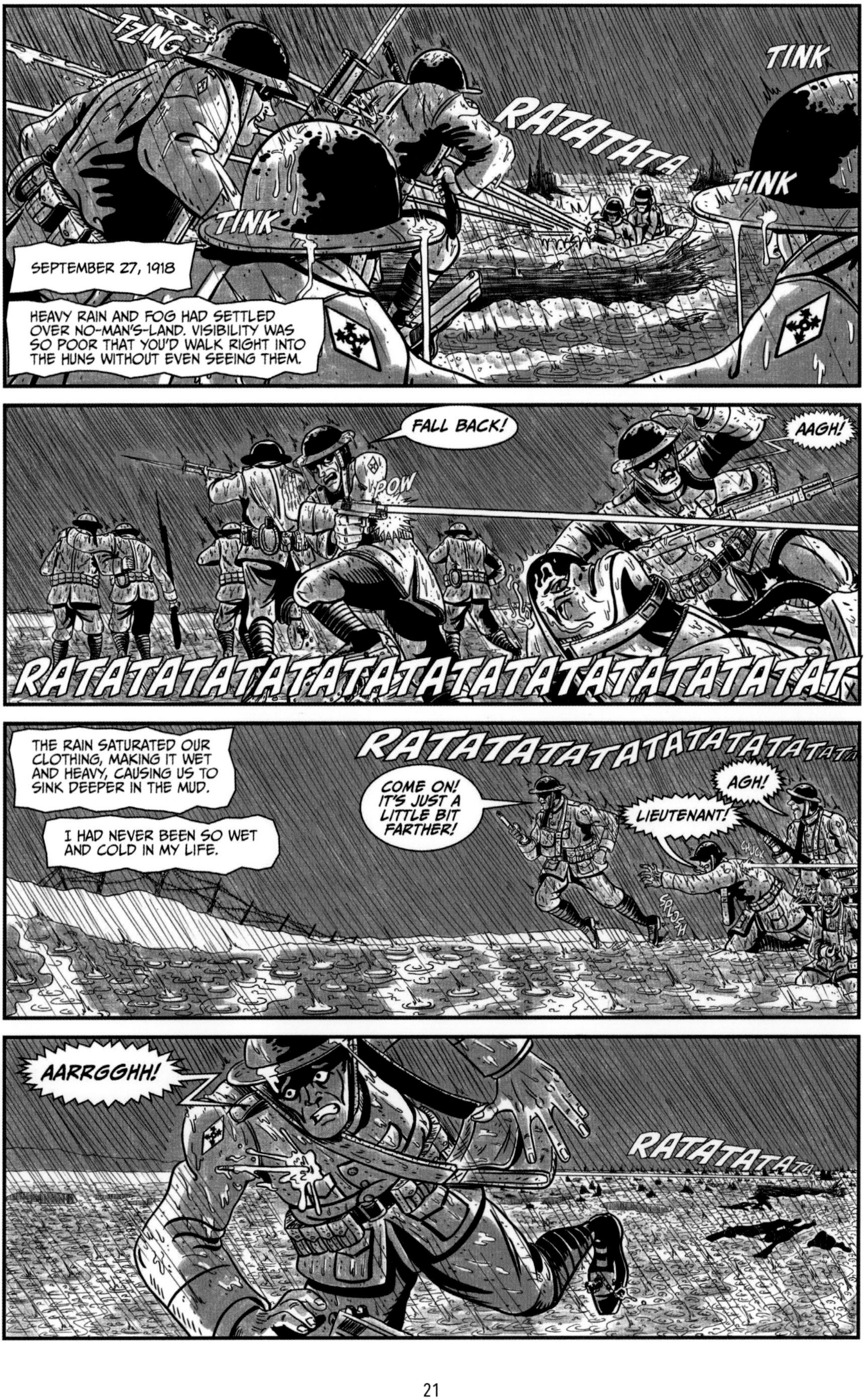
TZING
TINK
RATATATATA
TINK
TINK
SEPTEMBER 27, 1918
HEAVY RAIN AND FOG HAD SETTLED OVER NO-MAN'S-LAND. VISIBILITY WAS SO POOR THAT YOU'D WALK RIGHT INTO THE HUNS WITHOUT EVEN SEEING THEM.
FALL BACK!
AAGH!
POW
RATATATATATATATATATATATATATATATAT
THE RAIN SATURATED OUR CLOTHING, MAKING IT WET AND HEAVY, CAUSING US TO SINK DEEPER IN THE MUD.
I HAD NEVER BEEN SO WET AND COLD IN MY LIFE.
RATATATATATATATATATATA
COME ON! IT'S JUST A LITTLE BIT FARTHER!
AGH!
LIEUTENANT!
AARRGGHH!
RATATATATA

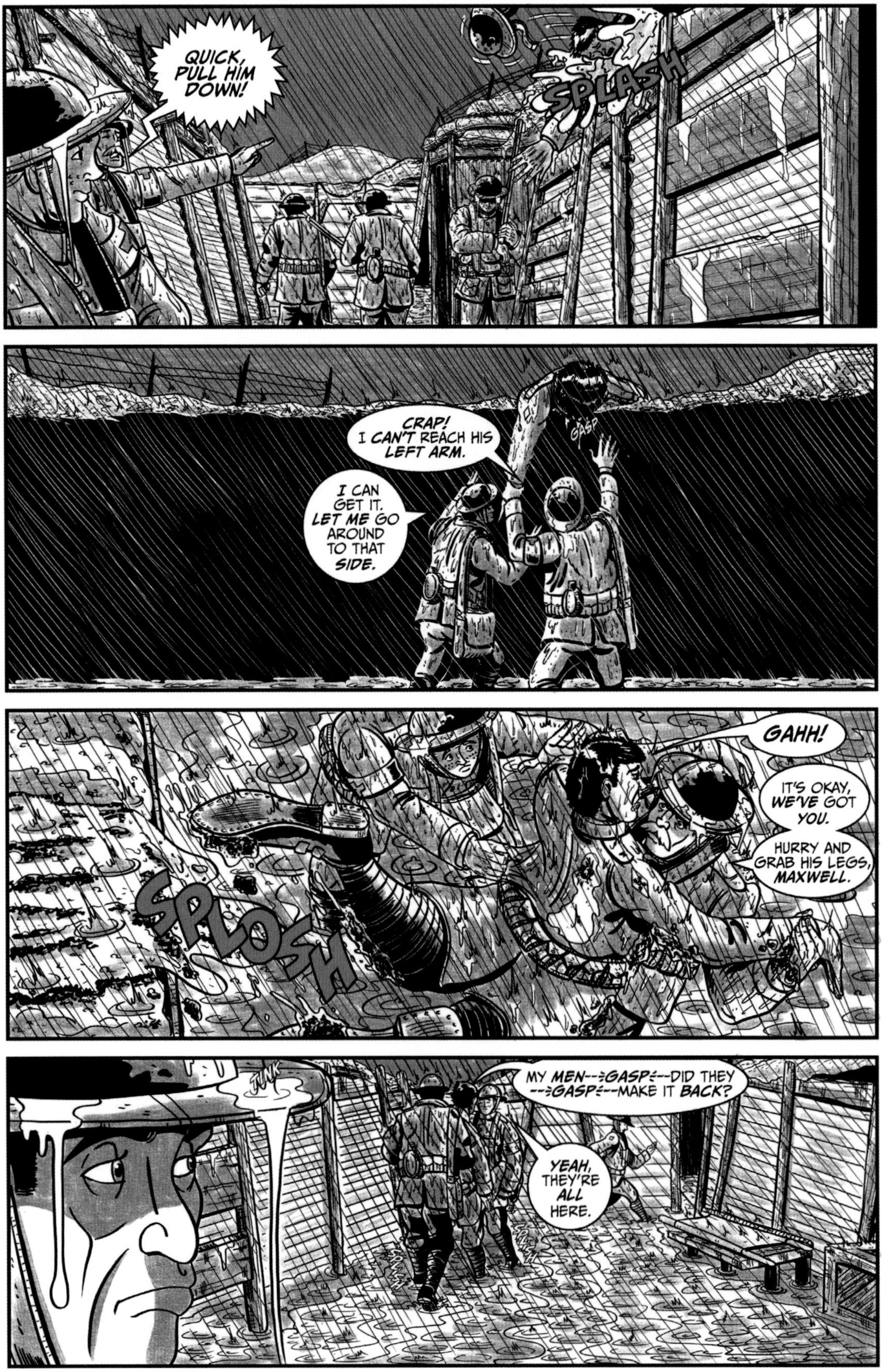
QUICK, PULL HIM DOWN!
SPLASH
CRAP! I CAN'T REACH HIS LEFT ARM.
GASP
I CAN GET IT. LET ME GO AROUND TO THAT SIDE.
GAHH!
IT'S OKAY, WE'VE GOT YOU.
HURRY AND GRAB HIS LEGS, MAXWELL.
SPLOSH
TUNK
MY MEN--GASP--DID THEY --GASP--MAKE IT BACK?
YEAH, THEY'RE ALL HERE.

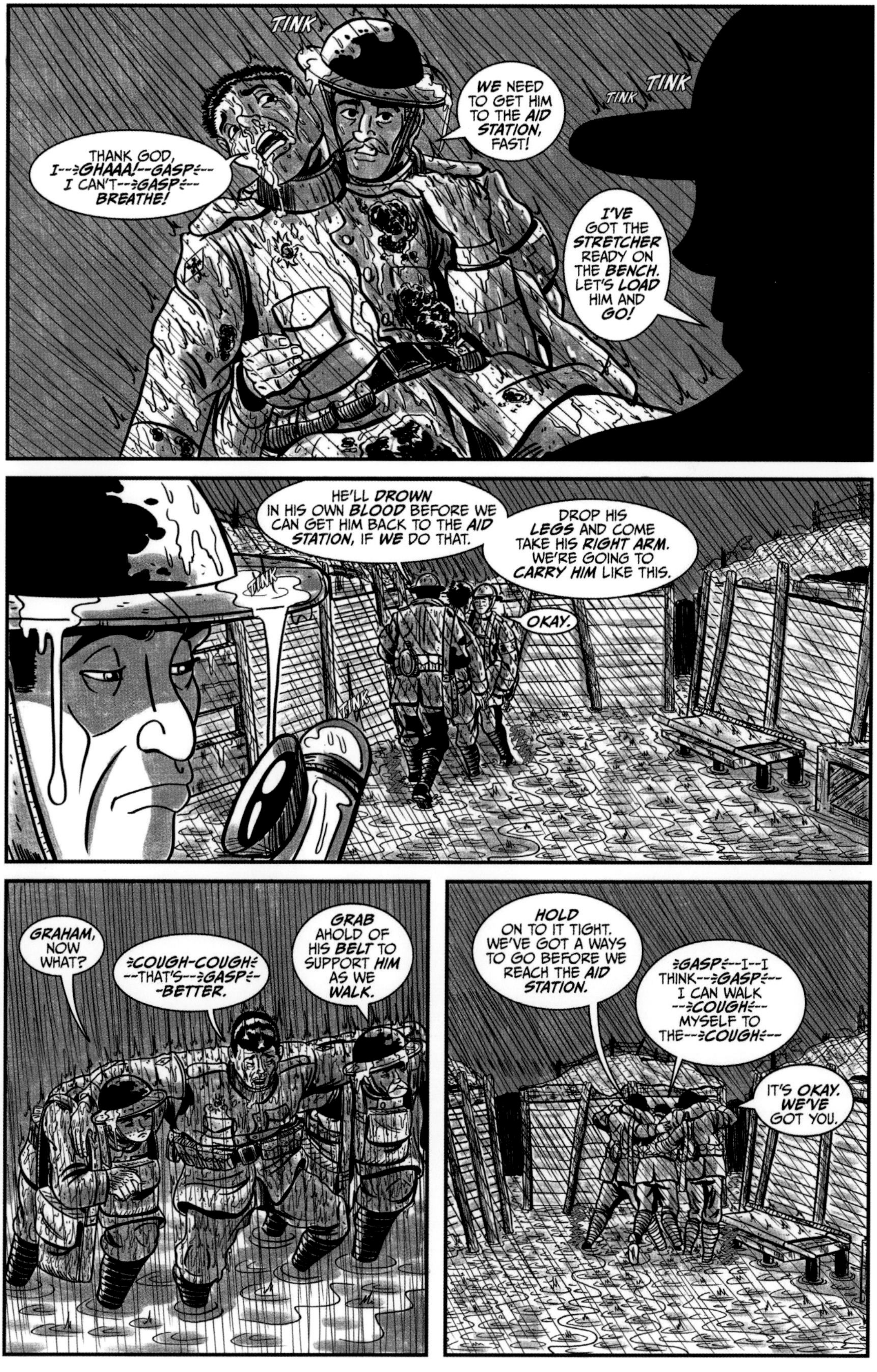
TINK
WE NEED TO GET HIM TO THE AID STATION, FAST!
TINK TINK
THANK GOD, I--⋛GHAAA!--GASP⋚-- I CAN'T--⋛GASP⋚-- BREATHE!
I'VE GOT THE STRETCHER READY ON THE BENCH. LET'S LOAD HIM AND GO!
HE'LL DROWN IN HIS OWN BLOOD BEFORE WE CAN GET HIM BACK TO THE AID STATION, IF WE DO THAT.
DROP HIS LEGS AND COME TAKE HIS RIGHT ARM. WE'RE GOING TO CARRY HIM LIKE THIS.
OKAY.
GRAHAM, NOW WHAT?
⋛COUGH-COUGH⋚ --THAT'S--⋛GASP⋚- -BETTER.
GRAB AHOLD OF HIS BELT TO SUPPORT HIM AS WE WALK.
HOLD ON TO IT TIGHT. WE'VE GOT A WAYS TO GO BEFORE WE REACH THE AID STATION.
⋛GASP⋚--I--I THINK--⋛GASP⋚-- I CAN WALK --⋛COUGH⋚-- MYSELF TO THE--⋛COUGH⋚--
IT'S OKAY. WE'VE GOT YOU.

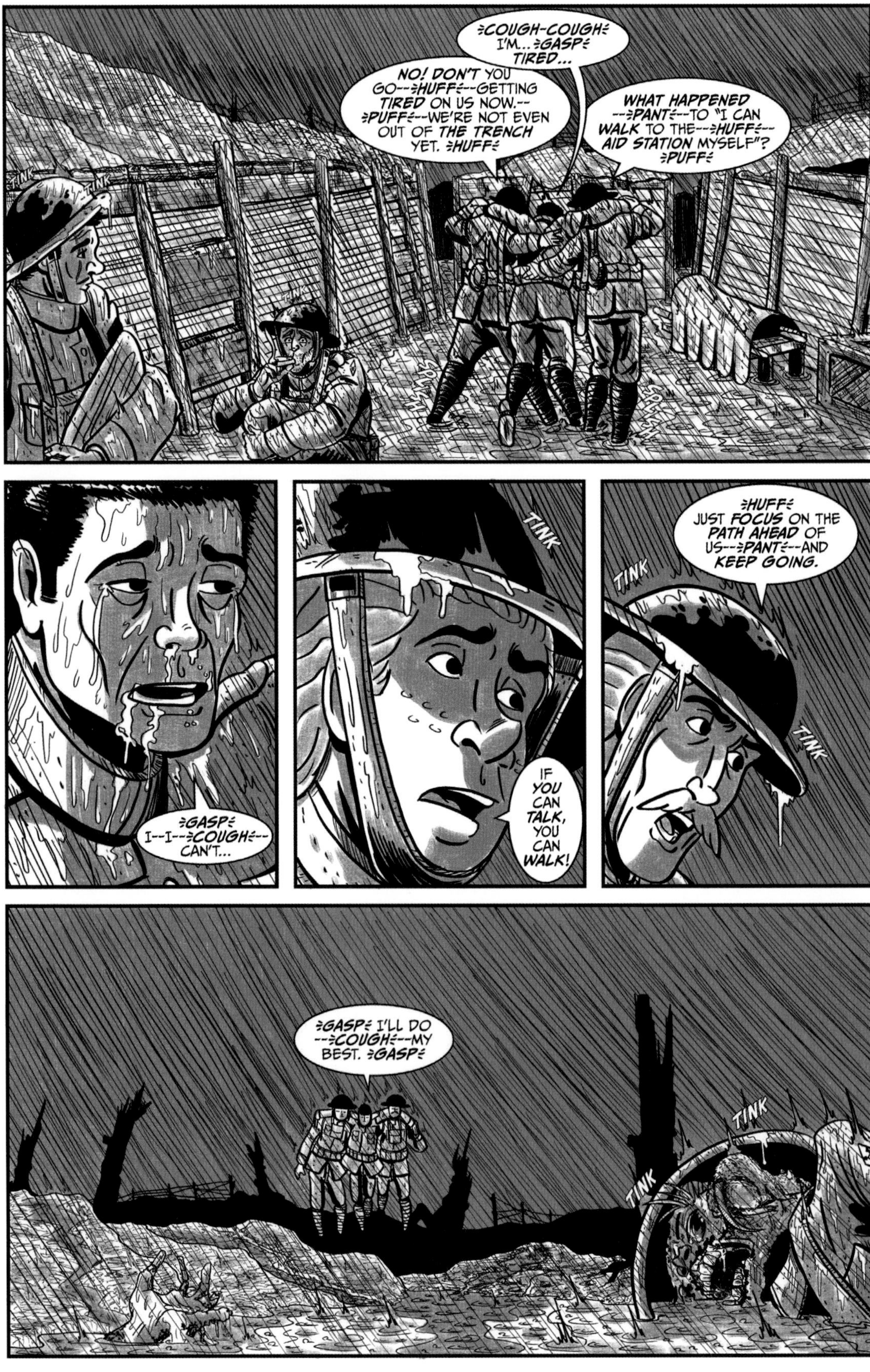
≷COUGH-COUGH≶ I'M... ≷GASP≶ TIRED...
NO! DON'T YOU GO--≷HUFF≶--GETTING TIRED ON US NOW.--≷PUFF≶--WE'RE NOT EVEN OUT OF THE TRENCH YET. ≷HUFF≶
WHAT HAPPENED --≷PANT≶--TO "I CAN WALK TO THE--≷HUFF≶--AID STATION MYSELF"? ≷PUFF≶
TINK
TINK
TINK
≷GASP≶ I--I--≷COUGH≶-- CAN'T...
TINK
IF YOU CAN TALK, YOU CAN WALK!
≷HUFF≶ JUST FOCUS ON THE PATH AHEAD OF US--≷PANT≶--AND KEEP GOING.
TINK
TINK
≷GASP≶ I'LL DO --≷COUGH≶--MY BEST. ≷GASP≶
TINK
TINK

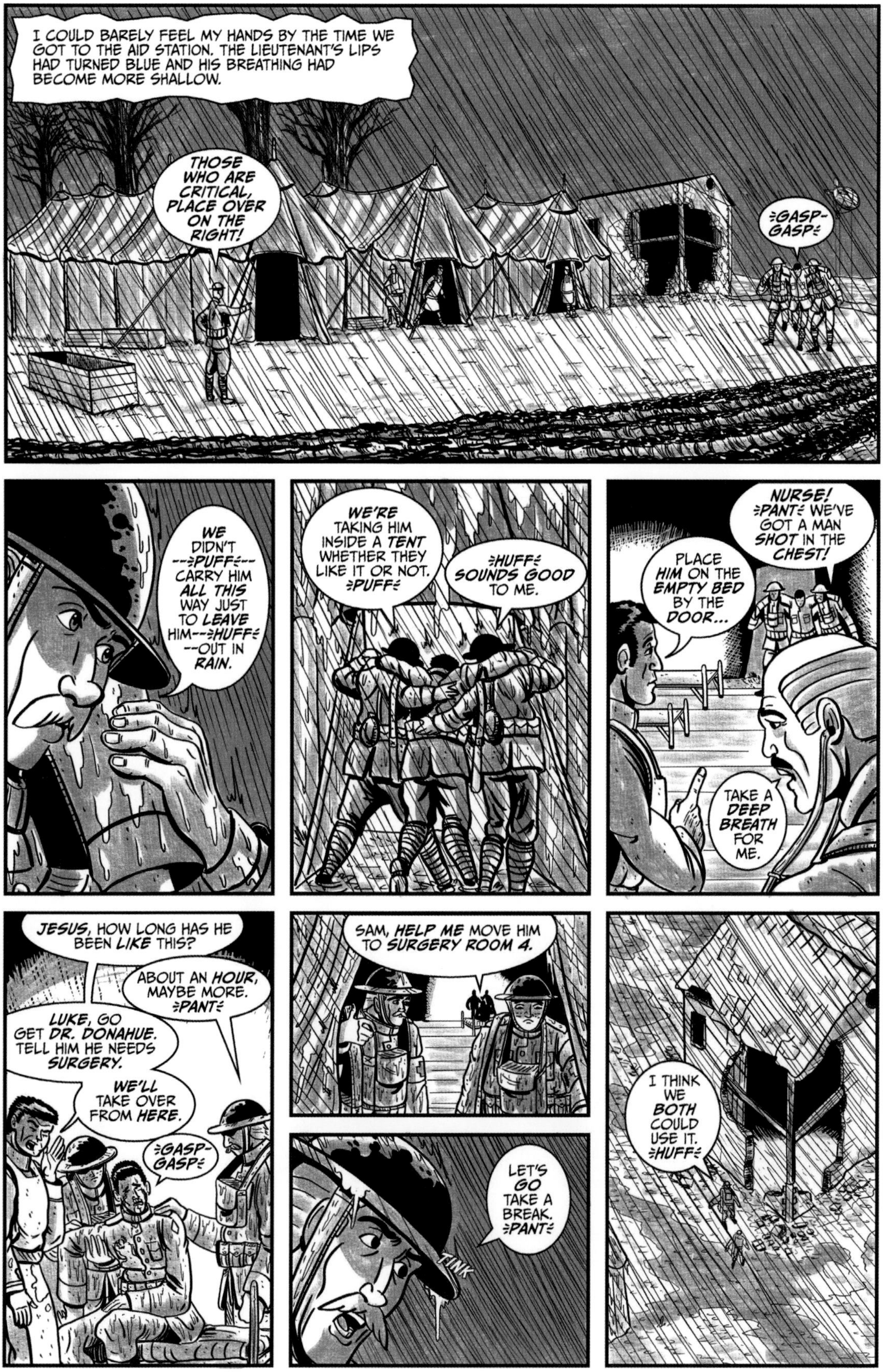
I COULD BARELY FEEL MY HANDS BY THE TIME WE GOT TO THE AID STATION. THE LIEUTENANT'S LIPS HAD TURNED BLUE AND HIS BREATHING HAD BECOME MORE SHALLOW.
THOSE WHO ARE CRITICAL, PLACE OVER ON THE RIGHT!
GASP-GASP
WE DIDN'T --PUFF-- CARRY HIM ALL THIS WAY JUST TO LEAVE HIM--HUFF --OUT IN RAIN.
WE'RE TAKING HIM INSIDE A TENT WHETHER THEY LIKE IT OR NOT. PUFF
HUFF SOUNDS GOOD TO ME.
NURSE! PANT WE'VE GOT A MAN SHOT IN THE CHEST!
PLACE HIM ON THE EMPTY BED BY THE DOOR...
TAKE A DEEP BREATH FOR ME.
JESUS, HOW LONG HAS HE BEEN LIKE THIS?
ABOUT AN HOUR, MAYBE MORE. PANT
LUKE, GO GET DR. DONAHUE. TELL HIM HE NEEDS SURGERY.
WE'LL TAKE OVER FROM HERE.
GASP-GASP
SAM, HELP ME MOVE HIM TO SURGERY ROOM 4.
LET'S GO TAKE A BREAK. PANT
TINK
I THINK WE BOTH COULD USE IT. HUFF

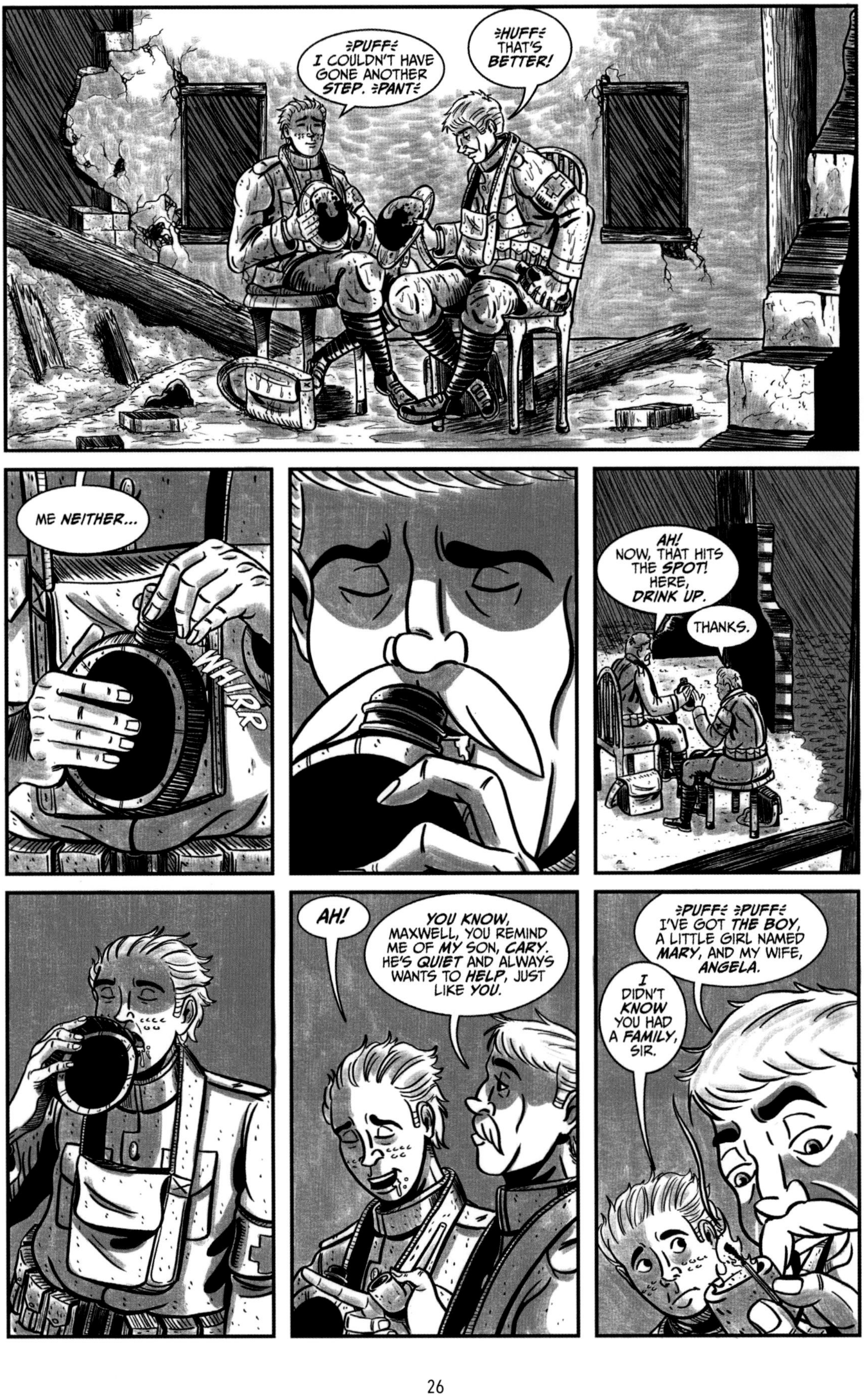

≈PUFF≈ I COULDN'T HAVE GONE ANOTHER STEP. ≈PANT≈
≈HUFF≈ THAT'S BETTER!
ME NEITHER...
WHIRR
AH! NOW, THAT HITS THE SPOT! HERE, DRINK UP.
THANKS.
AH!
YOU KNOW, MAXWELL, YOU REMIND ME OF MY SON, CARY. HE'S QUIET AND ALWAYS WANTS TO HELP, JUST LIKE YOU.
≈PUFF≈ ≈PUFF≈ I'VE GOT THE BOY, A LITTLE GIRL NAMED MARY, AND MY WIFE, ANGELA.
I DIDN'T KNOW YOU HAD A FAMILY, SIR.

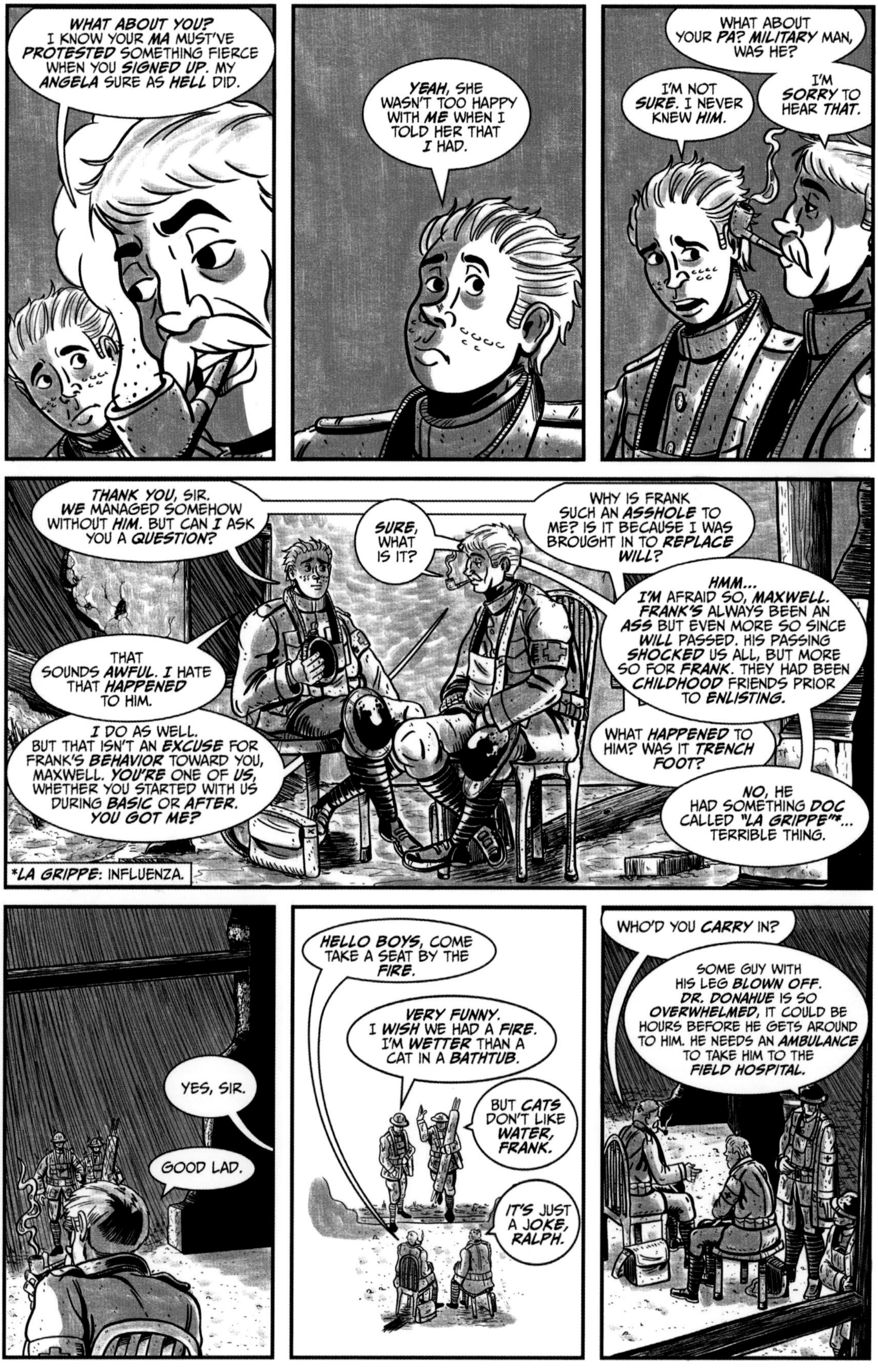
WHAT ABOUT YOU? I KNOW YOUR MA MUST'VE PROTESTED SOMETHING FIERCE WHEN YOU SIGNED UP. MY ANGELA SURE AS HELL DID.
YEAH, SHE WASN'T TOO HAPPY WITH ME WHEN I TOLD HER THAT I HAD.
WHAT ABOUT YOUR PA? MILITARY MAN, WAS HE?
I'M NOT SURE. I NEVER KNEW HIM.
I'M SORRY TO HEAR THAT.
THANK YOU, SIR. WE MANAGED SOMEHOW WITHOUT HIM. BUT CAN I ASK YOU A QUESTION?
SURE, WHAT IS IT?
WHY IS FRANK SUCH AN ASSHOLE TO ME? IS IT BECAUSE I WAS BROUGHT IN TO REPLACE WILL?
HMM... I'M AFRAID SO, MAXWELL. FRANK'S ALWAYS BEEN AN ASS BUT EVEN MORE SO SINCE WILL PASSED. HIS PASSING SHOCKED US ALL, BUT MORE SO FOR FRANK. THEY HAD BEEN CHILDHOOD FRIENDS PRIOR TO ENLISTING.
WHAT HAPPENED TO HIM? WAS IT TRENCH FOOT?
NO, HE HAD SOMETHING DOC CALLED "LA GRIPPE"*... TERRIBLE THING.
THAT SOUNDS AWFUL. I HATE THAT HAPPENED TO HIM.
I DO AS WELL. BUT THAT ISN'T AN EXCUSE FOR FRANK'S BEHAVIOR TOWARD YOU, MAXWELL. YOU'RE ONE OF US, WHETHER YOU STARTED WITH US DURING BASIC OR AFTER. YOU GOT ME?
*LA GRIPPE: INFLUENZA.
YES, SIR.
GOOD LAD.
HELLO BOYS, COME TAKE A SEAT BY THE FIRE.
VERY FUNNY. I WISH WE HAD A FIRE. I'M WETTER THAN A CAT IN A BATHTUB.
BUT CATS DON'T LIKE WATER, FRANK.
IT'S JUST A JOKE, RALPH.
WHO'D YOU CARRY IN?
SOME GUY WITH HIS LEG BLOWN OFF. DR. DONAHUE IS SO OVERWHELMED, IT COULD BE HOURS BEFORE HE GETS AROUND TO HIM. HE NEEDS AN AMBULANCE TO TAKE HIM TO THE FIELD HOSPITAL.

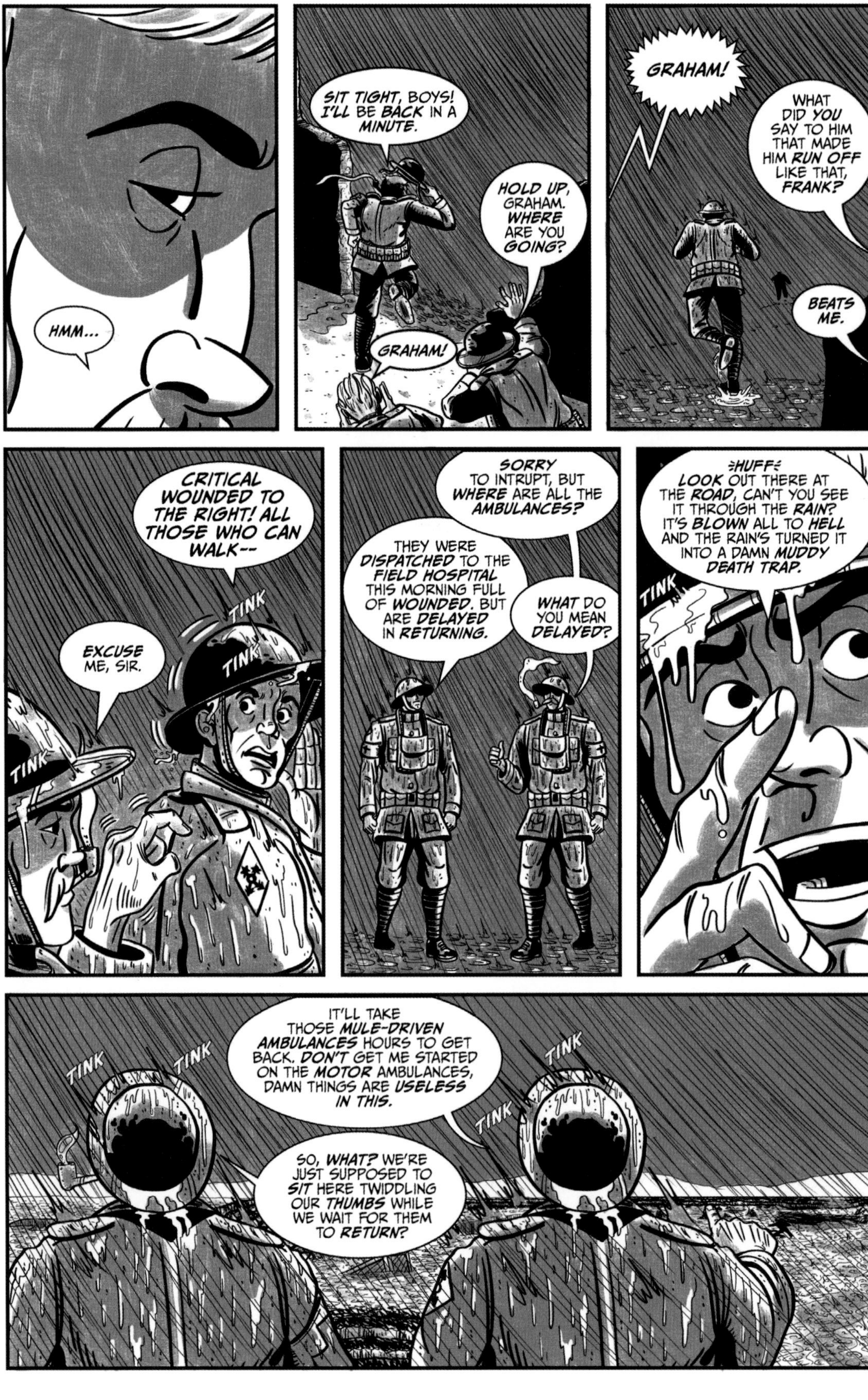
HMM...
SIT TIGHT, BOYS! I'LL BE BACK IN A MINUTE.
HOLD UP, GRAHAM. WHERE ARE YOU GOING?
GRAHAM!
GRAHAM!
WHAT DID YOU SAY TO HIM THAT MADE HIM RUN OFF LIKE THAT, FRANK?
BEATS ME.
CRITICAL WOUNDED TO THE RIGHT! ALL THOSE WHO CAN WALK--
TINK
TINK
EXCUSE ME, SIR.
TINK
SORRY TO INTRUPT, BUT WHERE ARE ALL THE AMBULANCES?
THEY WERE DISPATCHED TO THE FIELD HOSPITAL THIS MORNING FULL OF WOUNDED. BUT ARE DELAYED IN RETURNING.
WHAT DO YOU MEAN DELAYED?
HUFF
LOOK OUT THERE AT THE ROAD, CAN'T YOU SEE IT THROUGH THE RAIN? IT'S BLOWN ALL TO HELL AND THE RAIN'S TURNED IT INTO A DAMN MUDDY DEATH TRAP.
TINK
TINK
TINK
IT'LL TAKE THOSE MULE-DRIVEN AMBULANCES HOURS TO GET BACK. DON'T GET ME STARTED ON THE MOTOR AMBULANCES, DAMN THINGS ARE USELESS IN THIS.
TINK
TINK
SO, WHAT? WE'RE JUST SUPPOSED TO SIT HERE TWIDDLING OUR THUMBS WHILE WE WAIT FOR THEM TO RETURN?

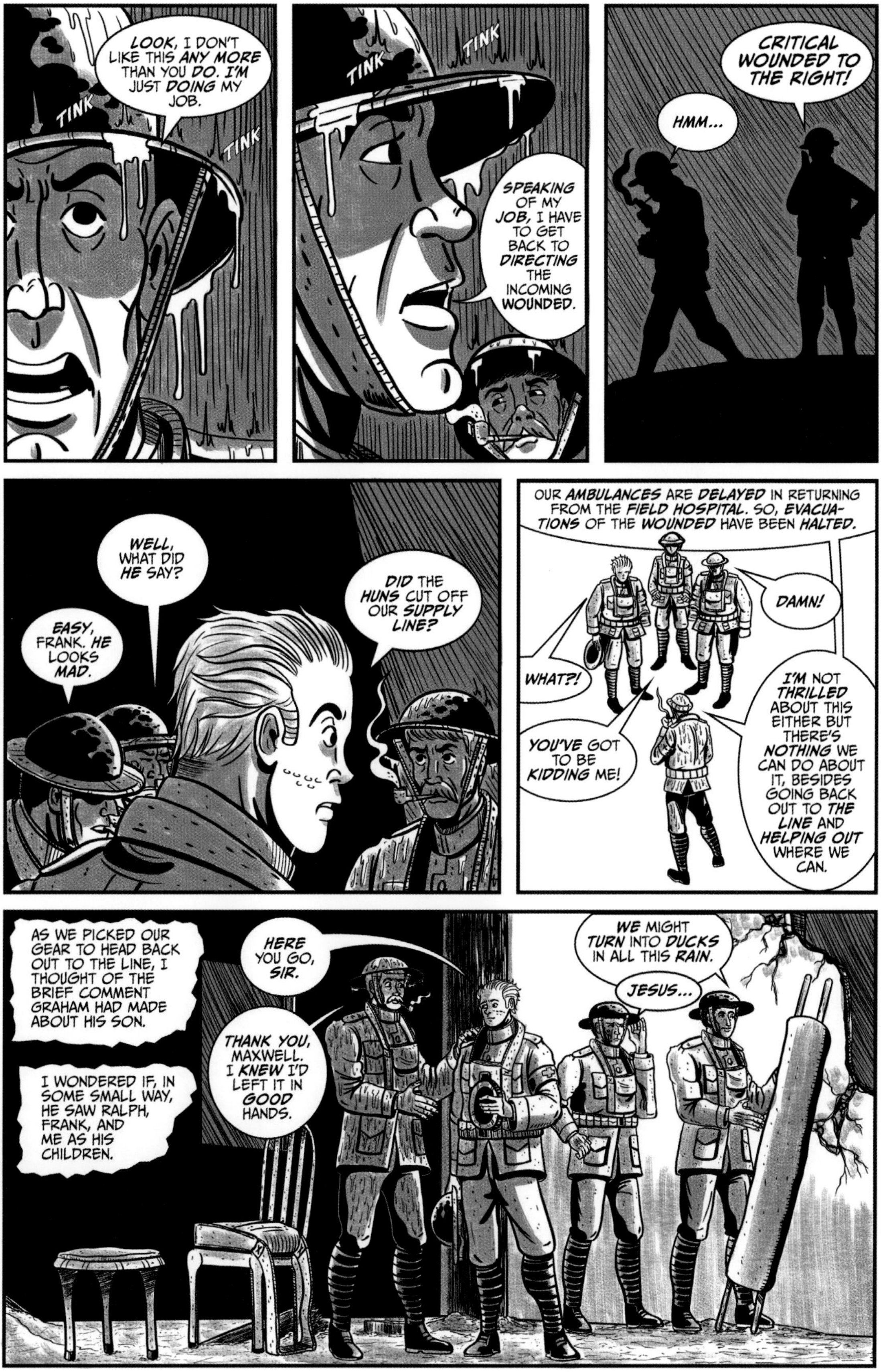

LOOK, I DON'T LIKE THIS ANY MORE THAN YOU DO. I'M JUST DOING MY JOB.
TINK
TINK
TINK
TINK
SPEAKING OF MY JOB, I HAVE TO GET BACK TO DIRECTING THE INCOMING WOUNDED.
CRITICAL WOUNDED TO THE RIGHT!
HMM...
WELL, WHAT DID HE SAY?
EASY, FRANK. HE LOOKS MAD.
DID THE HUNS CUT OFF OUR SUPPLY LINE?
OUR AMBULANCES ARE DELAYED IN RETURNING FROM THE FIELD HOSPITAL. SO, EVACUATIONS OF THE WOUNDED HAVE BEEN HALTED.
DAMN!
WHAT?!
YOU'VE GOT TO BE KIDDING ME!
I'M NOT THRILLED ABOUT THIS EITHER BUT THERE'S NOTHING WE CAN DO ABOUT IT, BESIDES GOING BACK OUT TO THE LINE AND HELPING OUT WHERE WE CAN.
AS WE PICKED OUR GEAR TO HEAD BACK OUT TO THE LINE, I THOUGHT OF THE BRIEF COMMENT GRAHAM HAD MADE ABOUT HIS SON.
I WONDERED IF, IN SOME SMALL WAY, HE SAW RALPH, FRANK, AND ME AS HIS CHILDREN.
HERE YOU GO, SIR.
THANK YOU, MAXWELL. I KNEW I'D LEFT IT IN GOOD HANDS.
WE MIGHT TURN INTO DUCKS IN ALL THIS RAIN.
JESUS...

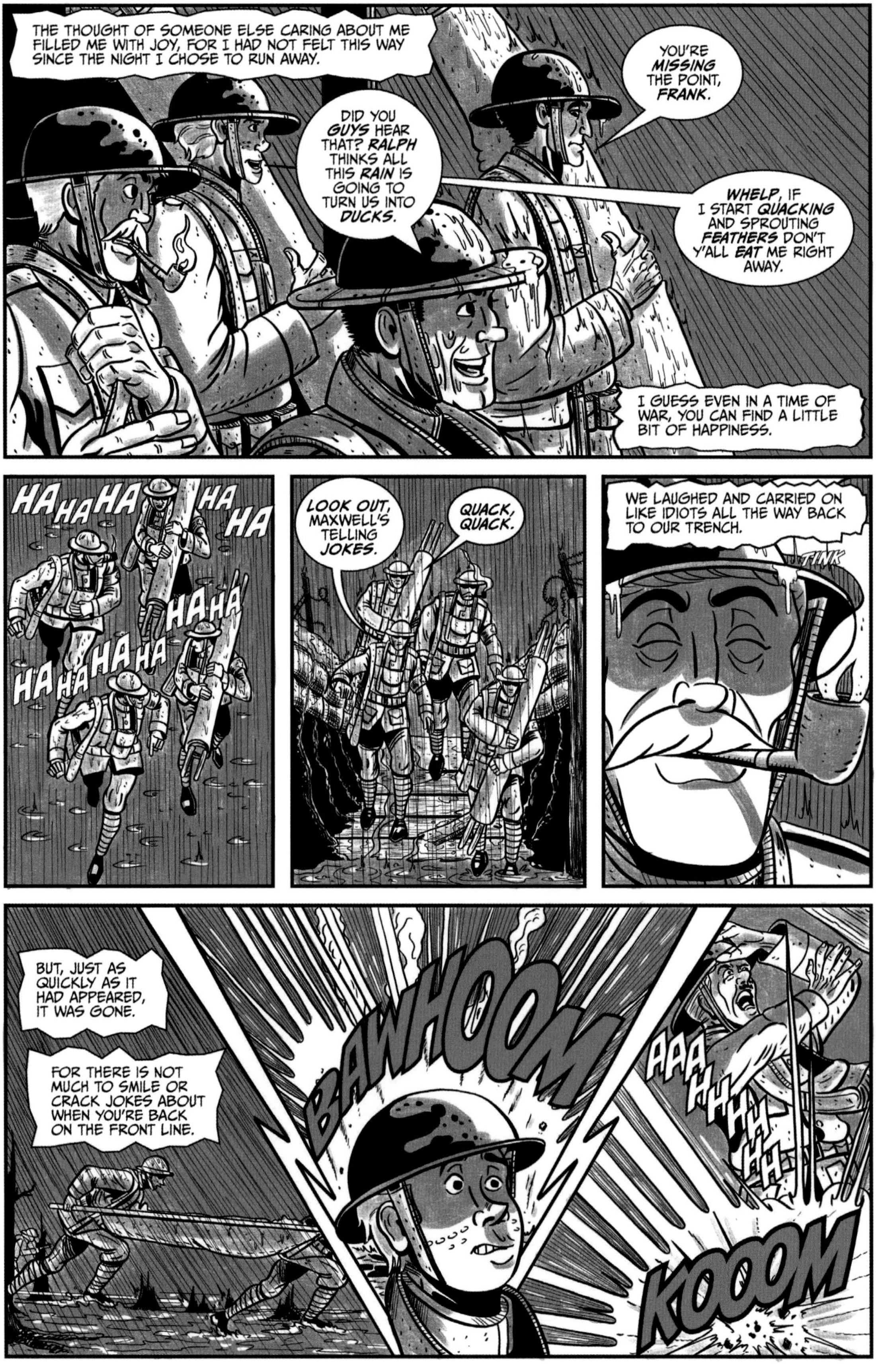

THE THOUGHT OF SOMEONE ELSE CARING ABOUT ME FILLED ME WITH JOY, FOR I HAD NOT FELT THIS WAY SINCE THE NIGHT I CHOSE TO RUN AWAY.
DID YOU GUYS HEAR THAT? RALPH THINKS ALL THIS RAIN IS GOING TO TURN US INTO DUCKS.
YOU'RE MISSING THE POINT, FRANK.
WHELP, IF I START QUACKING AND SPROUTING FEATHERS DON'T Y'ALL EAT ME RIGHT AWAY.
I GUESS EVEN IN A TIME OF WAR, YOU CAN FIND A LITTLE BIT OF HAPPINESS.
HA HA HA HA HA
HA HA
HA HA HA HA HA
LOOK OUT, MAXWELL'S TELLING JOKES.
QUACK, QUACK.
WE LAUGHED AND CARRIED ON LIKE IDIOTS ALL THE WAY BACK TO OUR TRENCH.
TINK
BUT, JUST AS QUICKLY AS IT HAD APPEARED, IT WAS GONE.
FOR THERE IS NOT MUCH TO SMILE OR CRACK JOKES ABOUT WHEN YOU'RE BACK ON THE FRONT LINE.
BAWHOOM
AAAHHHHHHH
KOOOM

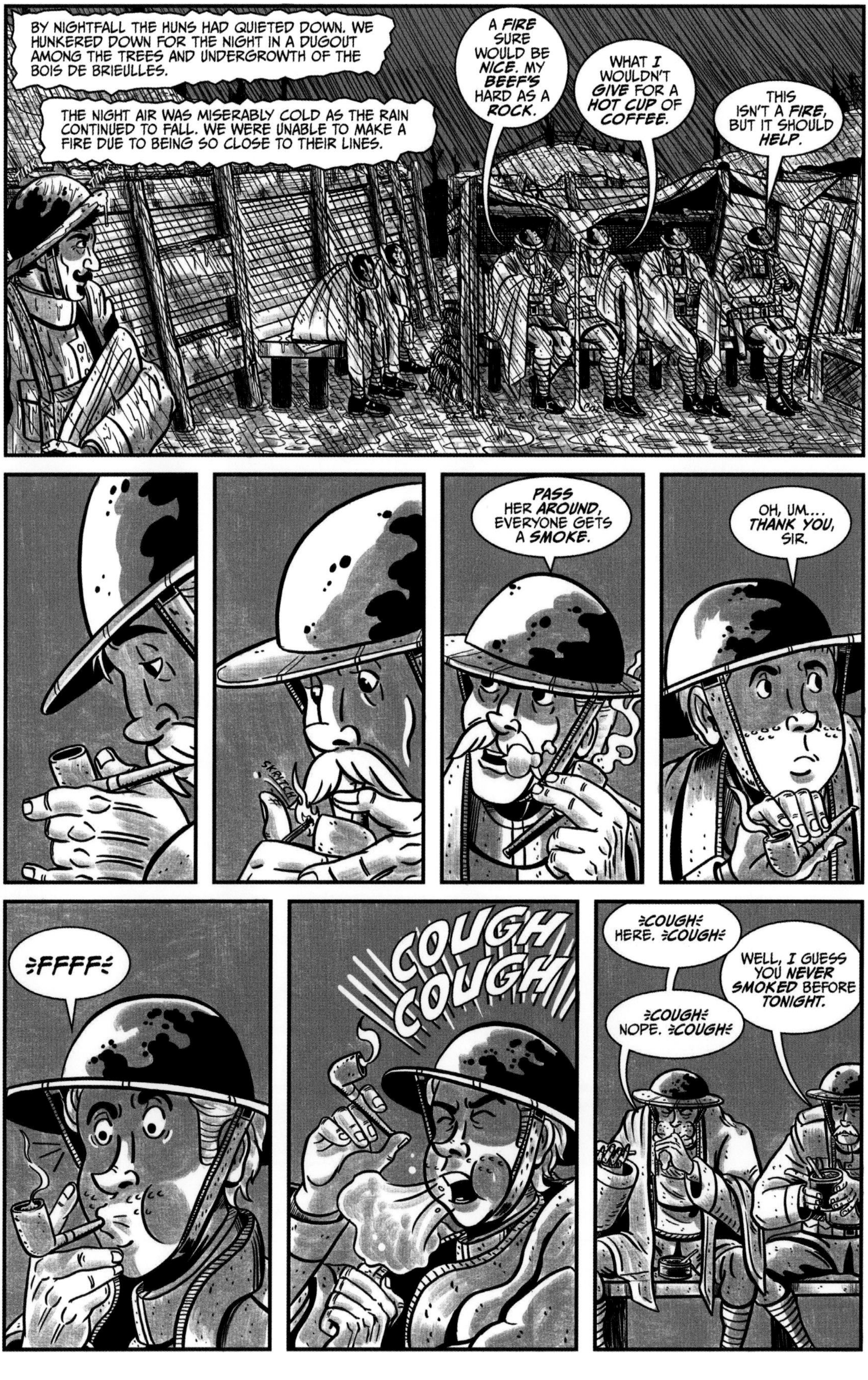
BY NIGHTFALL THE HUNS HAD QUIETED DOWN. WE HUNKERED DOWN FOR THE NIGHT IN A DUGOUT AMONG THE TREES AND UNDERGROWTH OF THE BOIS DE BRIEULLES.
THE NIGHT AIR WAS MISERABLY COLD AS THE RAIN CONTINUED TO FALL. WE WERE UNABLE TO MAKE A FIRE DUE TO BEING SO CLOSE TO THEIR LINES.
A FIRE SURE WOULD BE NICE. MY BEEF'S HARD AS A ROCK.
WHAT I WOULDN'T GIVE FOR A HOT CUP OF COFFEE.
THIS ISN'T A FIRE, BUT IT SHOULD HELP.
SKRITCH
PASS HER AROUND, EVERYONE GETS A SMOKE.
OH, UM.... THANK YOU, SIR.
FFFF
COUGH COUGH
COUGH HERE. COUGH
WELL, I GUESS YOU NEVER SMOKED BEFORE TONIGHT.
COUGH NOPE. COUGH

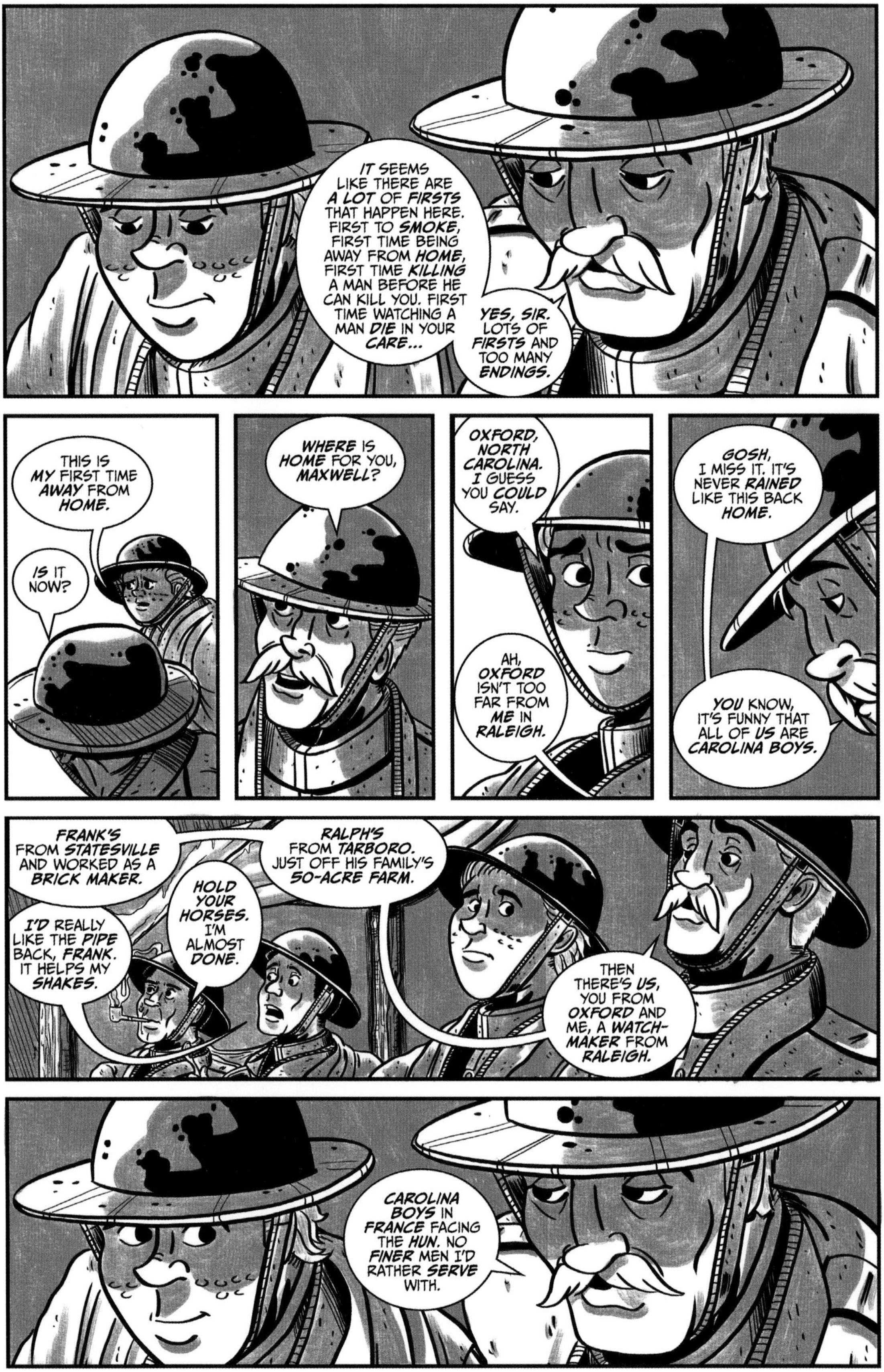
IT SEEMS LIKE THERE ARE A LOT OF FIRSTS THAT HAPPEN HERE. FIRST TO SMOKE, FIRST TIME BEING AWAY FROM HOME, FIRST TIME KILLING A MAN BEFORE HE CAN KILL YOU. FIRST TIME WATCHING A MAN DIE IN YOUR CARE...
YES, SIR. LOTS OF FIRSTS AND TOO MANY ENDINGS.
THIS IS MY FIRST TIME AWAY FROM HOME.
IS IT NOW?
WHERE IS HOME FOR YOU, MAXWELL?
OXFORD, NORTH CAROLINA. I GUESS YOU COULD SAY.
AH, OXFORD ISN'T TOO FAR FROM ME IN RALEIGH.
GOSH, I MISS IT. IT'S NEVER RAINED LIKE THIS BACK HOME.
YOU KNOW, IT'S FUNNY THAT ALL OF US ARE CAROLINA BOYS.
FRANK'S FROM STATESVILLE AND WORKED AS A BRICK MAKER.
RALPH'S FROM TARBORO. JUST OFF HIS FAMILY'S 50-ACRE FARM.
I'D REALLY LIKE THE PIPE BACK, FRANK. IT HELPS MY SHAKES.
HOLD YOUR HORSES. I'M ALMOST DONE.
THEN THERE'S US, YOU FROM OXFORD AND ME, A WATCH-MAKER FROM RALEIGH.
CAROLINA BOYS IN FRANCE FACING THE HUN. NO FINER MEN I'D RATHER SERVE WITH.

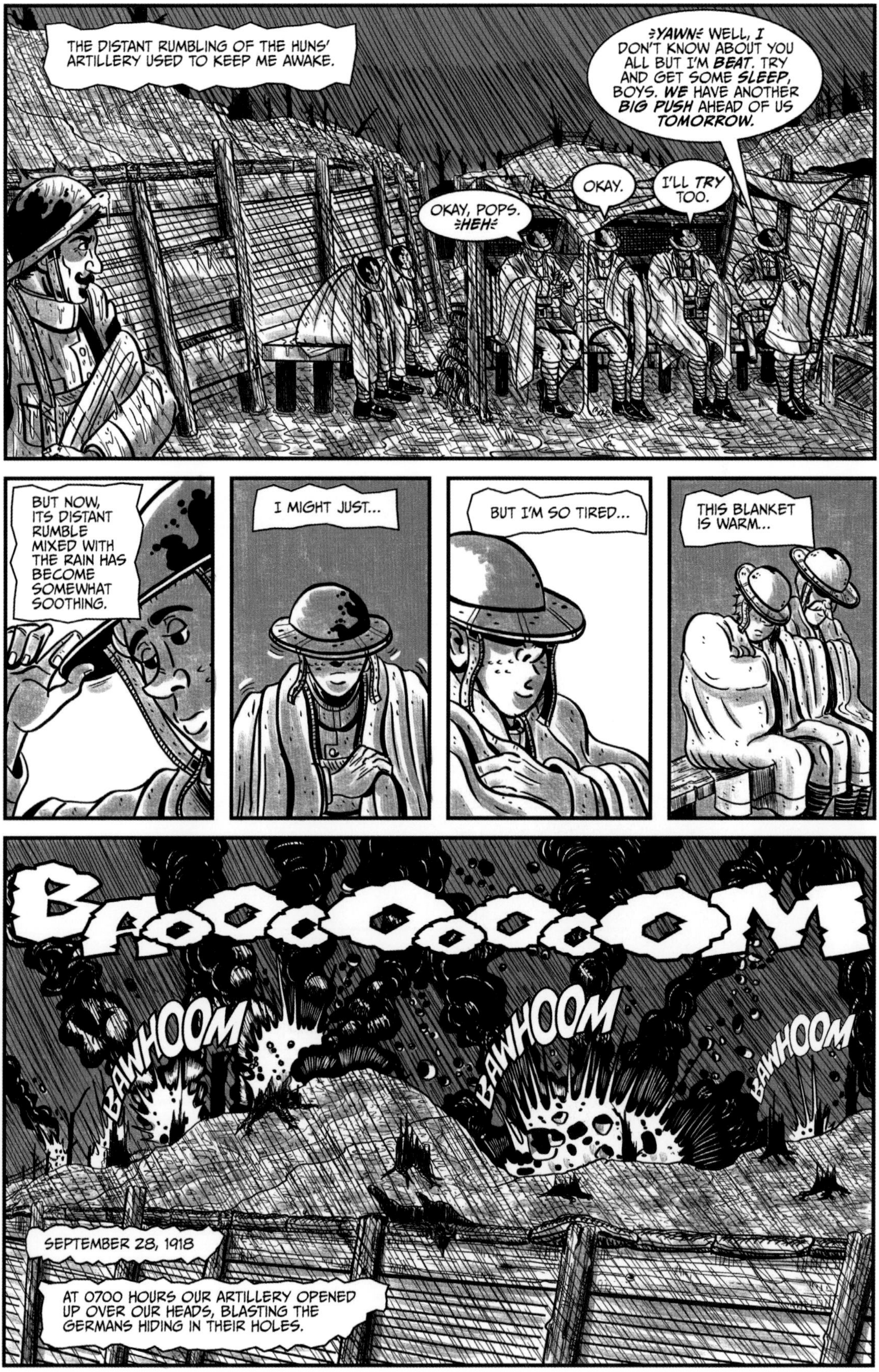
THE DISTANT RUMBLING OF THE HUNS' ARTILLERY USED TO KEEP ME AWAKE.
YAWN WELL, I DON'T KNOW ABOUT YOU ALL BUT I'M BEAT. TRY AND GET SOME SLEEP, BOYS. WE HAVE ANOTHER BIG PUSH AHEAD OF US TOMORROW.
OKAY, POPS. HEH
OKAY.
I'LL TRY TOO.
BUT NOW, ITS DISTANT RUMBLE MIXED WITH THE RAIN HAS BECOME SOMEWHAT SOOTHING.
I MIGHT JUST...
BUT I'M SO TIRED...
THIS BLANKET IS WARM...
BOOOOOOOM
BAWHOOM
BAWHOOM
BAWHOOM
SEPTEMBER 28, 1918
AT 0700 HOURS OUR ARTILLERY OPENED UP OVER OUR HEADS, BLASTING THE GERMANS HIDING IN THEIR HOLES.

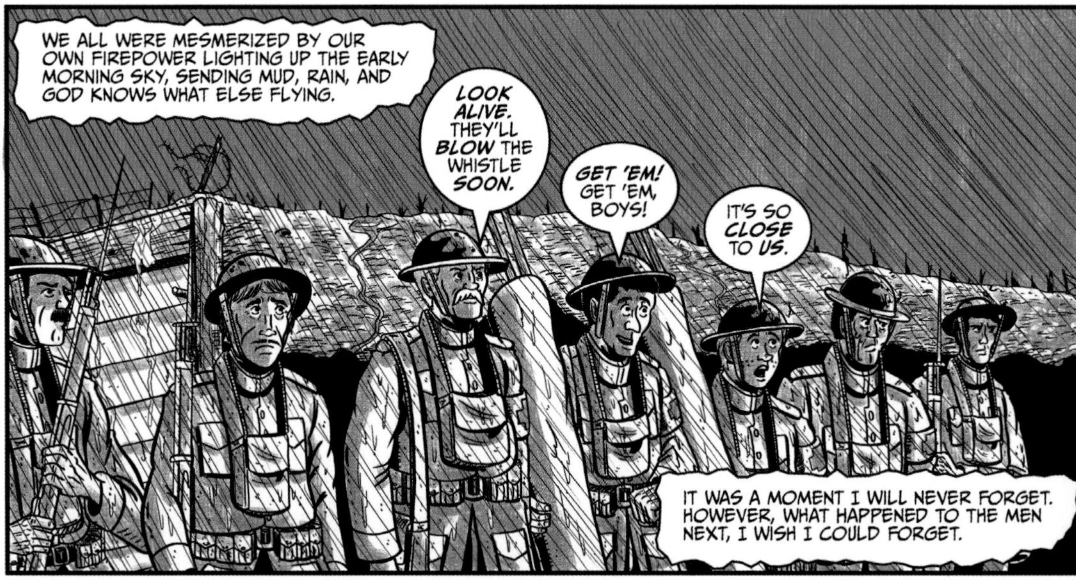
WE ALL WERE MESMERIZED BY OUR OWN FIREPOWER LIGHTING UP THE EARLY MORNING SKY, SENDING MUD, RAIN, AND GOD KNOWS WHAT ELSE FLYING.
LOOK ALIVE. THEY'LL BLOW THE WHISTLE SOON.
GET 'EM! GET 'EM, BOYS!
IT'S SO CLOSE TO US.
IT WAS A MOMENT I WILL NEVER FORGET. HOWEVER, WHAT HAPPENED TO THE MEN NEXT, I WISH I COULD FORGET.

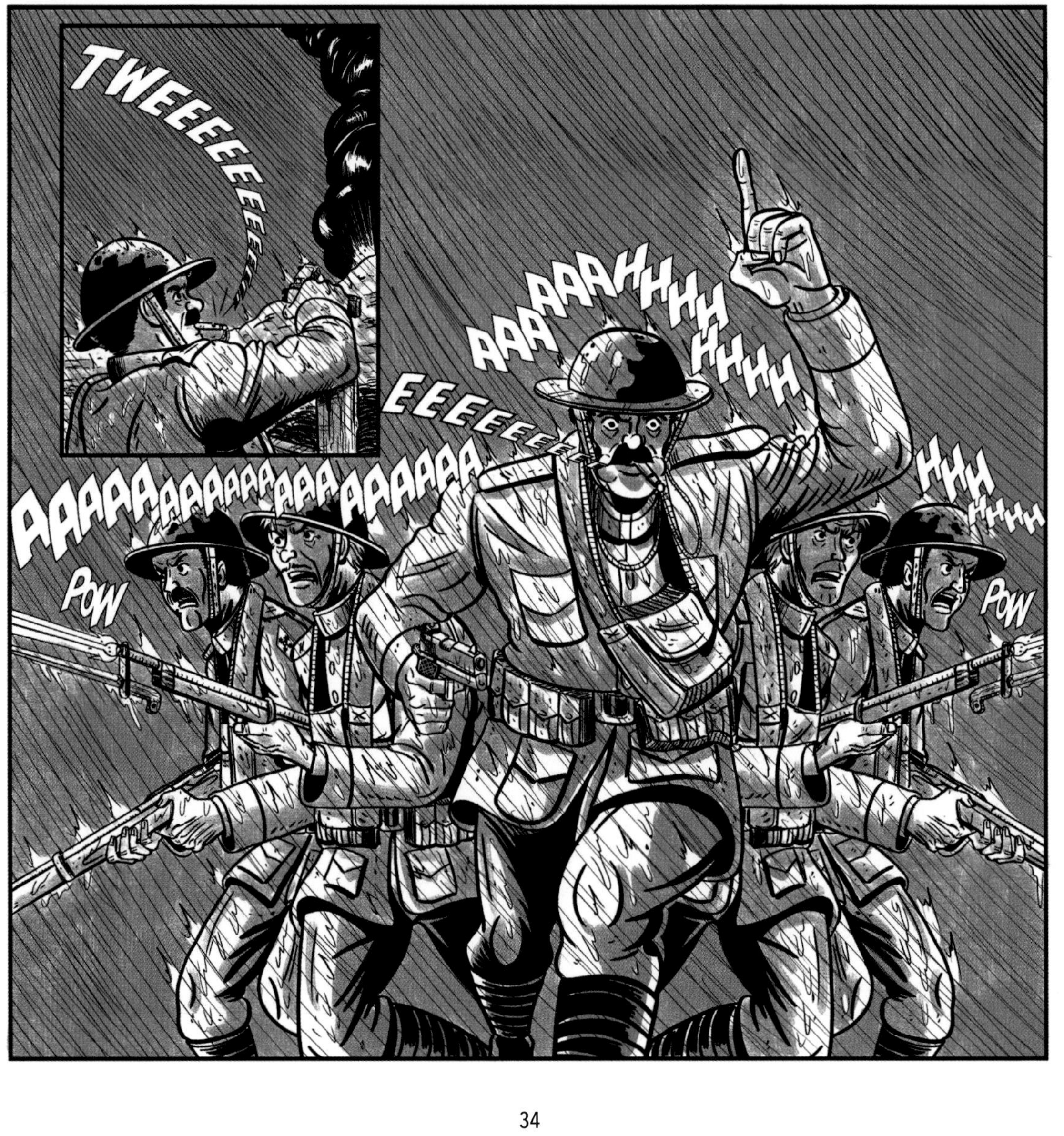
TWEEEEEEEEEEEEEE
EEEEEEEEEE
AAAAAAHHHHHHHHHHH
AAAAAAAAAAAAAAAAAA
HHHHHHH
POW
POW

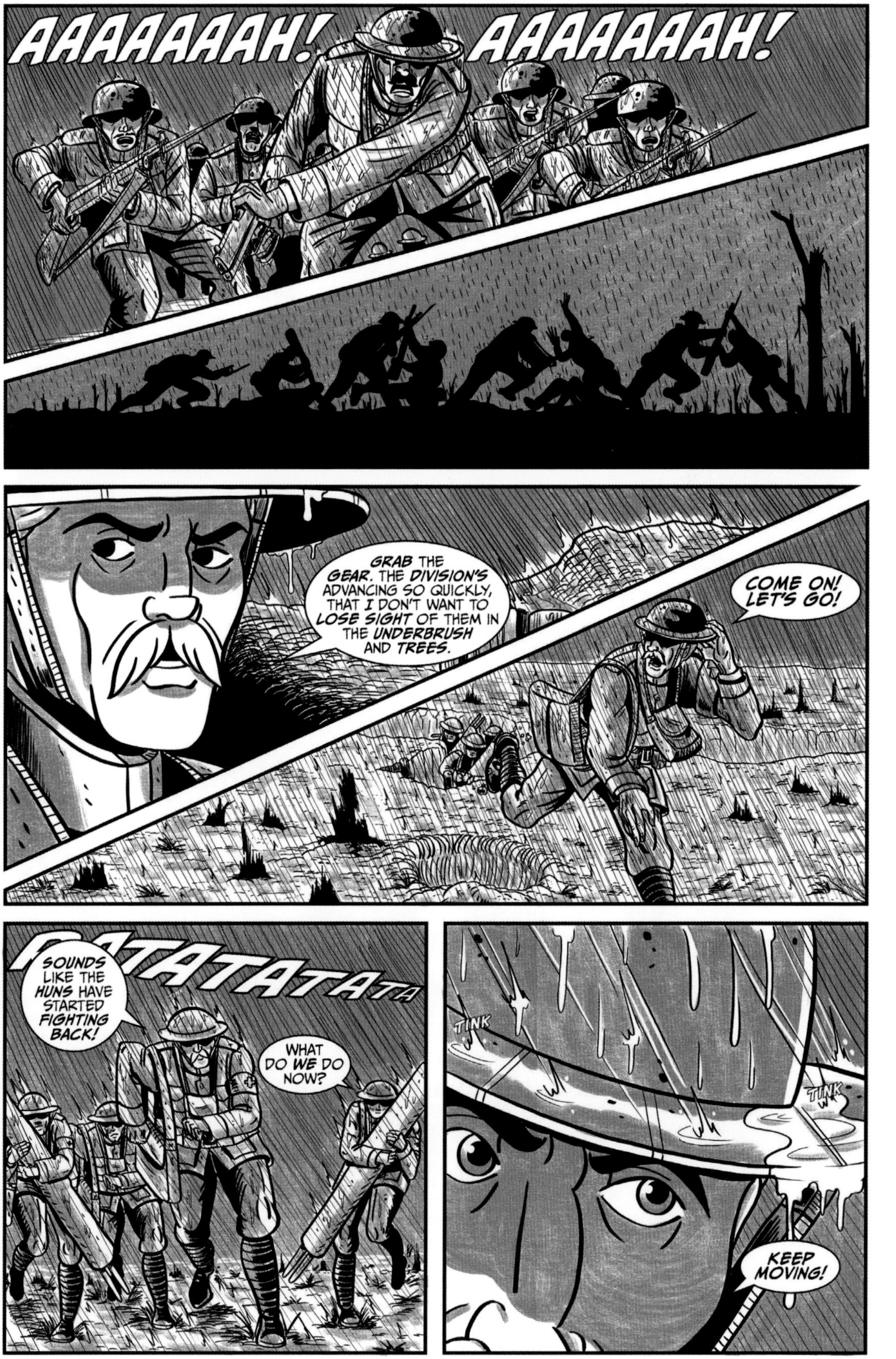
AAAAAAAH!
AAAAAAAAH!
GRAB THE GEAR. THE DIVISION'S ADVANCING SO QUICKLY, THAT I DON'T WANT TO LOSE SIGHT OF THEM IN THE UNDERBRUSH AND TREES.
COME ON! LET'S GO!
SOUNDS LIKE THE HUNS HAVE STARTED FIGHTING BACK!
WHAT DO WE DO NOW?
TINK
TINK
KEEP MOVING!

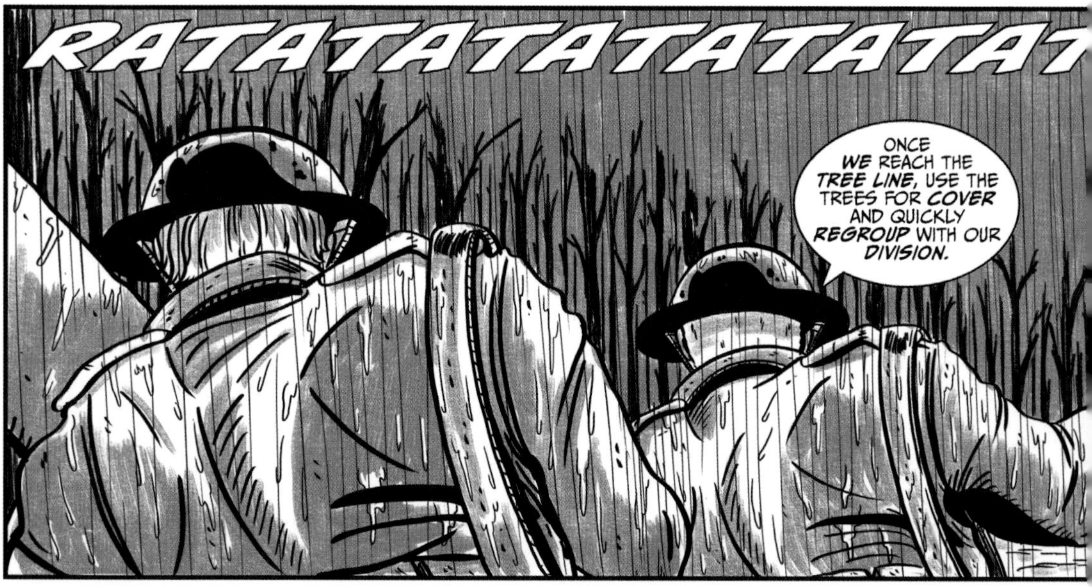
RATATATATATATATAT
ONCE WE REACH THE TREE LINE, USE THE TREES FOR COVER AND QUICKLY REGROUP WITH OUR DIVISION.

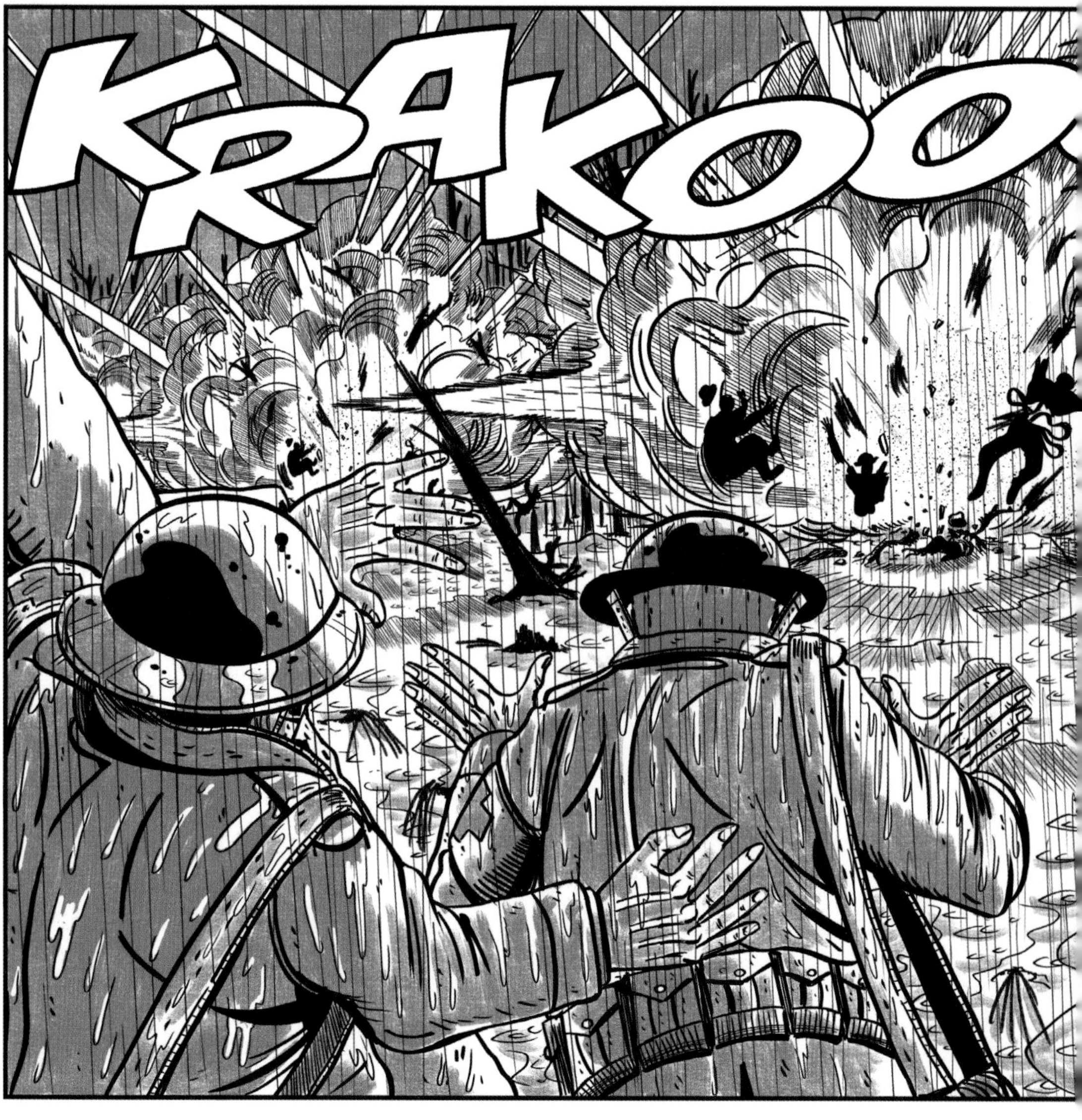
KRAKOO

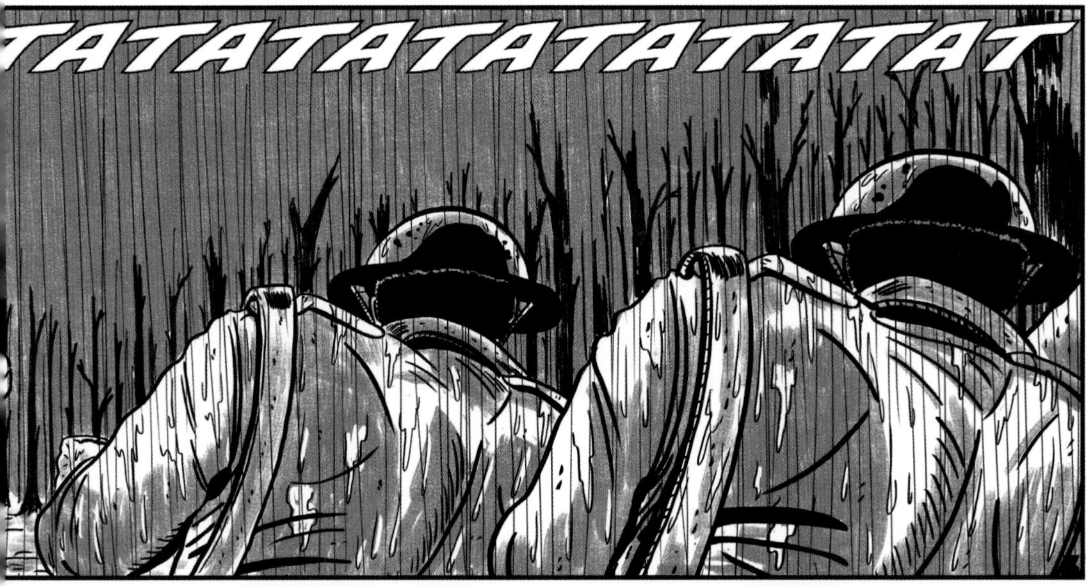
TATATATATATATATAT
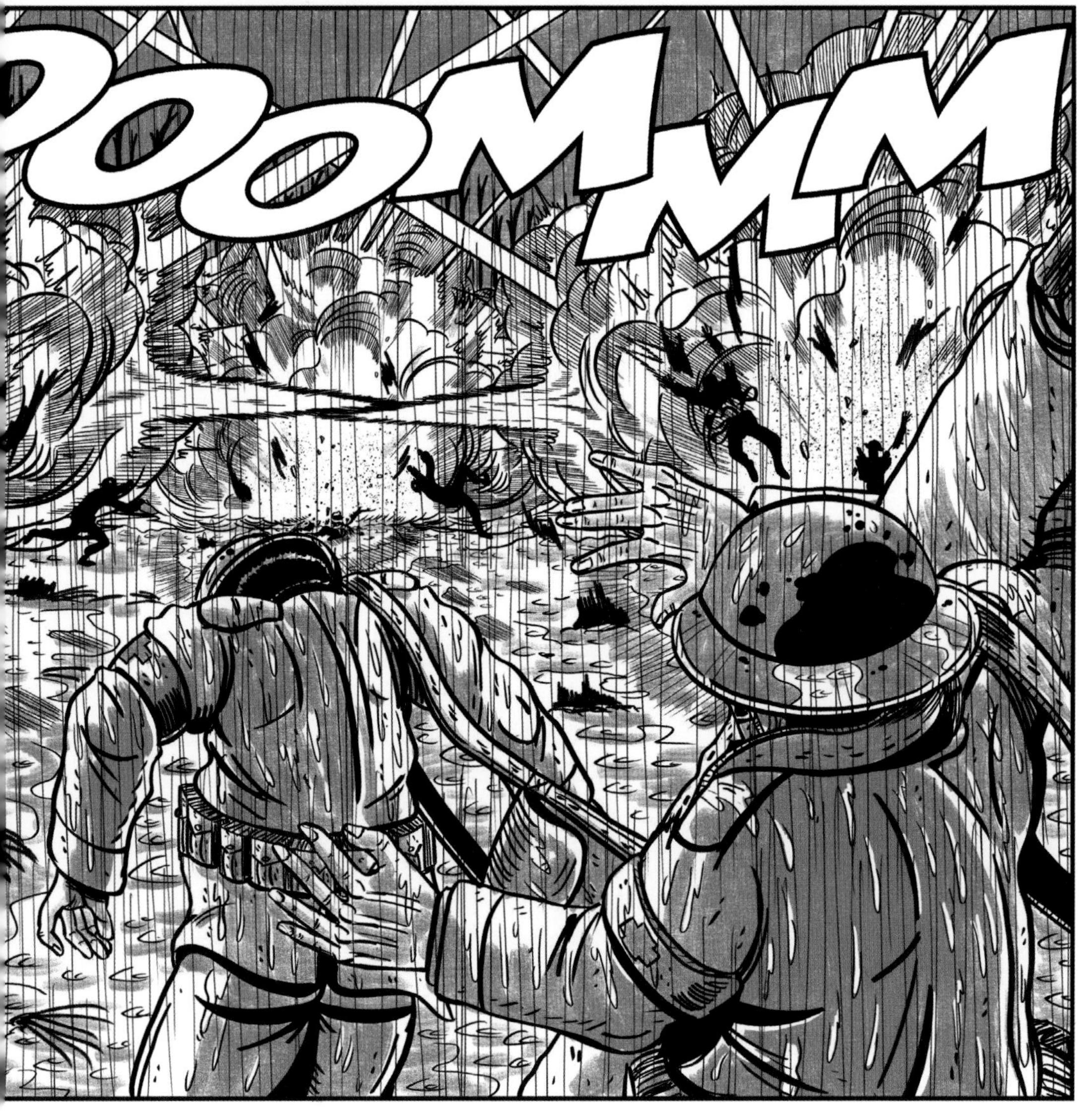
OOOMMM

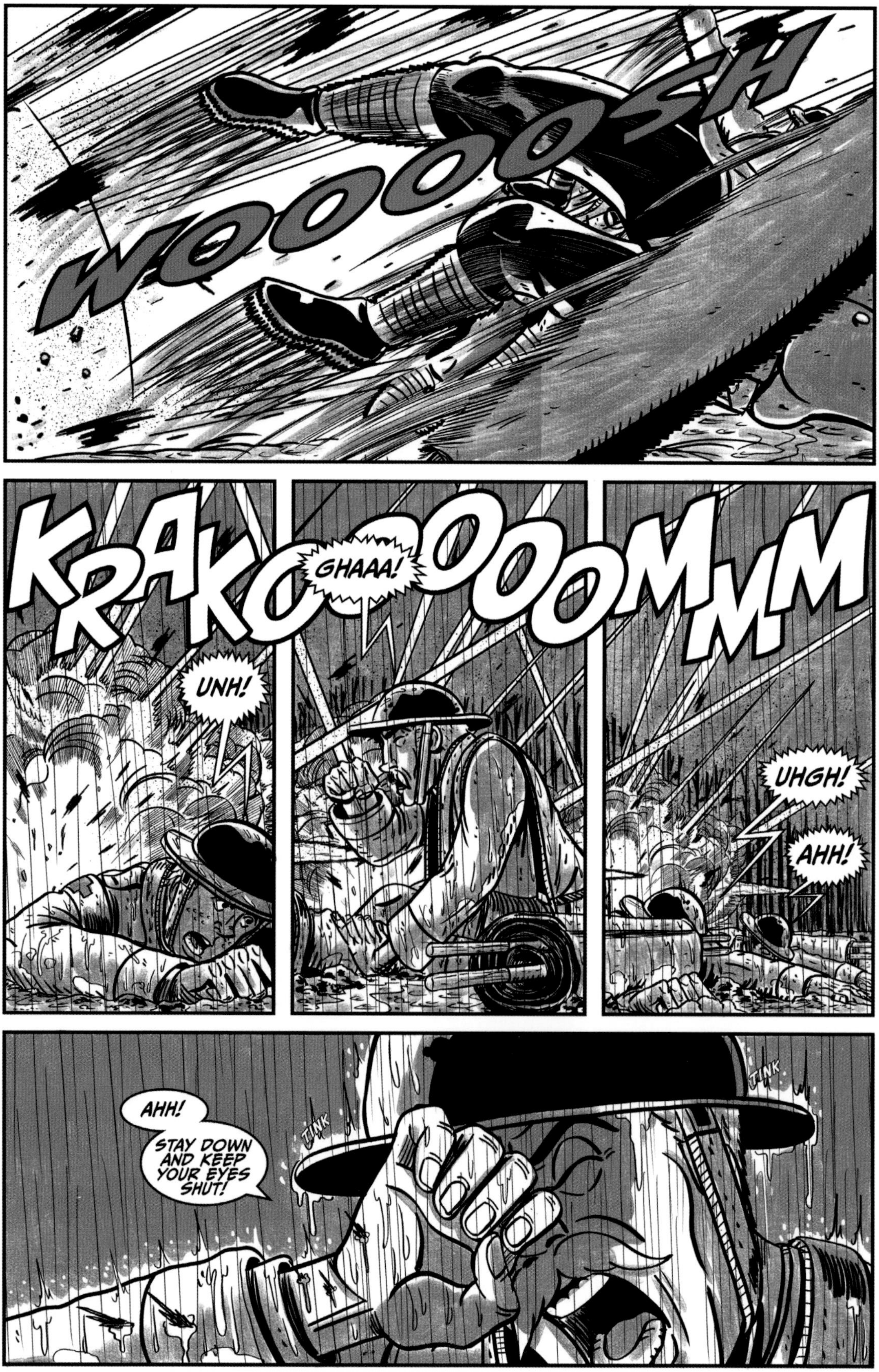
WOOOOOSH
KRAK
KRAKOOOOOMMMM
UNH!
GHAAA!
UHGH!
AHH!
AHH!
STAY DOWN AND KEEP YOUR EYES SHUT!
TINK
TINK

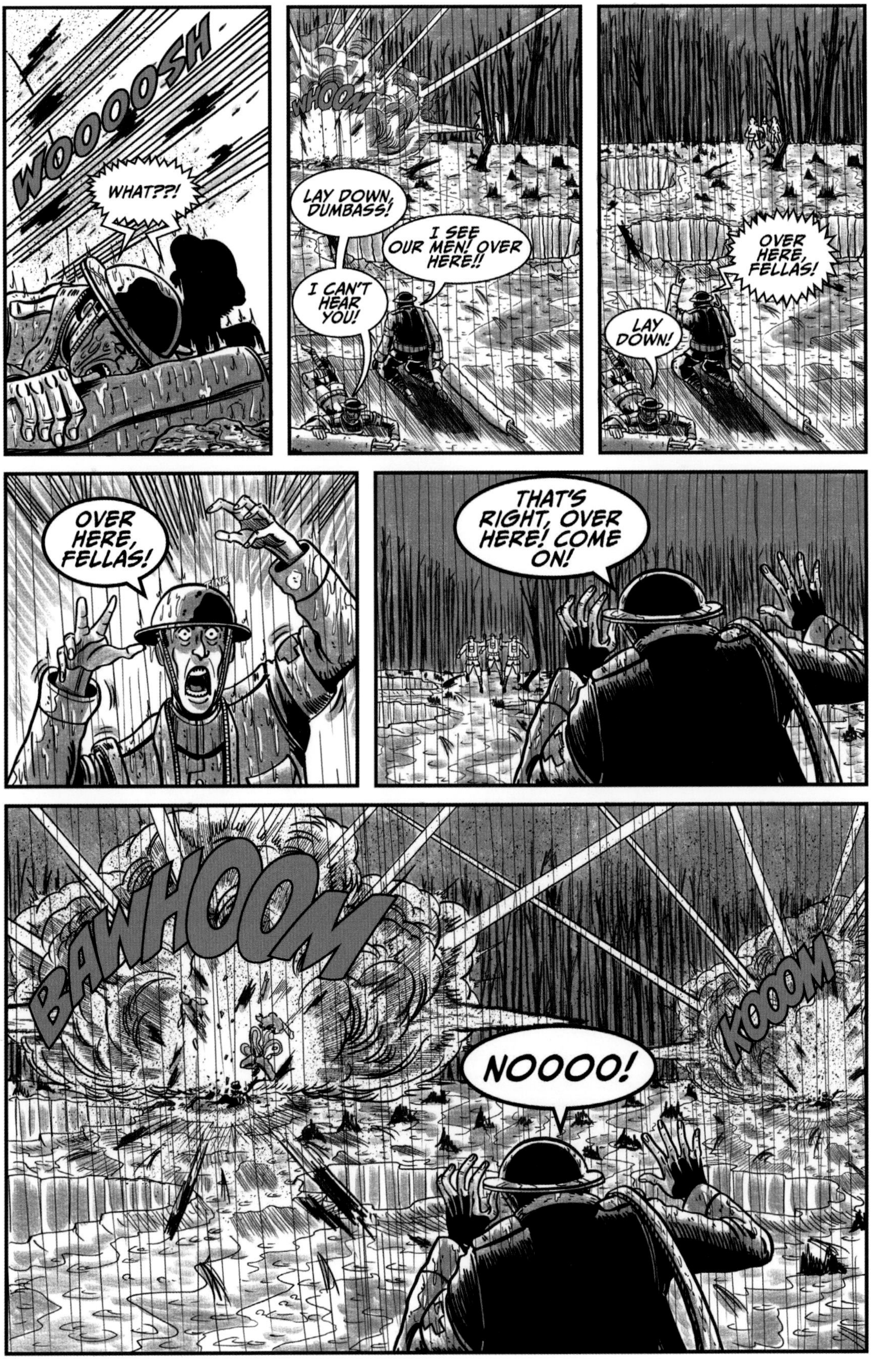
WOOOOSH
WHAT??!
WHOOM
LAY DOWN, DUMBASS!
I SEE OUR MEN! OVER HERE!!
I CAN'T HEAR YOU!
OVER HERE, FELLAS!
LAY DOWN!
OVER HERE, FELLAS!
THAT'S RIGHT, OVER HERE! COME ON!
BAWHOOM
KOOOM
NOOOO!

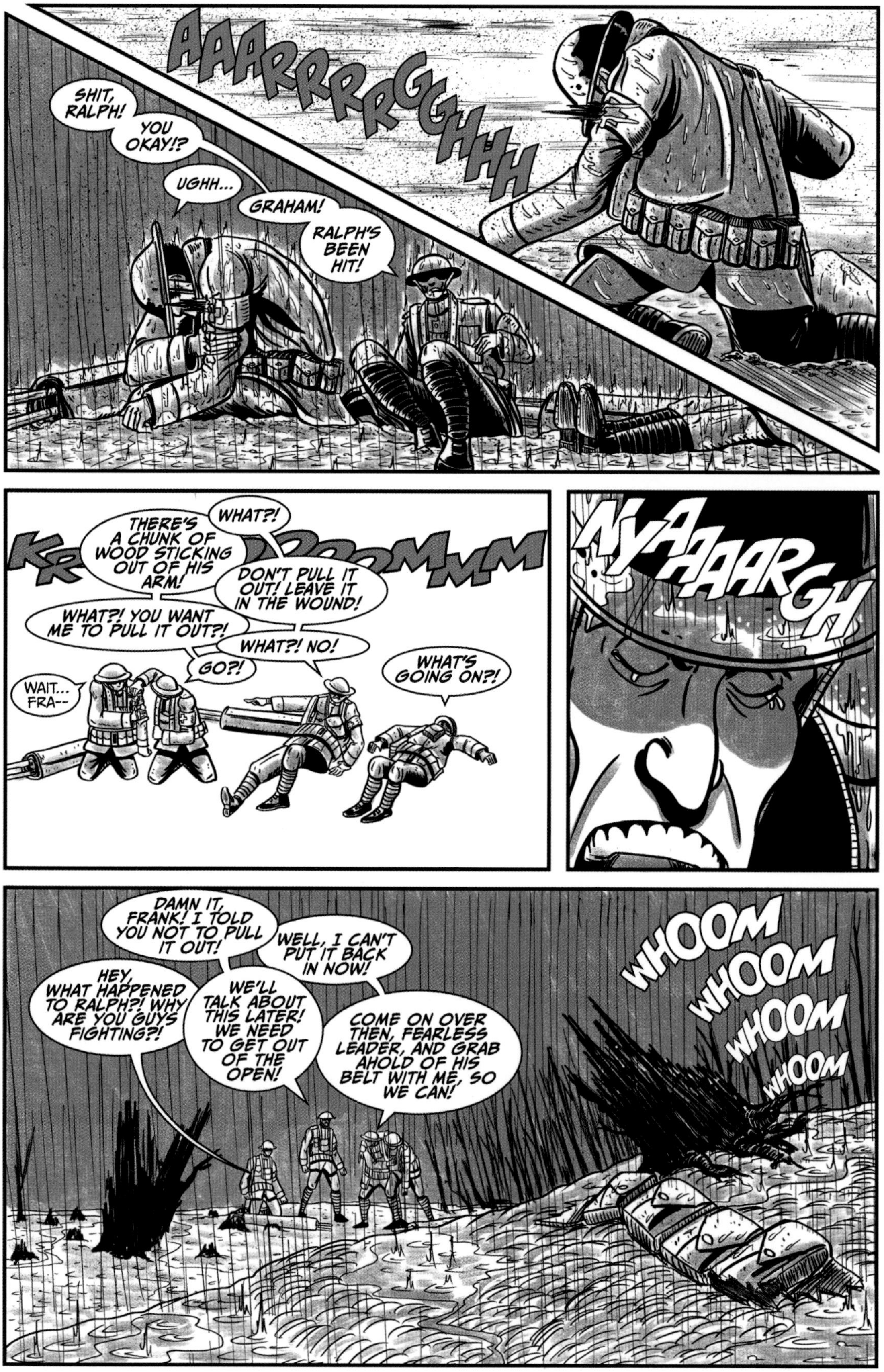
AAARRRRRGGHHHH
SHIT, RALPH!
YOU OKAY!?
UGHH...
GRAHAM!
RALPH'S BEEN HIT!
KRRRRRRROOOOOMMMM
THERE'S A CHUNK OF WOOD STICKING OUT OF HIS ARM!
WHAT?!
DON'T PULL IT OUT! LEAVE IT IN THE WOUND!
WHAT?! YOU WANT ME TO PULL IT OUT?!
WHAT?! NO!
GO?!
WAIT... FRA--
WHAT'S GOING ON?!
NYAAAARGH
DAMN IT, FRANK! I TOLD YOU NOT TO PULL IT OUT!
WELL, I CAN'T PUT IT BACK IN NOW!
HEY, WHAT HAPPENED TO RALPH?! WHY ARE YOU GUYS FIGHTING?!
WE'LL TALK ABOUT THIS LATER! WE NEED TO GET OUT OF THE OPEN!
COME ON OVER THEN, FEARLESS LEADER, AND GRAB AHOLD OF HIS BELT WITH ME, SO WE CAN!
WHOOM
WHOOM
WHOOM
WHOOM

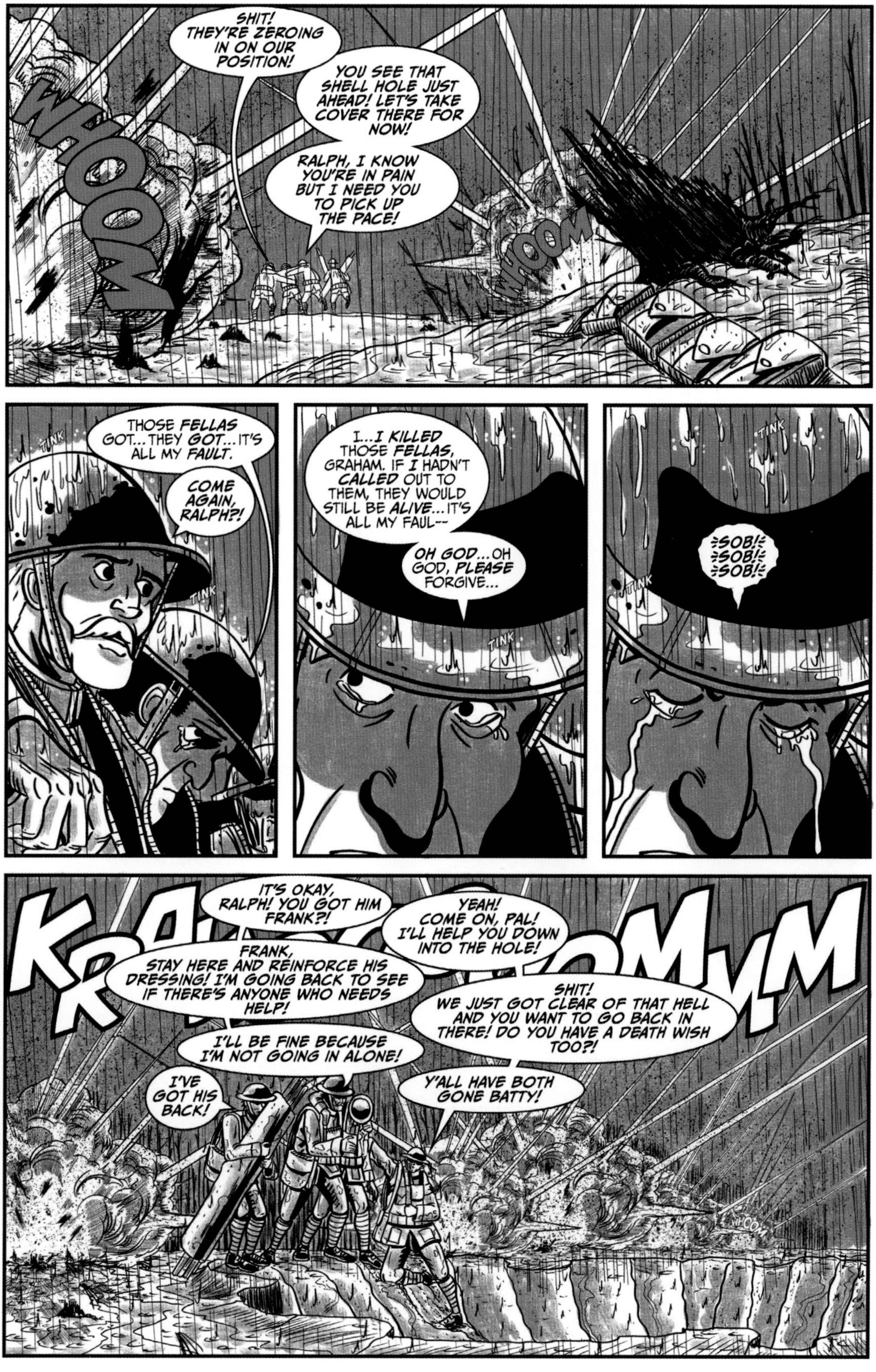
SHIT! THEY'RE ZEROING IN ON OUR POSITION!
YOU SEE THAT SHELL HOLE JUST AHEAD! LET'S TAKE COVER THERE FOR NOW!
RALPH, I KNOW YOU'RE IN PAIN BUT I NEED YOU TO PICK UP THE PACE!
WHOOM
WHOOM
TINK
THOSE FELLAS GOT... THEY GOT... IT'S ALL MY FAULT.
COME AGAIN, RALPH?!
TINK
I... I KILLED THOSE FELLAS, GRAHAM. IF I HADN'T CALLED OUT TO THEM, THEY WOULD STILL BE ALIVE... IT'S ALL MY FAUL--
OH GOD... OH GOD, PLEASE FORGIVE...
TINK
TINK
SOB! SOB! SOB!
TINK
IT'S OKAY, RALPH! YOU GOT HIM FRANK?!
YEAH! COME ON, PAL! I'LL HELP YOU DOWN INTO THE HOLE!
FRANK, STAY HERE AND REINFORCE HIS DRESSING! I'M GOING BACK TO SEE IF THERE'S ANYONE WHO NEEDS HELP!
SHIT! WE JUST GOT CLEAR OF THAT HELL AND YOU WANT TO GO BACK IN THERE! DO YOU HAVE A DEATH WISH TOO?!
I'LL BE FINE BECAUSE I'M NOT GOING IN ALONE!
I'VE GOT HIS BACK!
Y'ALL HAVE BOTH GONE BATTY!
WHOOM

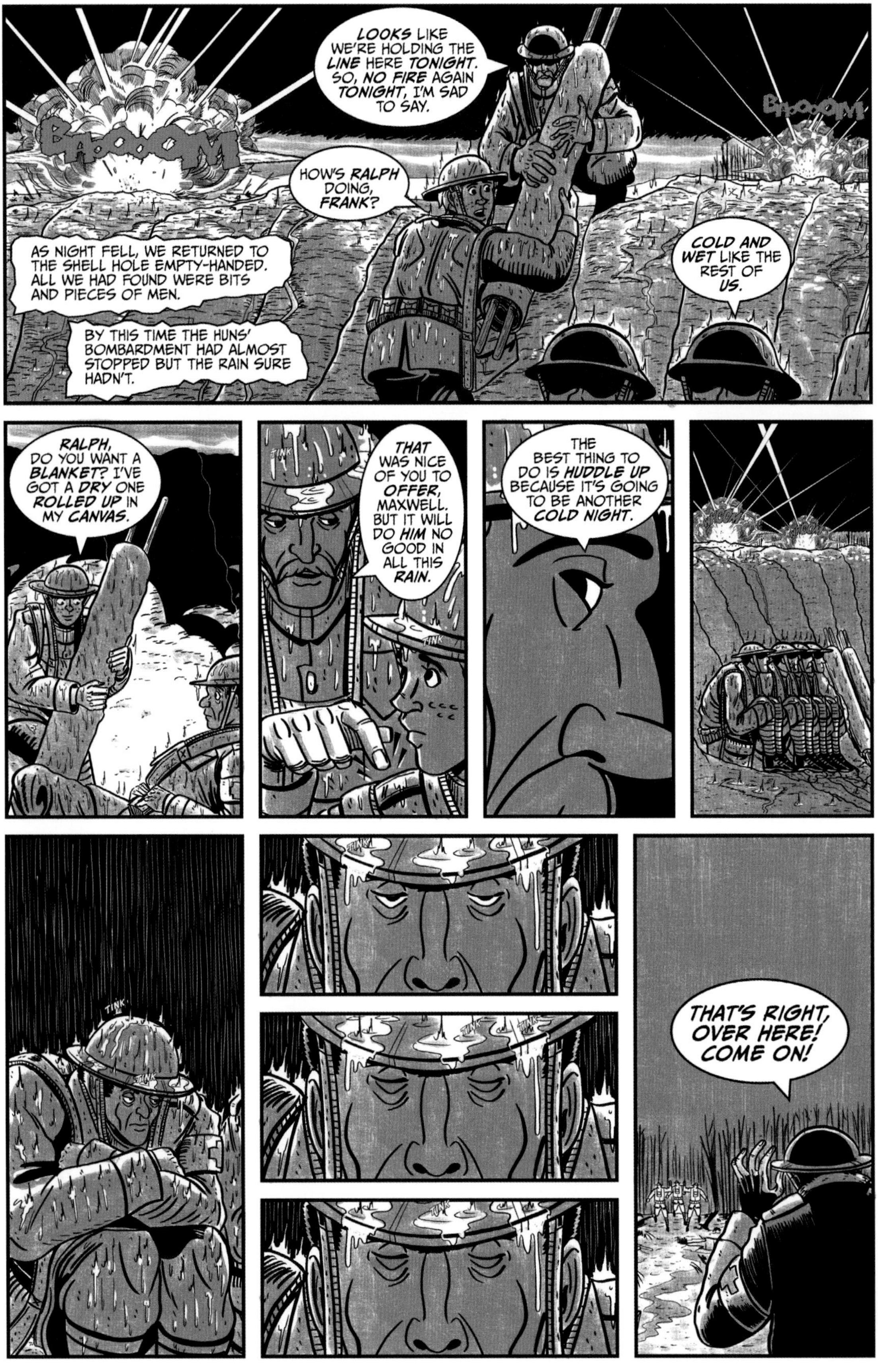

LOOKS LIKE WE'RE HOLDING THE LINE HERE TONIGHT. SO, NO FIRE AGAIN TONIGHT, I'M SAD TO SAY.
HOW'S RALPH DOING, FRANK?
AS NIGHT FELL, WE RETURNED TO THE SHELL HOLE EMPTY-HANDED. ALL WE HAD FOUND WERE BITS AND PIECES OF MEN.
BY THIS TIME THE HUNS' BOMBARDMENT HAD ALMOST STOPPED BUT THE RAIN SURE HADN'T.
COLD AND WET LIKE THE REST OF US.
RALPH, DO YOU WANT A BLANKET? I'VE GOT A DRY ONE ROLLED UP IN MY CANVAS.
THAT WAS NICE OF YOU TO OFFER, MAXWELL. BUT IT WILL DO HIM NO GOOD IN ALL THIS RAIN.
THE BEST THING TO DO IS HUDDLE UP BECAUSE IT'S GOING TO BE ANOTHER COLD NIGHT.
THAT'S RIGHT, OVER HERE! COME ON!

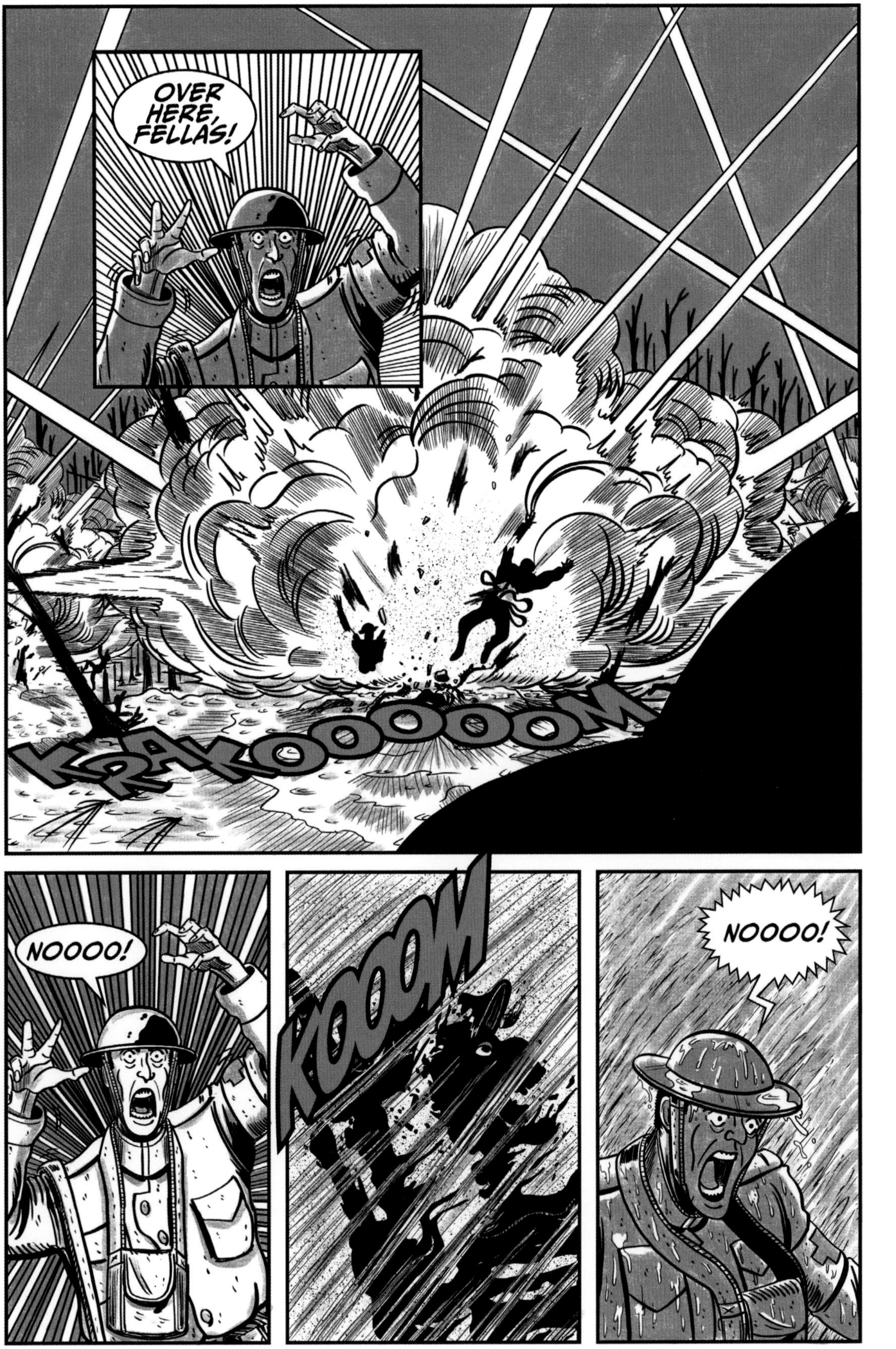
OVER HERE, FELLAS!
KRAKOOOOOM
NOOOO!
KOOOM
NOOOO!

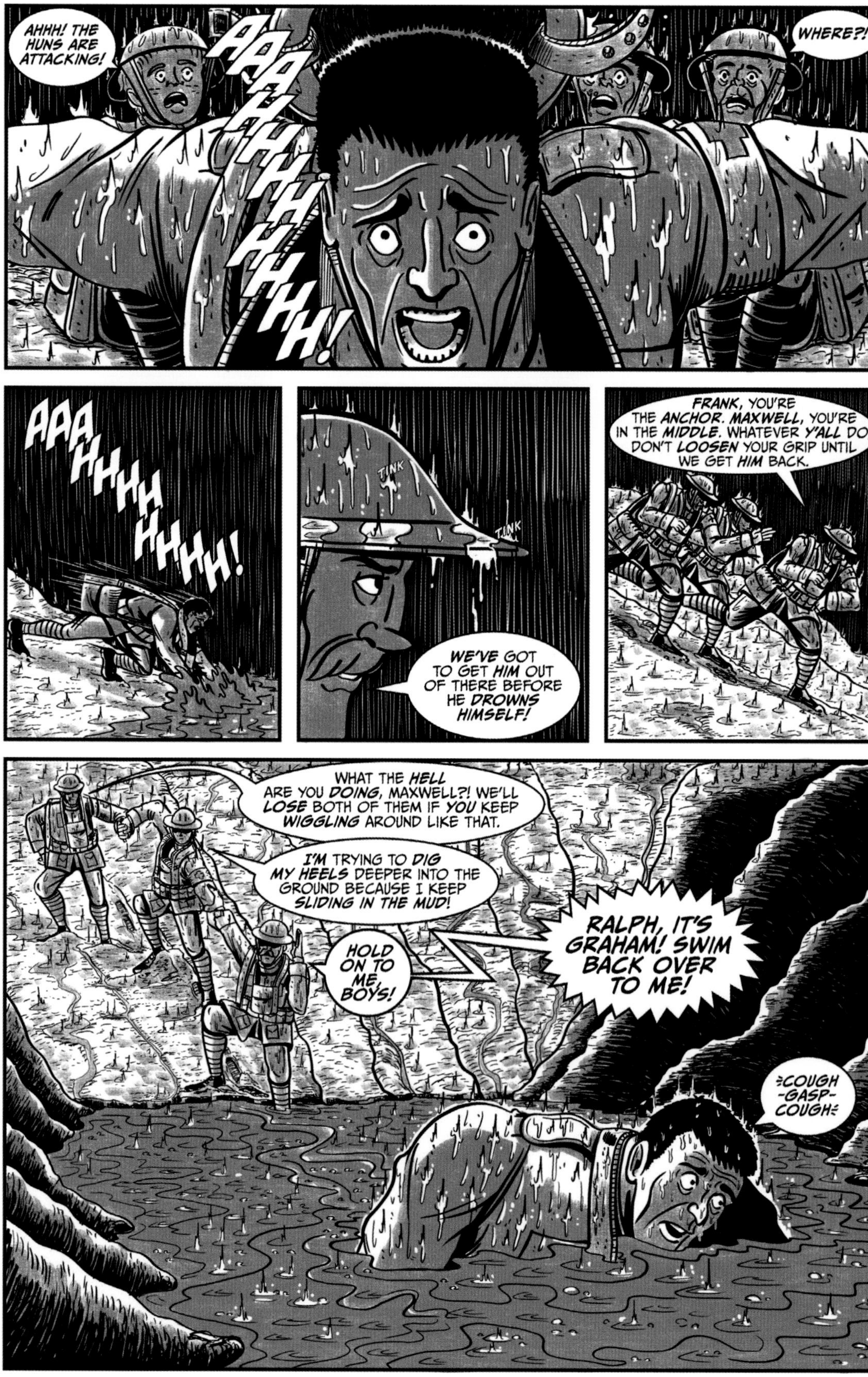
AHHH! THE HUNS ARE ATTACKING!
AAAHHHHHHHHHH!
WHERE?!
AAAHHHHHHHHH!
TINK
TINK
WE'VE GOT TO GET HIM OUT OF THERE BEFORE HE DROWNS HIMSELF!
FRANK, YOU'RE THE ANCHOR. MAXWELL, YOU'RE IN THE MIDDLE. WHATEVER Y'ALL DO, DON'T LOOSEN YOUR GRIP UNTIL WE GET HIM BACK.
WHAT THE HELL ARE YOU DOING, MAXWELL?! WE'LL LOSE BOTH OF THEM IF YOU KEEP WIGGLING AROUND LIKE THAT.
I'M TRYING TO DIG MY HEELS DEEPER INTO THE GROUND BECAUSE I KEEP SLIDING IN THE MUD!
HOLD ON TO ME, BOYS!
RALPH, IT'S GRAHAM! SWIM BACK OVER TO ME!
-COUGH-GASP-COUGH-

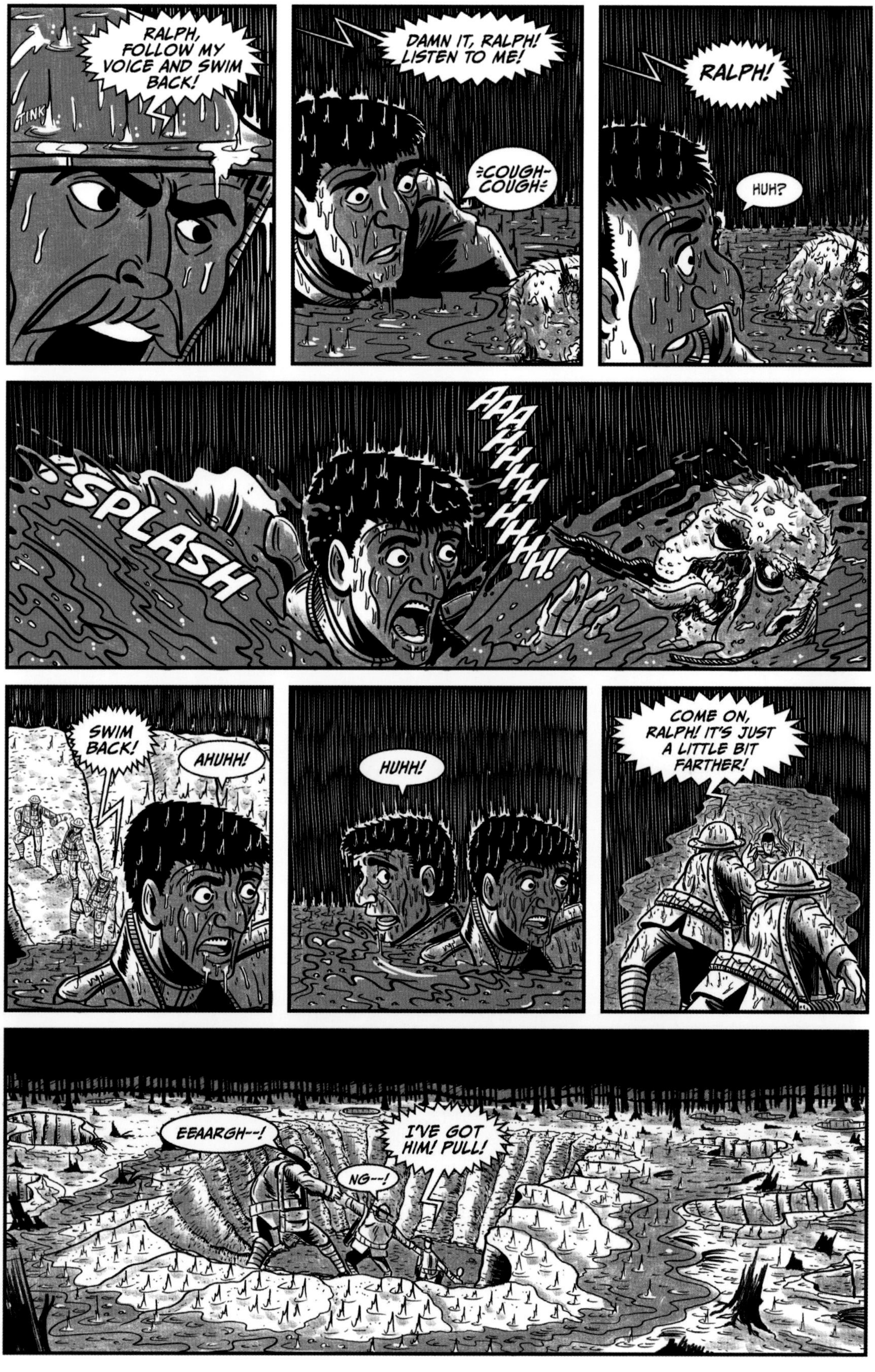
RALPH, FOLLOW MY VOICE AND SWIM BACK!
TINK
DAMN IT, RALPH! LISTEN TO ME!
COUGH-COUGH
RALPH!
HUH?
SPLASH
AAAHHHHHHHHH!
SWIM BACK!
AHUHH!
HUHH!
COME ON, RALPH! IT'S JUST A LITTLE BIT FARTHER!
EEAARGH--!
I'VE GOT HIM! PULL!
NG--!

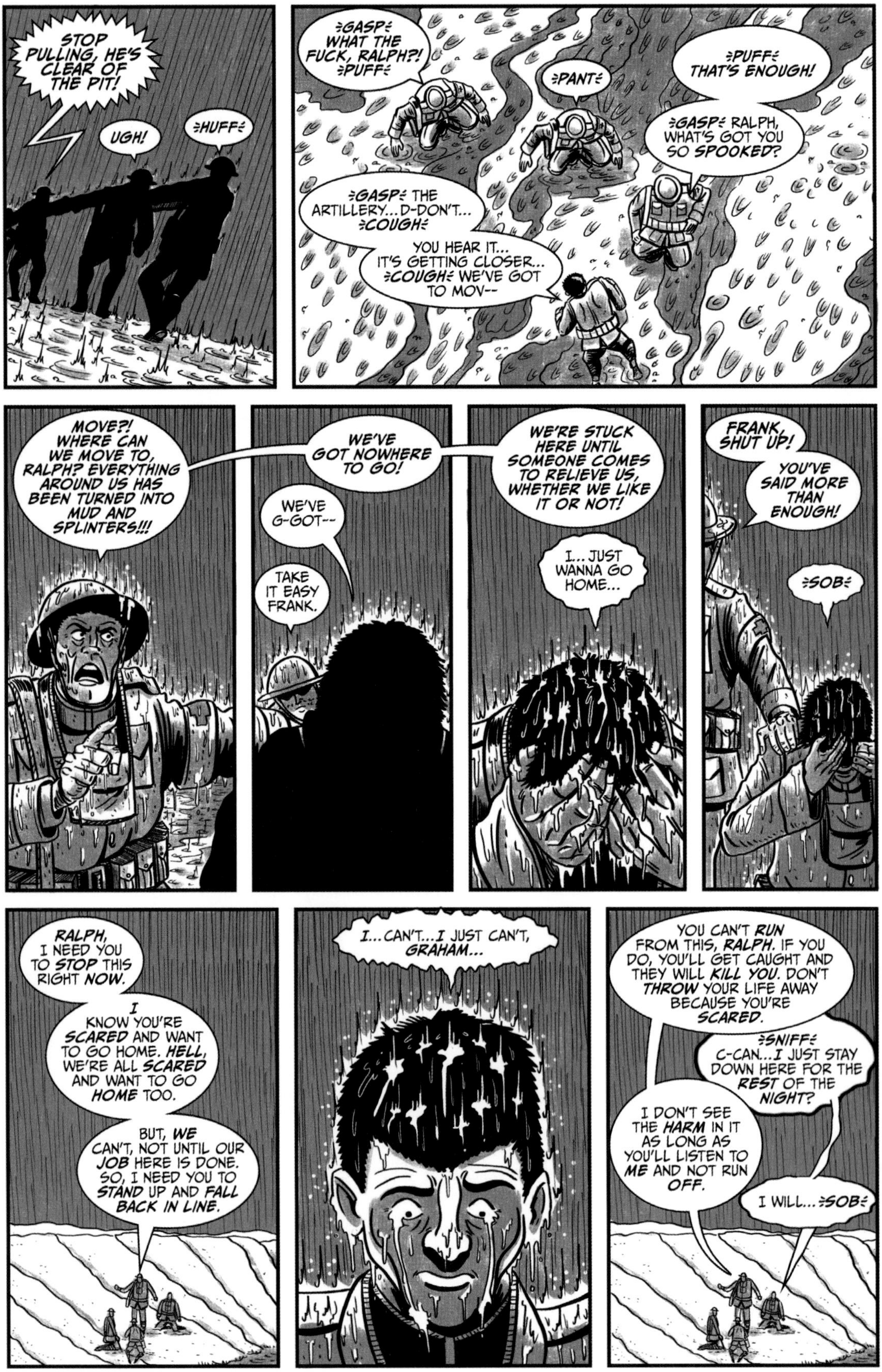
STOP PULLING, HE'S CLEAR OF THE PIT!
UGH!
HUFF
GASP WHAT THE FUCK, RALPH?! PUFF
PANT
PUFF THAT'S ENOUGH!
GASP RALPH, WHAT'S GOT YOU SO SPOOKED?
GASP THE ARTILLERY...D-DON'T... COUGH
YOU HEAR IT... IT'S GETTING CLOSER... COUGH WE'VE GOT TO MOV--
MOVE?! WHERE CAN WE MOVE TO, RALPH? EVERYTHING AROUND US HAS BEEN TURNED INTO MUD AND SPLINTERS!!!
WE'VE GOT NOWHERE TO GO!
WE'RE STUCK HERE UNTIL SOMEONE COMES TO RELIEVE US, WHETHER WE LIKE IT OR NOT!
WE'VE G-GOT--
TAKE IT EASY FRANK.
I... JUST WANNA GO HOME...
FRANK, SHUT UP!
YOU'VE SAID MORE THAN ENOUGH!
SOB
RALPH, I NEED YOU TO STOP THIS RIGHT NOW.
I KNOW YOU'RE SCARED AND WANT TO GO HOME. HELL, WE'RE ALL SCARED AND WANT TO GO HOME TOO.
BUT, WE CAN'T, NOT UNTIL OUR JOB HERE IS DONE. SO, I NEED YOU TO STAND UP AND FALL BACK IN LINE.
I...CAN'T...I JUST CAN'T, GRAHAM...
YOU CAN'T RUN FROM THIS, RALPH. IF YOU DO, YOU'LL GET CAUGHT AND THEY WILL KILL YOU. DON'T THROW YOUR LIFE AWAY BECAUSE YOU'RE SCARED.
SNIFF C-CAN...I JUST STAY DOWN HERE FOR THE REST OF THE NIGHT?
I DON'T SEE THE HARM IN IT AS LONG AS YOU'LL LISTEN TO ME AND NOT RUN OFF.
I WILL... SOB

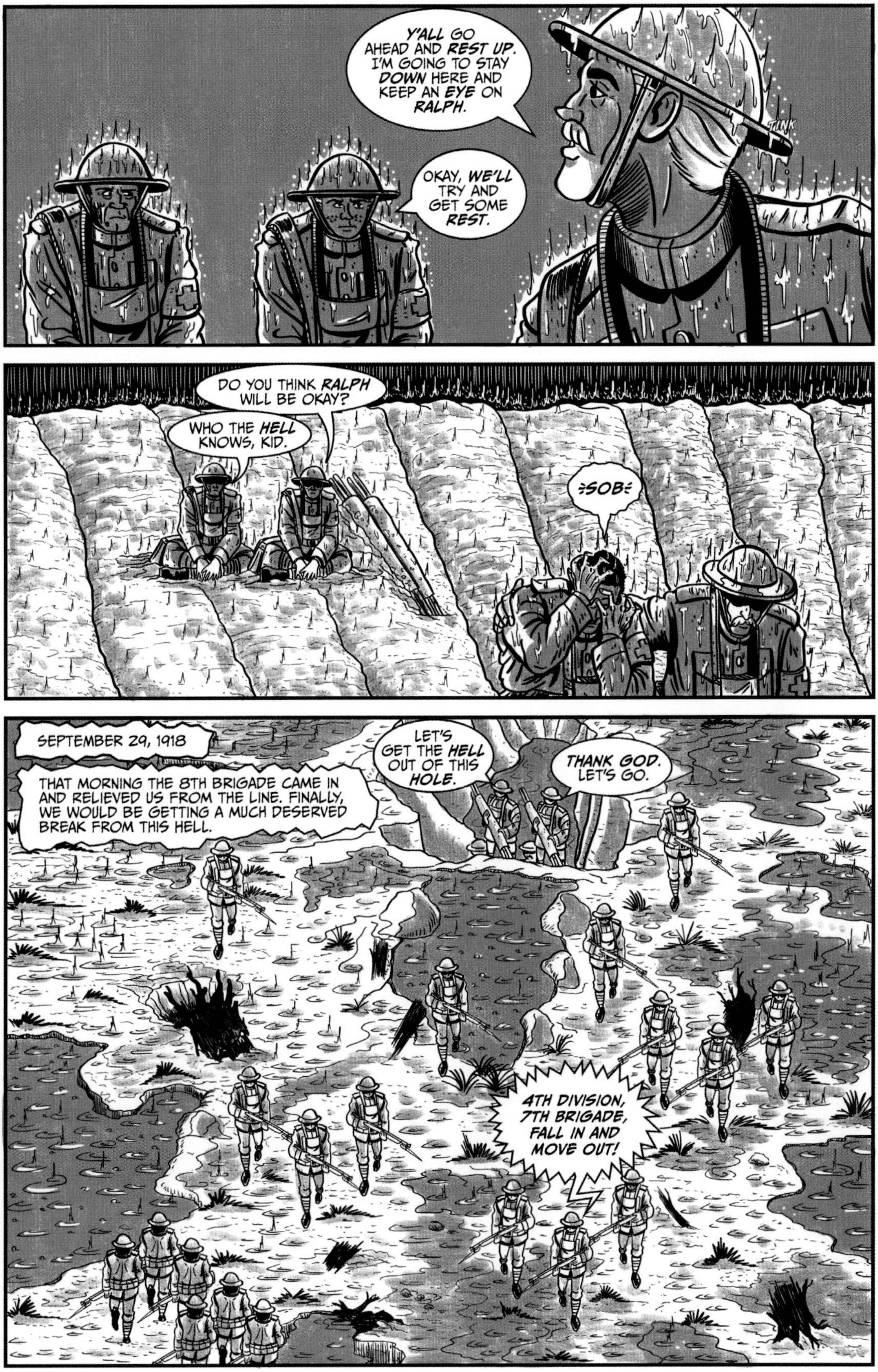
Y'ALL GO AHEAD AND REST UP. I'M GOING TO STAY DOWN HERE AND KEEP AN EYE ON RALPH.
OKAY, WE'LL TRY AND GET SOME REST.
TINK
DO YOU THINK RALPH WILL BE OKAY?
WHO THE HELL KNOWS, KID.
SOB
SEPTEMBER 29, 1918
THAT MORNING THE 8TH BRIGADE CAME IN AND RELIEVED US FROM THE LINE. FINALLY, WE WOULD BE GETTING A MUCH DESERVED BREAK FROM THIS HELL.
LET'S GET THE HELL OUT OF THIS HOLE.
THANK GOD. LET'S GO.
4TH DIVISION, 7TH BRIGADE, FALL IN AND MOVE OUT!

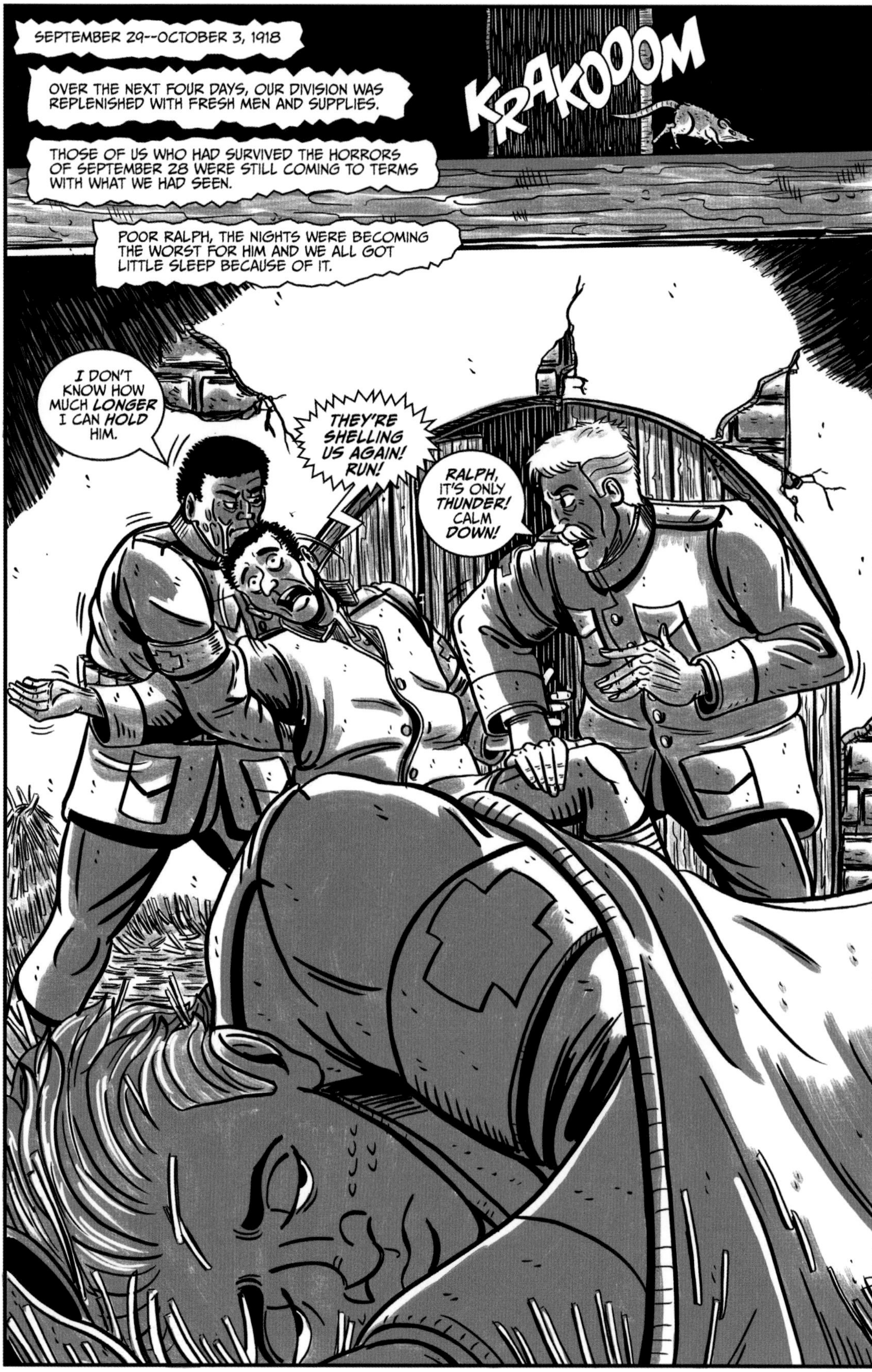
SEPTEMBER 29--OCTOBER 3, 1918
OVER THE NEXT FOUR DAYS, OUR DIVISION WAS REPLENISHED WITH FRESH MEN AND SUPPLIES.
THOSE OF US WHO HAD SURVIVED THE HORRORS OF SEPTEMBER 28 WERE STILL COMING TO TERMS WITH WHAT WE HAD SEEN.
KRAKOOOM
POOR RALPH, THE NIGHTS WERE BECOMING THE WORST FOR HIM AND WE ALL GOT LITTLE SLEEP BECAUSE OF IT.
I DON'T KNOW HOW MUCH LONGER I CAN HOLD HIM.
THEY'RE SHELLING US AGAIN! RUN!
RALPH, IT'S ONLY THUNDER! CALM DOWN!

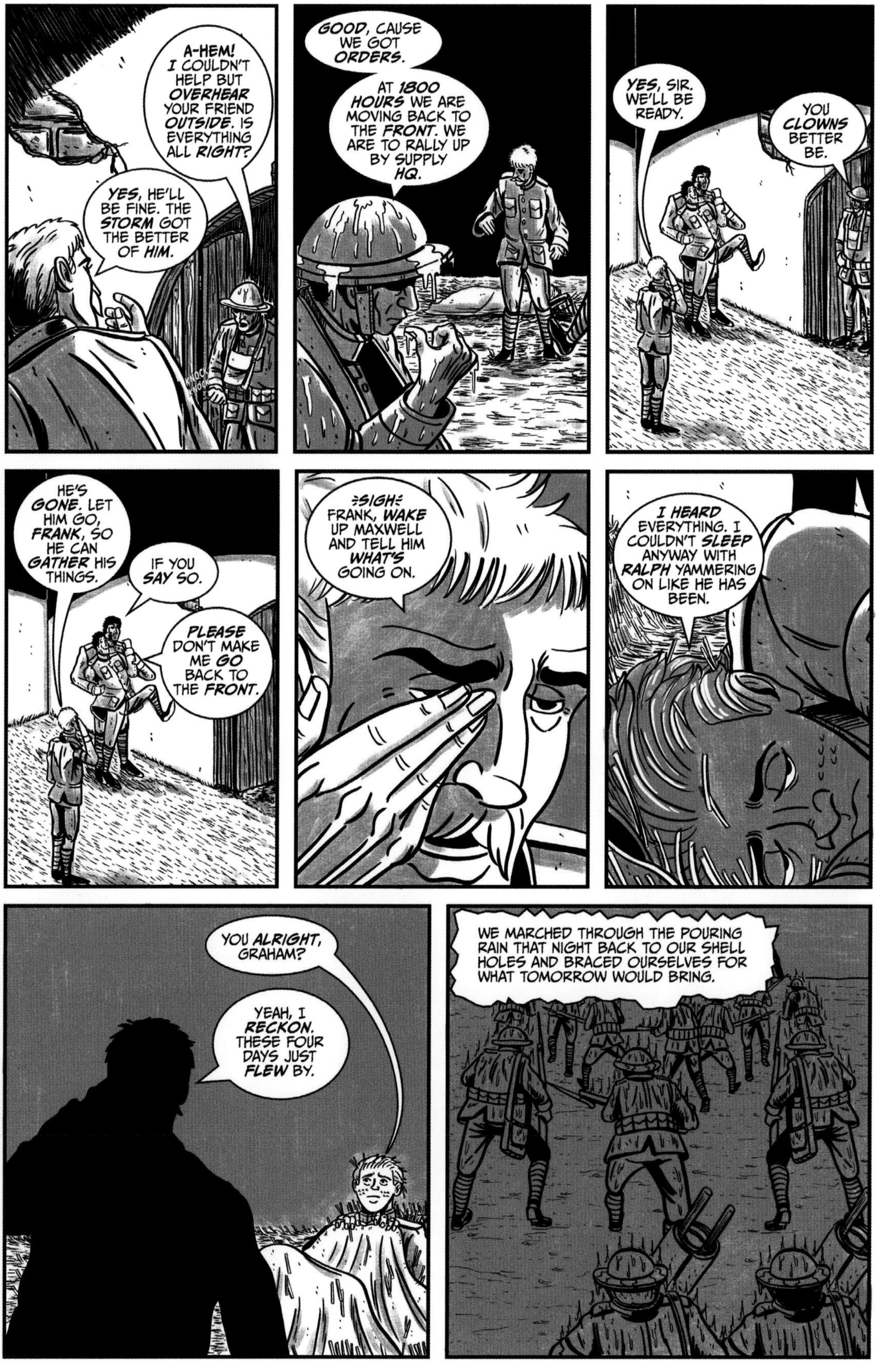
A-HEM! I COULDN'T HELP BUT OVERHEAR YOUR FRIEND OUTSIDE. IS EVERYTHING ALL RIGHT?
YES, HE'LL BE FINE. THE STORM GOT THE BETTER OF HIM.
KNOCK KNOCK
GOOD, CAUSE WE GOT ORDERS.
AT 1800 HOURS WE ARE MOVING BACK TO THE FRONT. WE ARE TO RALLY UP BY SUPPLY HQ.
YES, SIR. WE'LL BE READY.
YOU CLOWNS BETTER BE.
HE'S GONE. LET HIM GO, FRANK, SO HE CAN GATHER HIS THINGS.
IF YOU SAY SO.
PLEASE DON'T MAKE ME GO BACK TO THE FRONT.
SIGH FRANK, WAKE UP MAXWELL AND TELL HIM WHAT'S GOING ON.
I HEARD EVERYTHING. I COULDN'T SLEEP ANYWAY WITH RALPH YAMMERING ON LIKE HE HAS BEEN.
YOU ALRIGHT, GRAHAM?
YEAH, I RECKON. THESE FOUR DAYS JUST FLEW BY.
WE MARCHED THROUGH THE POURING RAIN THAT NIGHT BACK TO OUR SHELL HOLES AND BRACED OURSELVES FOR WHAT TOMORROW WOULD BRING.

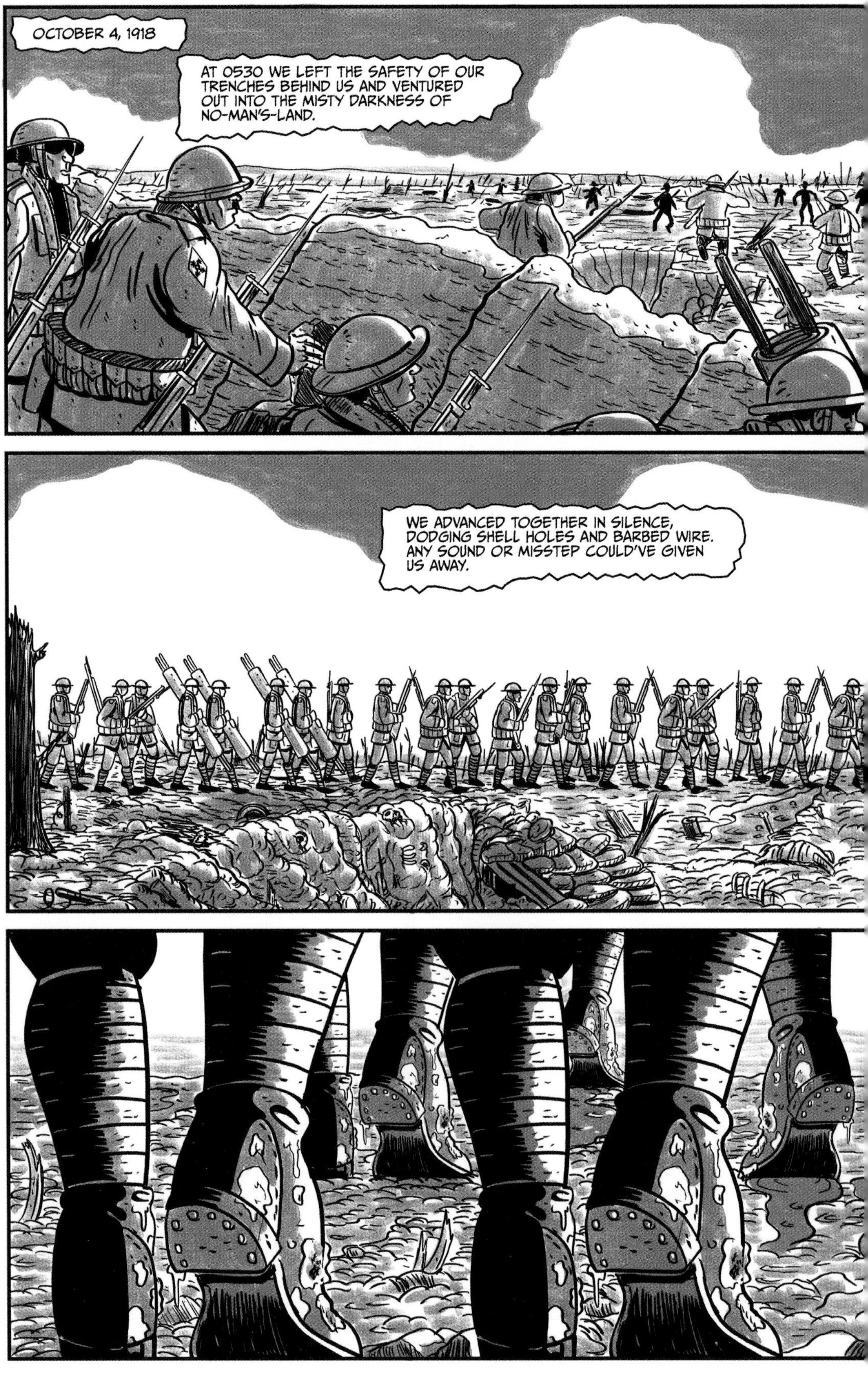
OCTOBER 4, 1918
AT 0530 WE LEFT THE SAFETY OF OUR TRENCHES BEHIND US AND VENTURED OUT INTO THE MISTY DARKNESS OF NO-MAN'S-LAND.
WE ADVANCED TOGETHER IN SILENCE, DODGING SHELL HOLES AND BARBED WIRE. ANY SOUND OR MISSTEP COULD'VE GIVEN US AWAY.

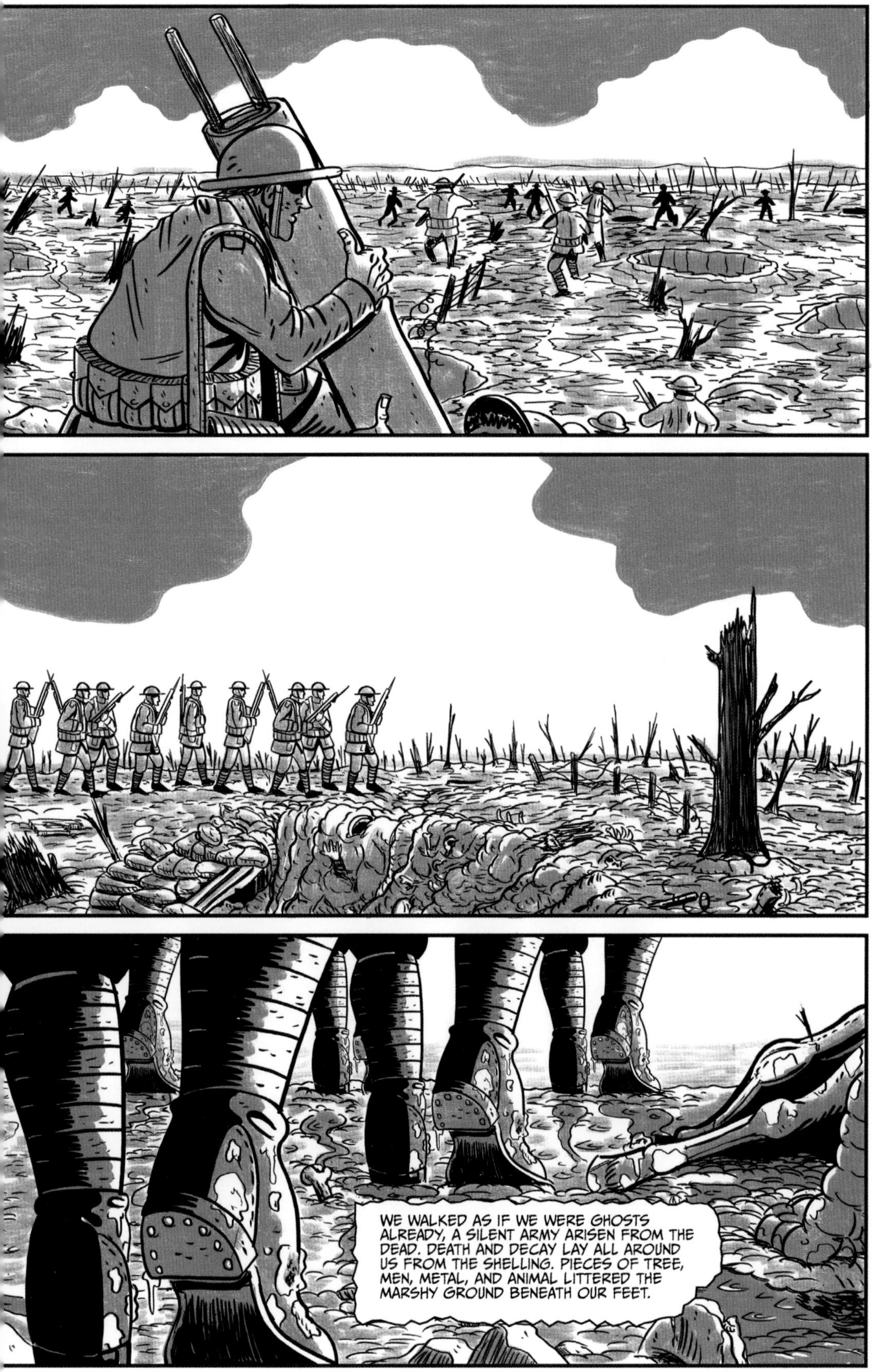
WE WALKED AS IF WE WERE GHOSTS ALREADY, A SILENT ARMY ARISEN FROM THE DEAD. DEATH AND DECAY LAY ALL AROUND US FROM THE SHELLING. PIECES OF TREE, MEN, METAL, AND ANIMAL LITTERED THE MARSHY GROUND BENEATH OUR FEET.

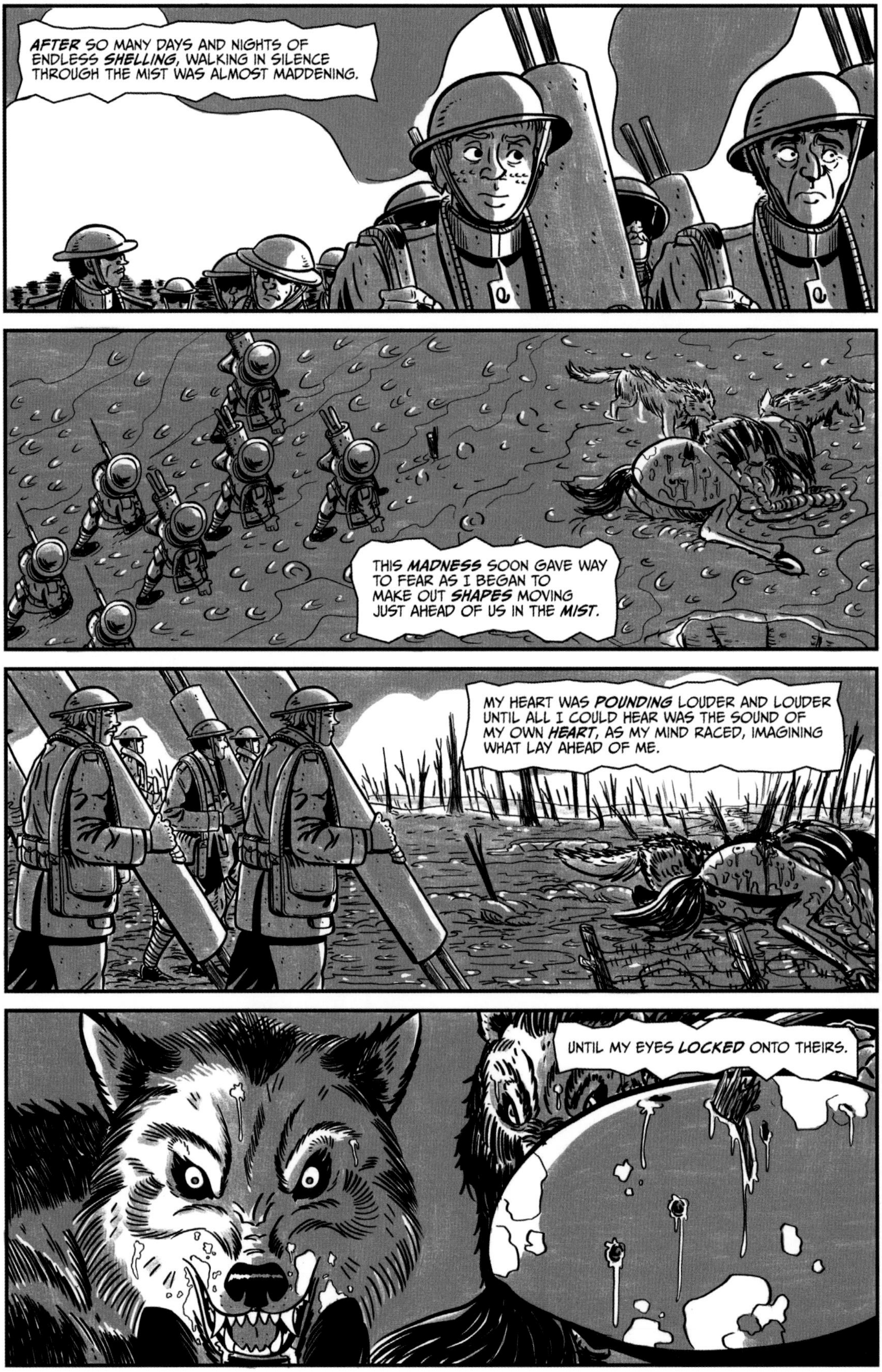
AFTER SO MANY DAYS AND NIGHTS OF ENDLESS SHELLING, WALKING IN SILENCE THROUGH THE MIST WAS ALMOST MADDENING.
THIS MADNESS SOON GAVE WAY TO FEAR AS I BEGAN TO MAKE OUT SHAPES MOVING JUST AHEAD OF US IN THE MIST.
MY HEART WAS POUNDING LOUDER AND LOUDER UNTIL ALL I COULD HEAR WAS THE SOUND OF MY OWN HEART, AS MY MIND RACED, IMAGINING WHAT LAY AHEAD OF ME.
UNTIL MY EYES LOCKED ONTO THEIRS.

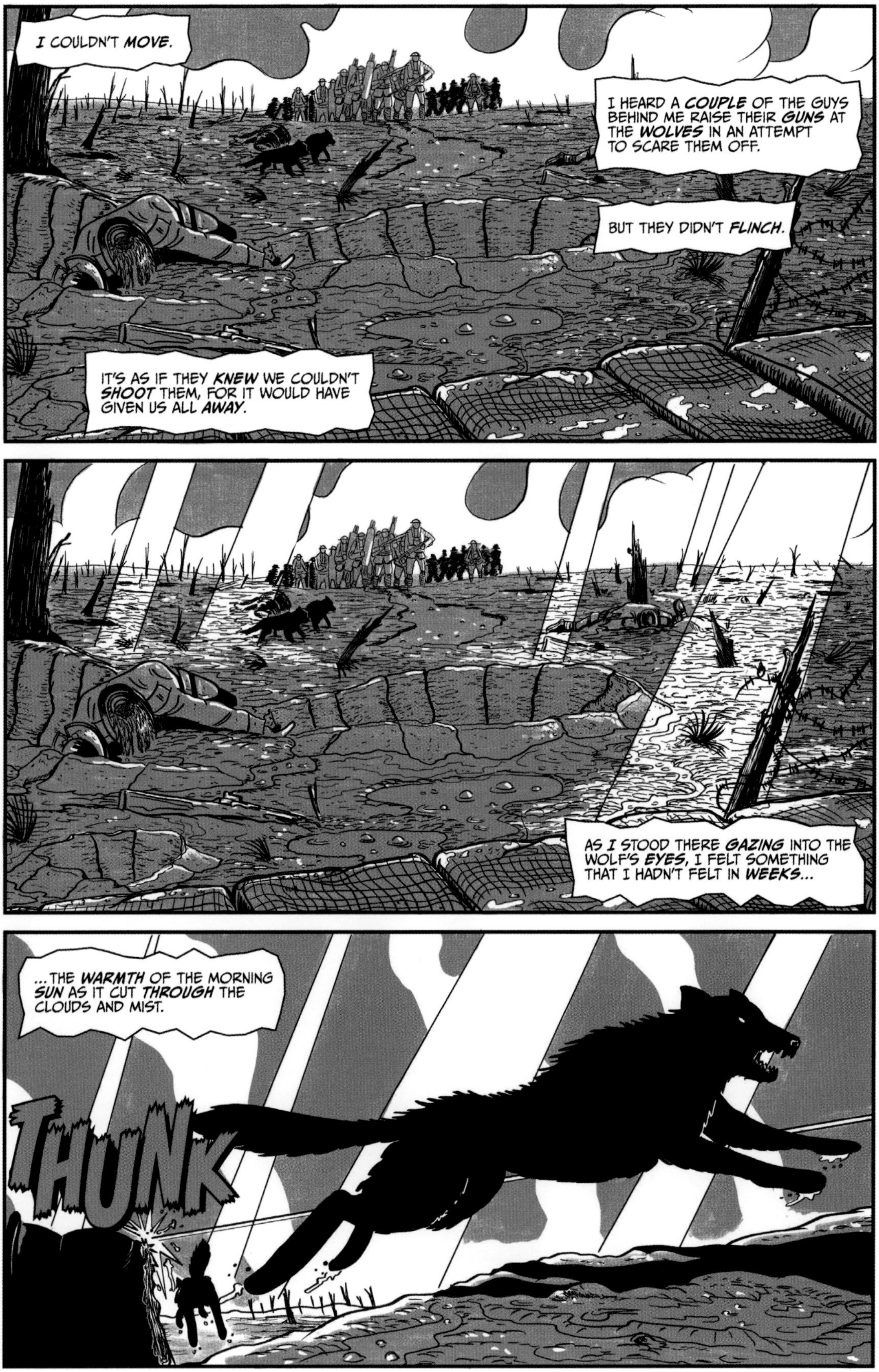
I COULDN'T MOVE.
I HEARD A COUPLE OF THE GUYS BEHIND ME RAISE THEIR GUNS AT THE WOLVES IN AN ATTEMPT TO SCARE THEM OFF.
BUT THEY DIDN'T FLINCH.
IT'S AS IF THEY KNEW WE COULDN'T SHOOT THEM, FOR IT WOULD HAVE GIVEN US ALL AWAY.
AS I STOOD THERE GAZING INTO THE WOLF'S EYES, I FELT SOMETHING THAT I HADN'T FELT IN WEEKS...
...THE WARMTH OF THE MORNING SUN AS IT CUT THROUGH THE CLOUDS AND MIST.
THUNK

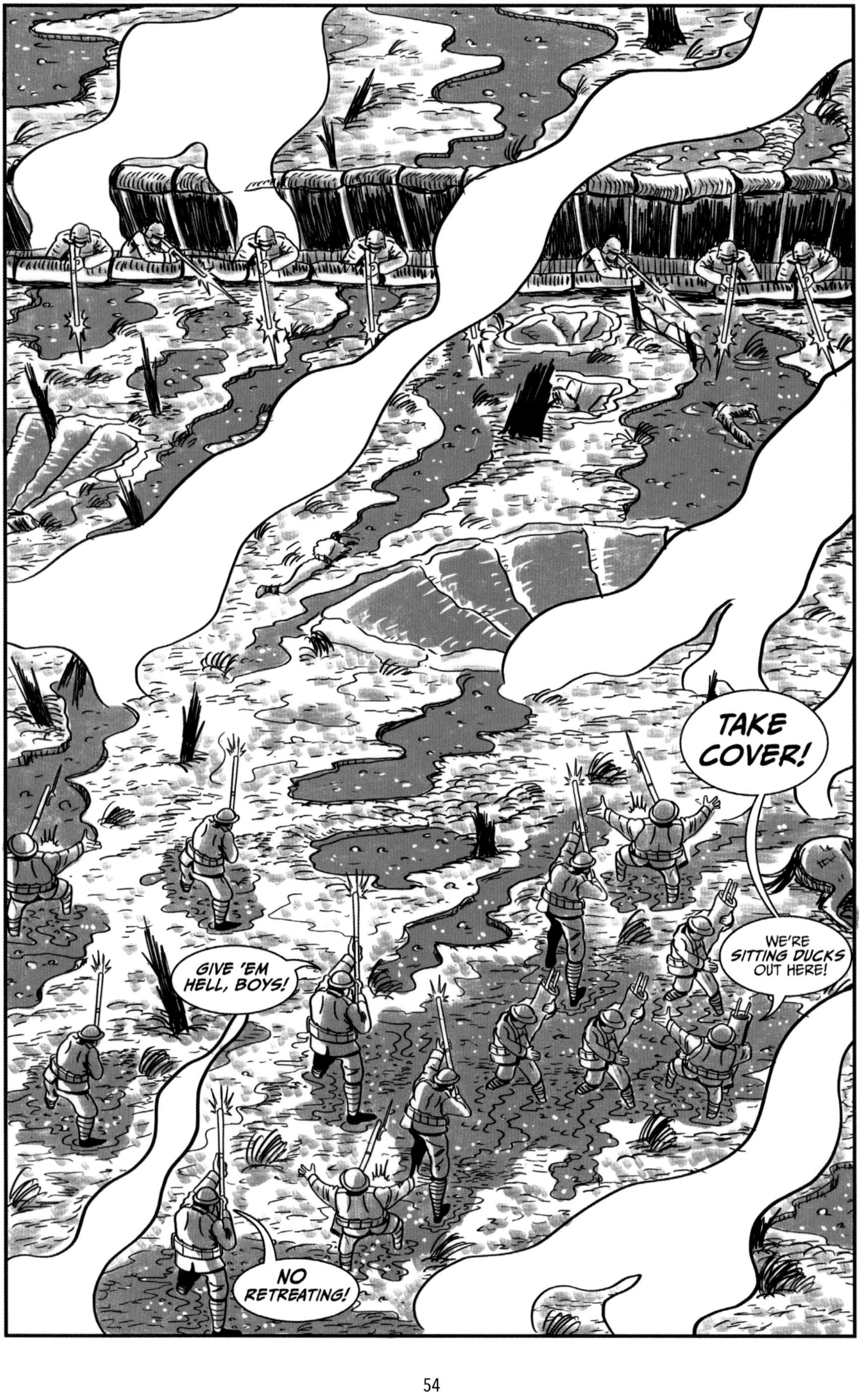
TAKE COVER!
WE'RE SITTING DUCKS OUT HERE!
GIVE 'EM HELL, BOYS!
NO RETREATING!

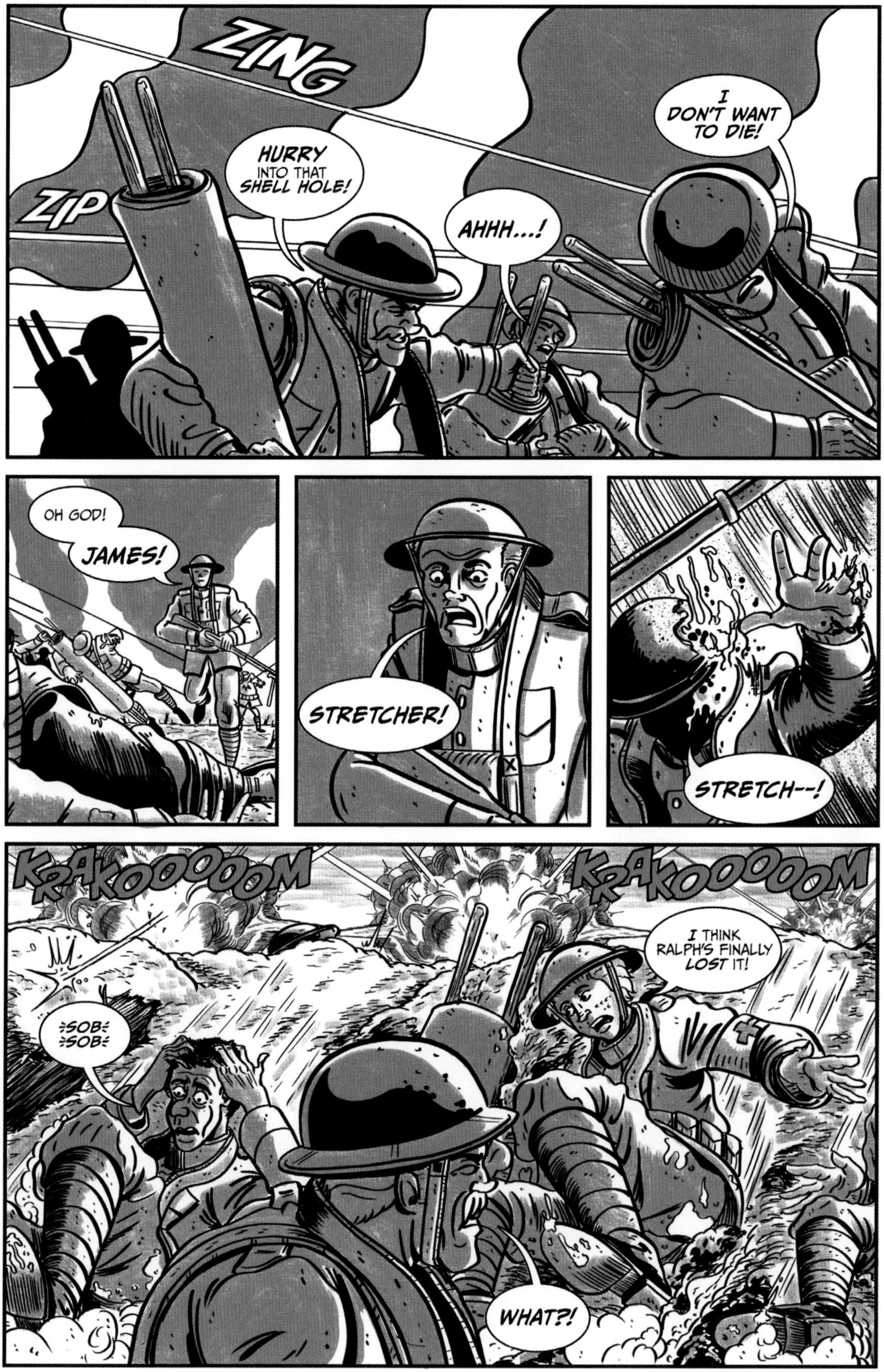
ZING
ZIP
HURRY INTO THAT SHELL HOLE!
AHHH...!
I DON'T WANT TO DIE!
OH GOD!
JAMES!
STRETCHER!
STRETCH--!
KRAKOOOOOOM
KRAKOOOOOOM
I THINK RALPH'S FINALLY LOST IT!
SOB SOB
WHAT?!

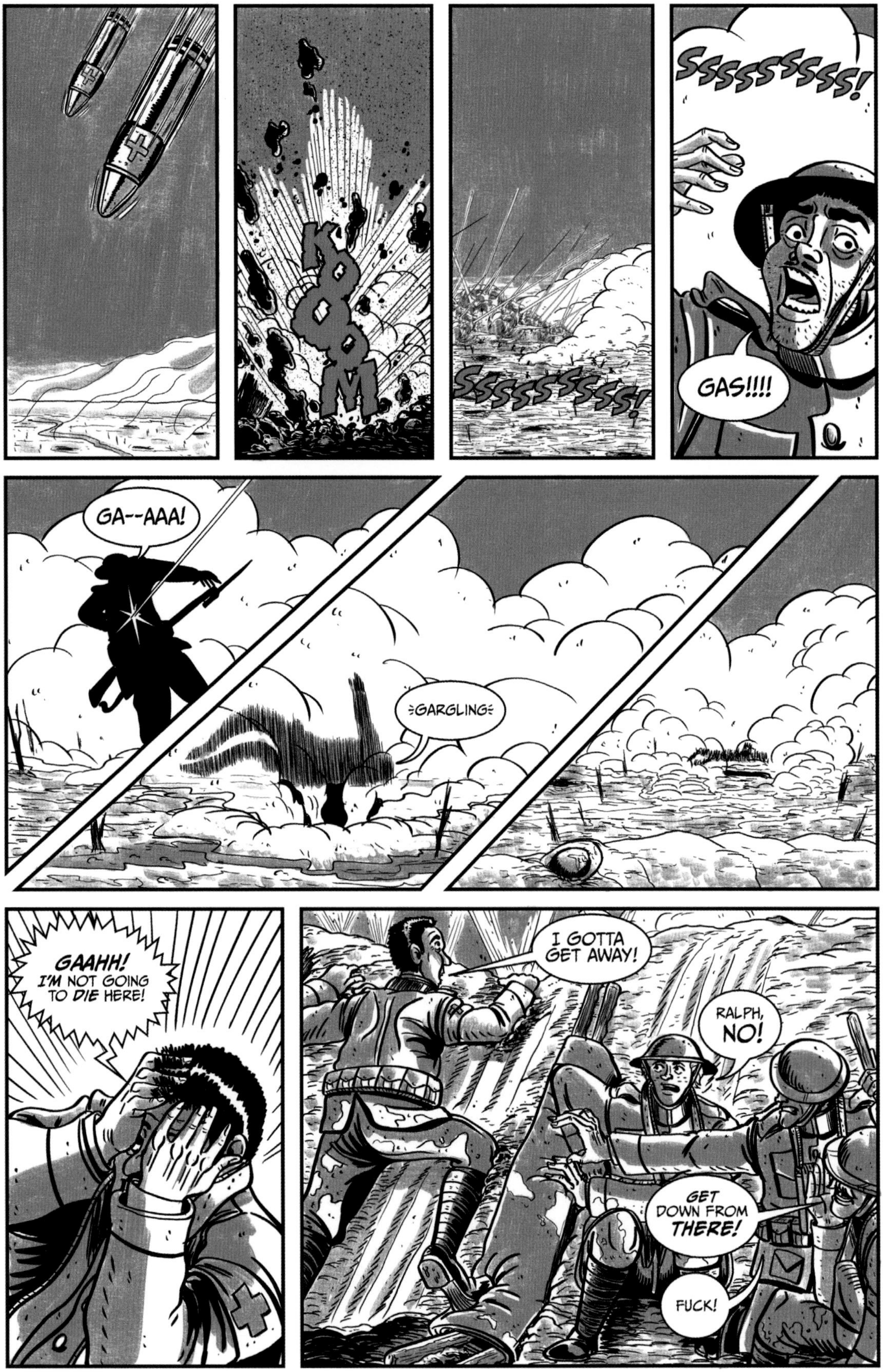
BOOM
SSSSSSSSSS!
SSSSSSSSS!
GAS!!!!
GA--AAA!
GARGLING
GAAHH! I'M NOT GOING TO DIE HERE!
I GOTTA GET AWAY!
RALPH, NO!
GET DOWN FROM THERE!
FUCK!

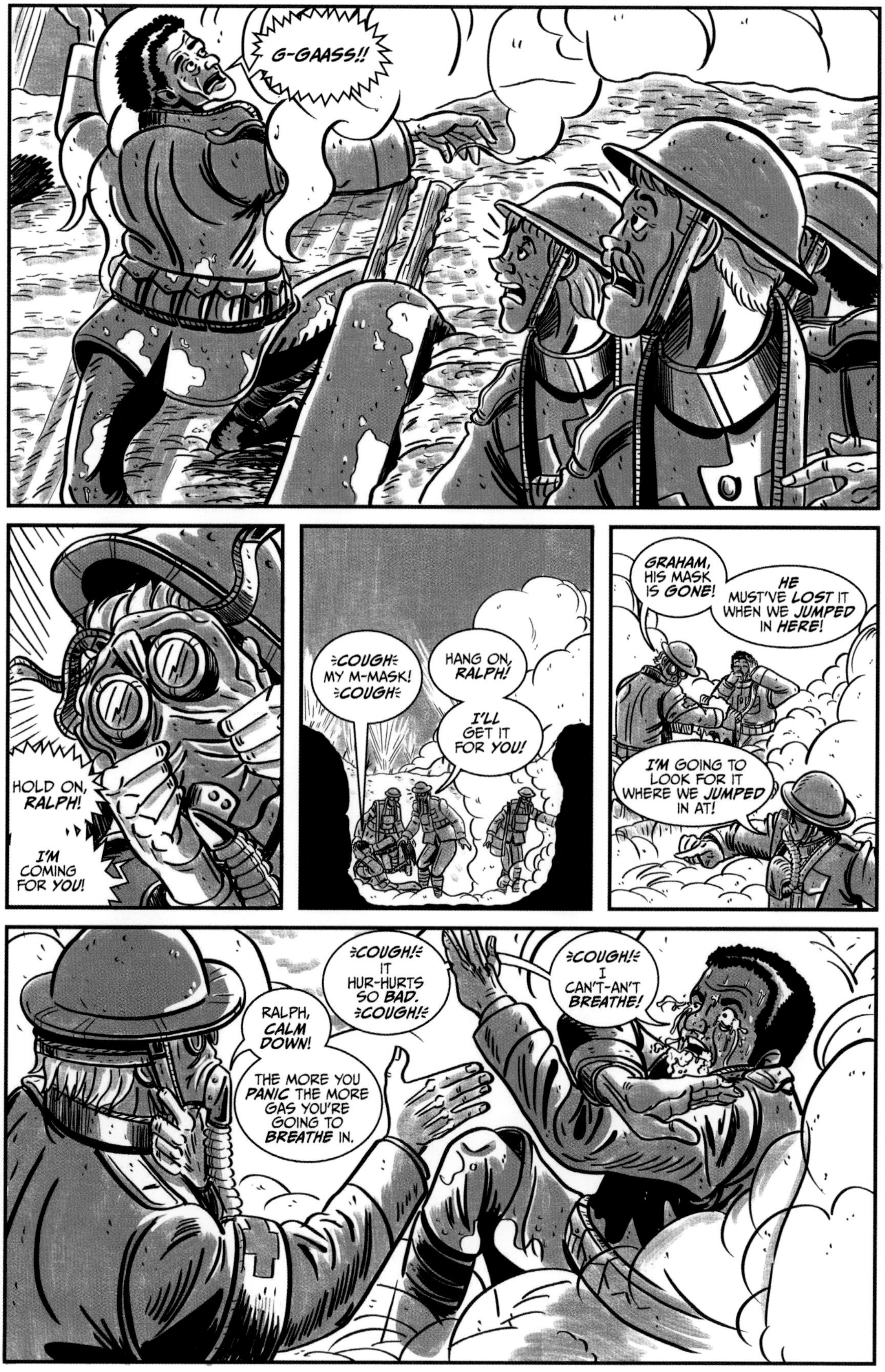
G-GAASS!!
GRAHAM, HIS MASK IS GONE!
HE MUST'VE LOST IT WHEN WE JUMPED IN HERE!
I'M GOING TO LOOK FOR IT WHERE WE JUMPED IN AT!
COUGH MY M-MASK! COUGH
HANG ON, RALPH!
I'LL GET IT FOR YOU!
HOLD ON, RALPH!
I'M COMING FOR YOU!
COUGH! IT HUR-HURTS SO BAD. COUGH!
COUGH! I CAN'T-AN'T BREATHE!
RALPH, CALM DOWN!
THE MORE YOU PANIC THE MORE GAS YOU'RE GOING TO BREATHE IN.

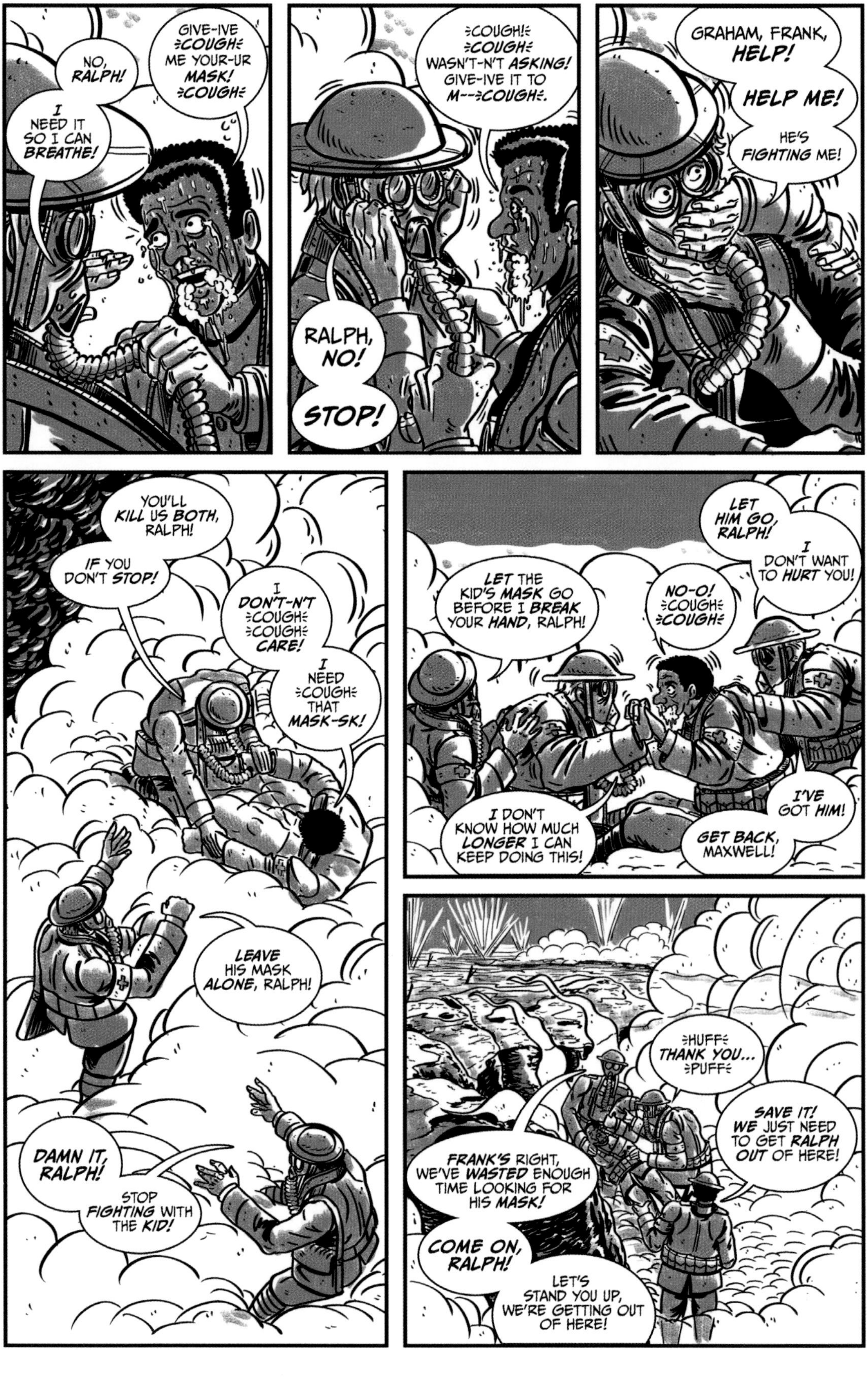
NO, RALPH!
I NEED IT SO I CAN BREATHE!
GIVE-IVE ≷COUGH≶ ME YOUR-UR MASK! ≷COUGH≶
≷COUGH!≶ ≷COUGH≶ WASN'T-N'T ASKING! GIVE-IVE IT TO M--≷COUGH≶.
RALPH, NO!
STOP!
GRAHAM, FRANK, HELP!
HELP ME!
HE'S FIGHTING ME!
YOU'LL KILL US BOTH, RALPH!
IF YOU DON'T STOP!
I DON'T-N'T ≷COUGH≶ ≷COUGH≶ CARE!
I NEED ≷COUGH≶ THAT MASK-SK!
LEAVE HIS MASK ALONE, RALPH!
DAMN IT, RALPH!
STOP FIGHTING WITH THE KID!
LET HIM GO, RALPH!
I DON'T WANT TO HURT YOU!
LET THE KID'S MASK GO BEFORE I BREAK YOUR HAND, RALPH!
NO-O! ≷COUGH≶ ≷COUGH≶
I DON'T KNOW HOW MUCH LONGER I CAN KEEP DOING THIS!
I'VE GOT HIM!
GET BACK, MAXWELL!
≷HUFF≶ THANK YOU... ≷PUFF≶
SAVE IT! WE JUST NEED TO GET RALPH OUT OF HERE!
FRANK'S RIGHT, WE'VE WASTED ENOUGH TIME LOOKING FOR HIS MASK!
COME ON, RALPH!
LET'S STAND YOU UP, WE'RE GETTING OUT OF HERE!

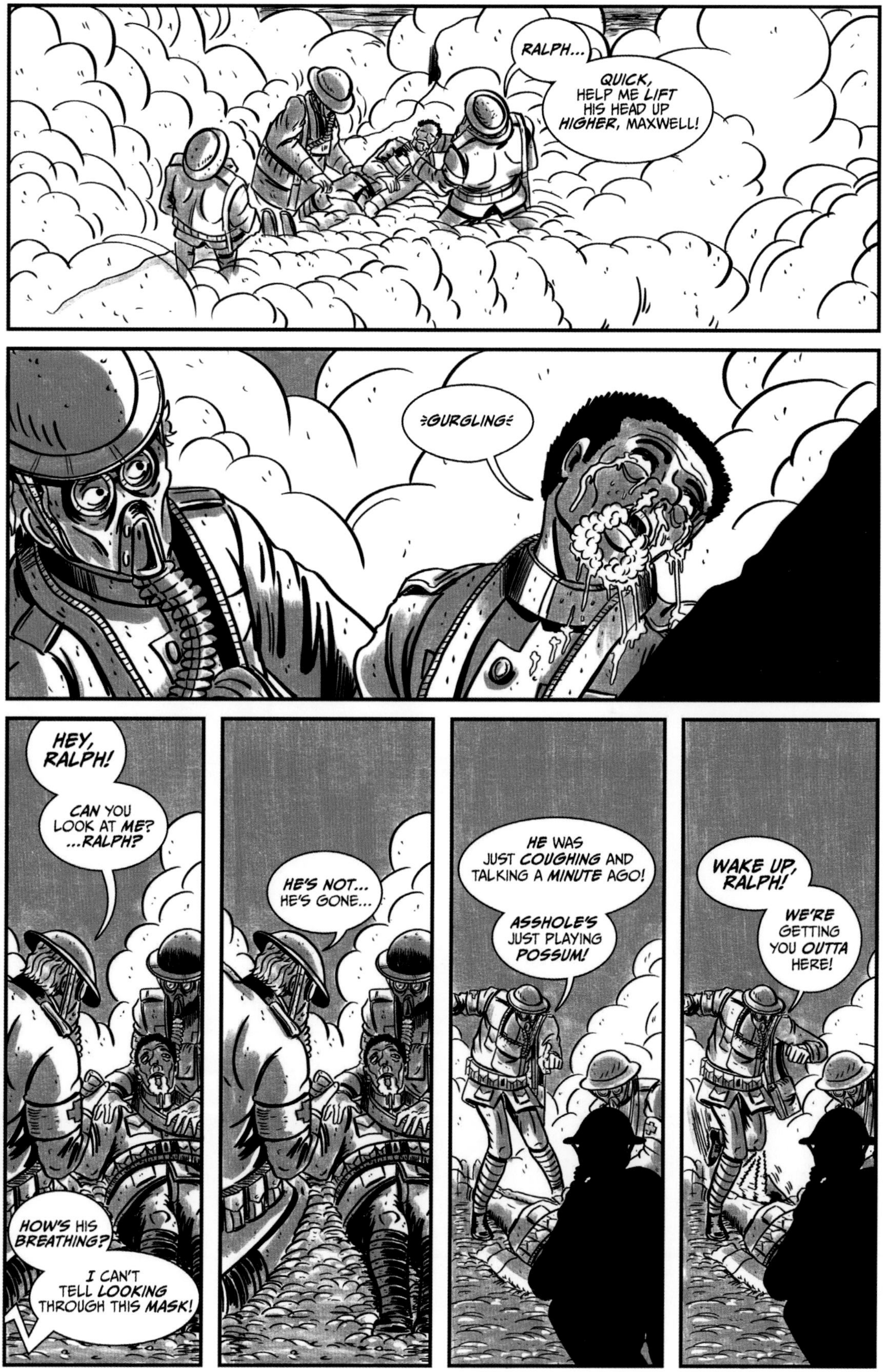
RALPH...
QUICK, HELP ME LIFT HIS HEAD UP HIGHER, MAXWELL!
GURGLING
HEY, RALPH!
CAN YOU LOOK AT ME? ...RALPH?
HOW'S HIS BREATHING?
I CAN'T TELL LOOKING THROUGH THIS MASK!
HE'S NOT... HE'S GONE...
HE WAS JUST COUGHING AND TALKING A MINUTE AGO!
ASSHOLE'S JUST PLAYING POSSUM!
WAKE UP, RALPH!
WE'RE GETTING YOU OUTTA HERE!

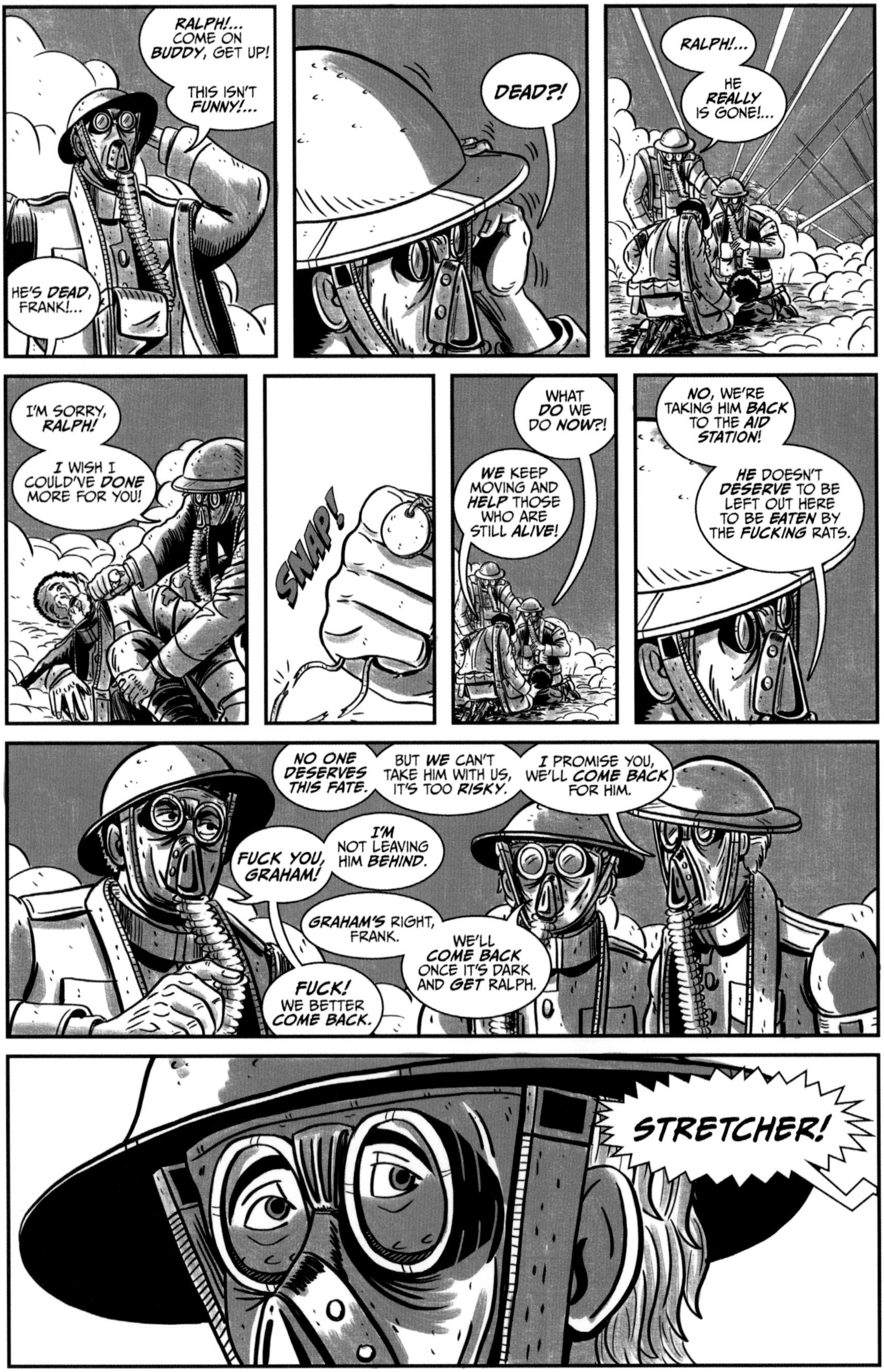
RALPH!... COME ON BUDDY, GET UP!
THIS ISN'T FUNNY!...
HE'S DEAD, FRANK!...
DEAD?!
RALPH!...
HE REALLY IS GONE!...
I'M SORRY, RALPH!
I WISH I COULD'VE DONE MORE FOR YOU!
SNAP!
WHAT DO WE DO NOW?!
WE KEEP MOVING AND HELP THOSE WHO ARE STILL ALIVE!
NO, WE'RE TAKING HIM BACK TO THE AID STATION!
HE DOESN'T DESERVE TO BE LEFT OUT HERE TO BE EATEN BY THE FUCKING RATS.
NO ONE DESERVES THIS FATE.
BUT WE CAN'T TAKE HIM WITH US, IT'S TOO RISKY.
I PROMISE YOU, WE'LL COME BACK FOR HIM.
FUCK YOU, GRAHAM!
I'M NOT LEAVING HIM BEHIND.
GRAHAM'S RIGHT, FRANK.
WE'LL COME BACK ONCE IT'S DARK AND GET RALPH.
FUCK! WE BETTER COME BACK.
STRETCHER!

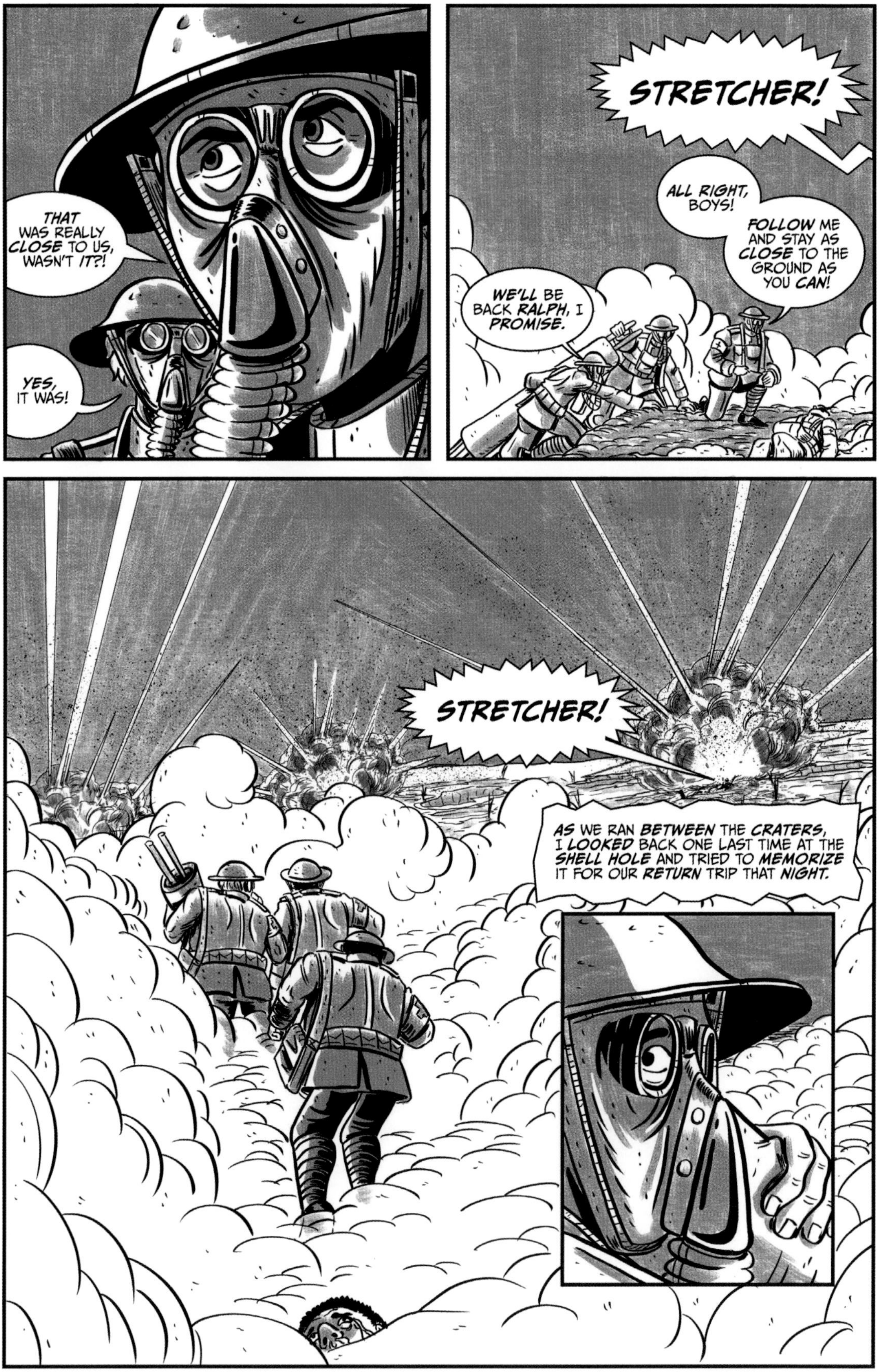
THAT WAS REALLY CLOSE TO US, WASN'T IT?!
YES, IT WAS!
STRETCHER!
ALL RIGHT, BOYS!
FOLLOW ME AND STAY AS CLOSE TO THE GROUND AS YOU CAN!
WE'LL BE BACK RALPH, I PROMISE.
STRETCHER!
AS WE RAN BETWEEN THE CRATERS, I LOOKED BACK ONE LAST TIME AT THE SHELL HOLE AND TRIED TO MEMORIZE IT FOR OUR RETURN TRIP THAT NIGHT.

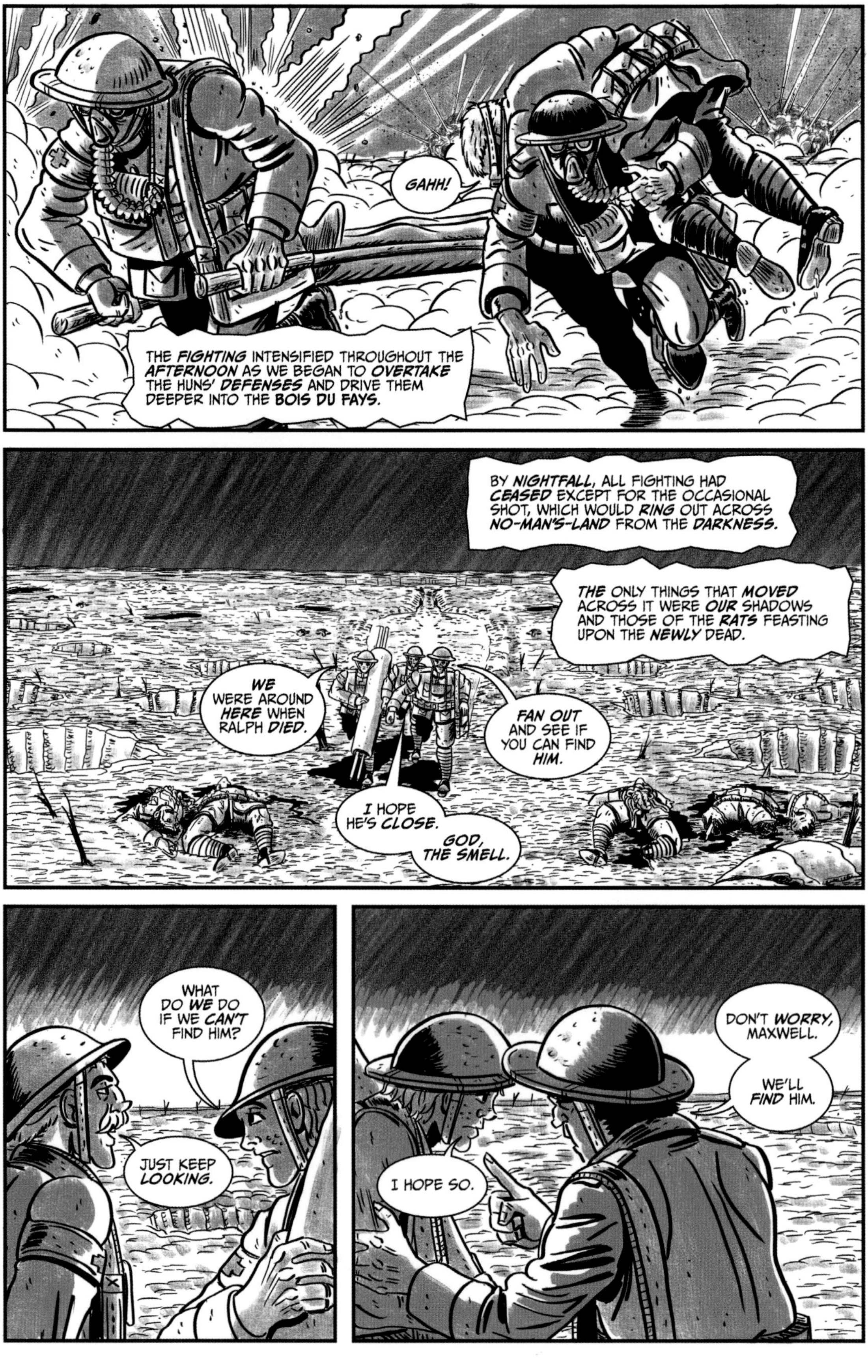
GAHH!
THE FIGHTING INTENSIFIED THROUGHOUT THE AFTERNOON AS WE BEGAN TO OVERTAKE THE HUNS' DEFENSES AND DRIVE THEM DEEPER INTO THE BOIS DU FAYS.
BY NIGHTFALL, ALL FIGHTING HAD CEASED EXCEPT FOR THE OCCASIONAL SHOT, WHICH WOULD RING OUT ACROSS NO-MAN'S-LAND FROM THE DARKNESS.
THE ONLY THINGS THAT MOVED ACROSS IT WERE OUR SHADOWS AND THOSE OF THE RATS FEASTING UPON THE NEWLY DEAD.
WE WERE AROUND HERE WHEN RALPH DIED.
FAN OUT AND SEE IF YOU CAN FIND HIM.
I HOPE HE'S CLOSE.
GOD, THE SMELL.
WHAT DO WE DO IF WE CAN'T FIND HIM?
JUST KEEP LOOKING.
DON'T WORRY, MAXWELL.
WE'LL FIND HIM.
I HOPE SO.

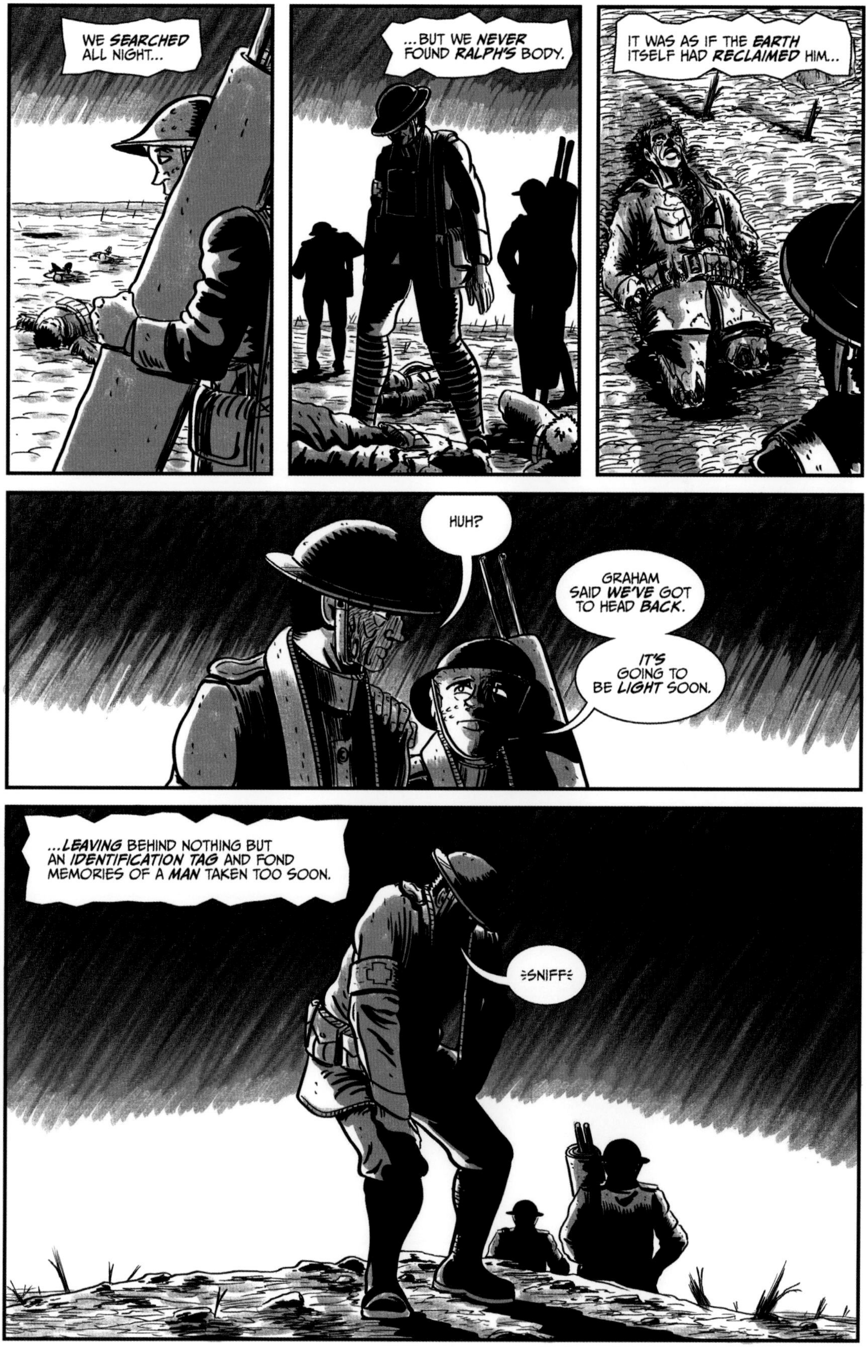
WE SEARCHED ALL NIGHT...
...BUT WE NEVER FOUND RALPH'S BODY.
IT WAS AS IF THE EARTH ITSELF HAD RECLAIMED HIM...
HUH?
GRAHAM SAID WE'VE GOT TO HEAD BACK.
IT'S GOING TO BE LIGHT SOON.
...LEAVING BEHIND NOTHING BUT AN IDENTIFICATION TAG AND FOND MEMORIES OF A MAN TAKEN TOO SOON.
≈SNIFF≈

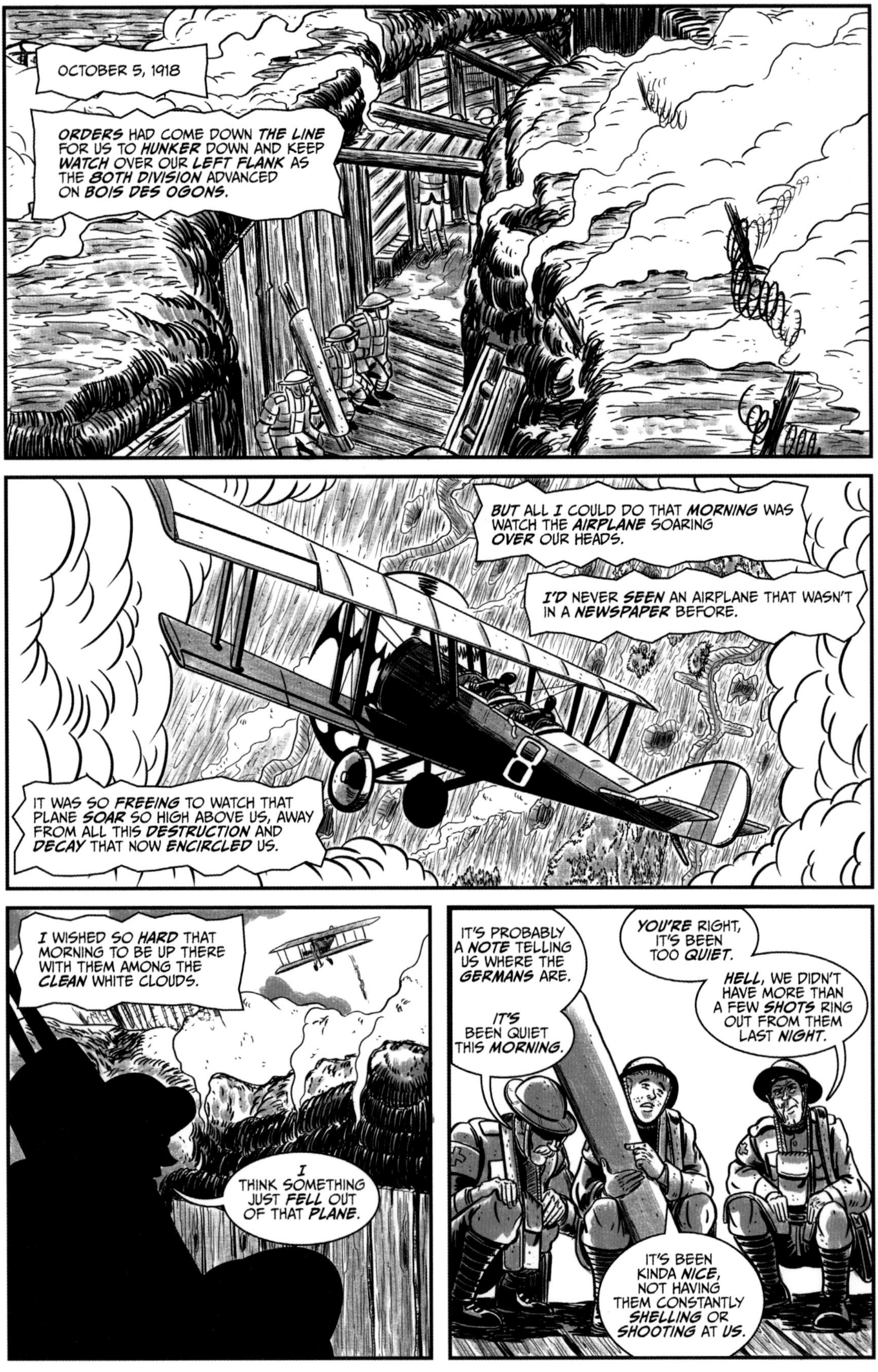

OCTOBER 5, 1918
ORDERS HAD COME DOWN THE LINE FOR US TO HUNKER DOWN AND KEEP WATCH OVER OUR LEFT FLANK AS THE 80TH DIVISION ADVANCED ON BOIS DES OGONS.
BUT ALL I COULD DO THAT MORNING WAS WATCH THE AIRPLANE SOARING OVER OUR HEADS.
I'D NEVER SEEN AN AIRPLANE THAT WASN'T IN A NEWSPAPER BEFORE.
IT WAS SO FREEING TO WATCH THAT PLANE SOAR SO HIGH ABOVE US, AWAY FROM ALL THIS DESTRUCTION AND DECAY THAT NOW ENCIRCLED US.
I WISHED SO HARD THAT MORNING TO BE UP THERE WITH THEM AMONG THE CLEAN WHITE CLOUDS.
I THINK SOMETHING JUST FELL OUT OF THAT PLANE.
IT'S PROBABLY A NOTE TELLING US WHERE THE GERMANS ARE.
IT'S BEEN QUIET THIS MORNING.
YOU'RE RIGHT, IT'S BEEN TOO QUIET.
HELL, WE DIDN'T HAVE MORE THAN A FEW SHOTS RING OUT FROM THEM LAST NIGHT.
IT'S BEEN KINDA NICE, NOT HAVING THEM CONSTANTLY SHELLING OR SHOOTING AT US.

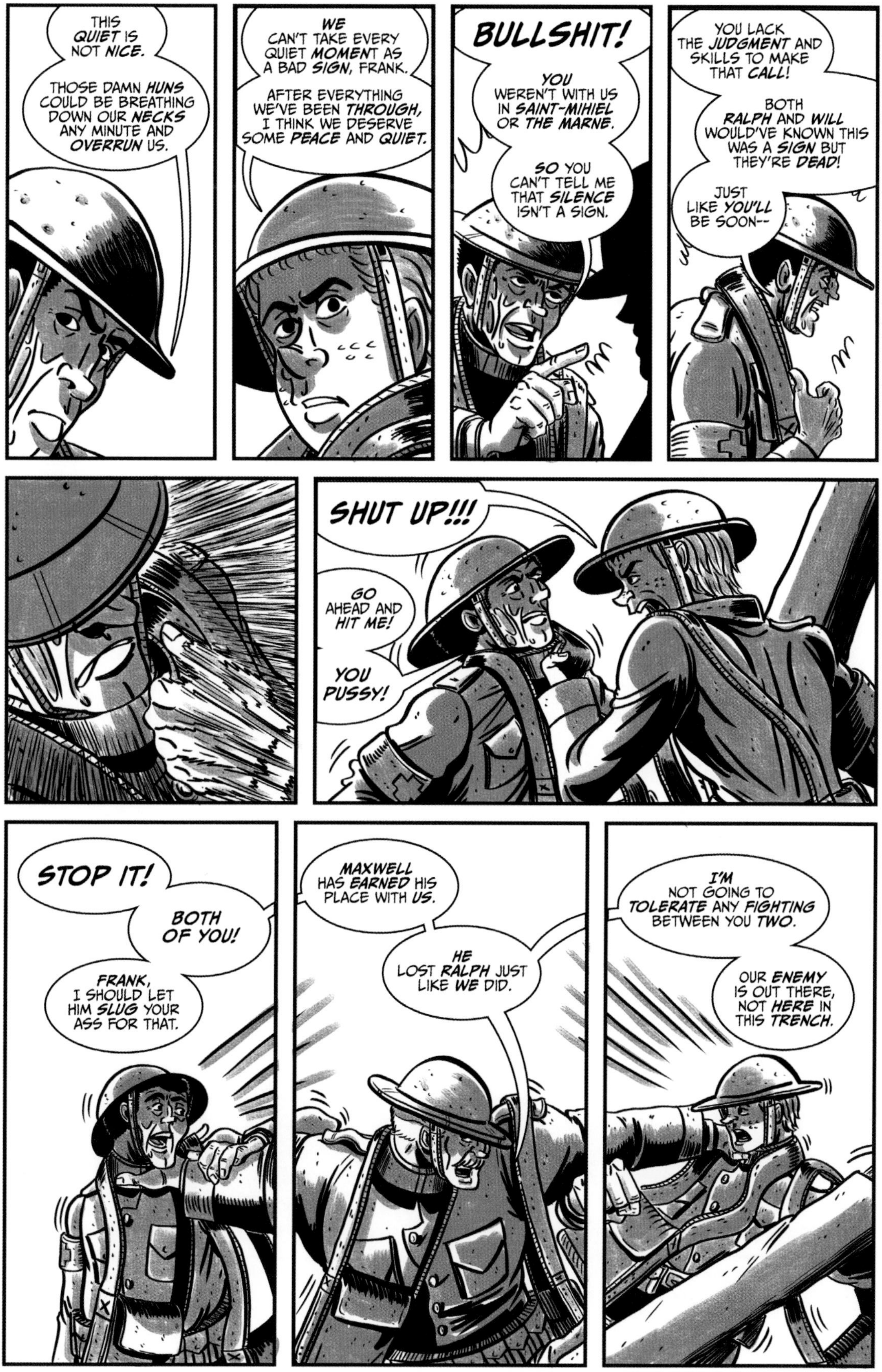
THIS QUIET IS NOT NICE.
THOSE DAMN HUNS COULD BE BREATHING DOWN OUR NECKS ANY MINUTE AND OVERRUN US.
WE CAN'T TAKE EVERY QUIET MOMENT AS A BAD SIGN, FRANK.
AFTER EVERYTHING WE'VE BEEN THROUGH, I THINK WE DESERVE SOME PEACE AND QUIET.
BULLSHIT!
YOU WEREN'T WITH US IN SAINT-MIHIEL OR THE MARNE.
SO YOU CAN'T TELL ME THAT SILENCE ISN'T A SIGN.
YOU LACK THE JUDGMENT AND SKILLS TO MAKE THAT CALL!
BOTH RALPH AND WILL WOULD'VE KNOWN THIS WAS A SIGN BUT THEY'RE DEAD!
JUST LIKE YOU'LL BE SOON--
SHUT UP!!!
GO AHEAD AND HIT ME!
YOU PUSSY!
STOP IT!
BOTH OF YOU!
FRANK, I SHOULD LET HIM SLUG YOUR ASS FOR THAT.
MAXWELL HAS EARNED HIS PLACE WITH US.
HE LOST RALPH JUST LIKE WE DID.
I'M NOT GOING TO TOLERATE ANY FIGHTING BETWEEN YOU TWO.
OUR ENEMY IS OUT THERE, NOT HERE IN THIS TRENCH.

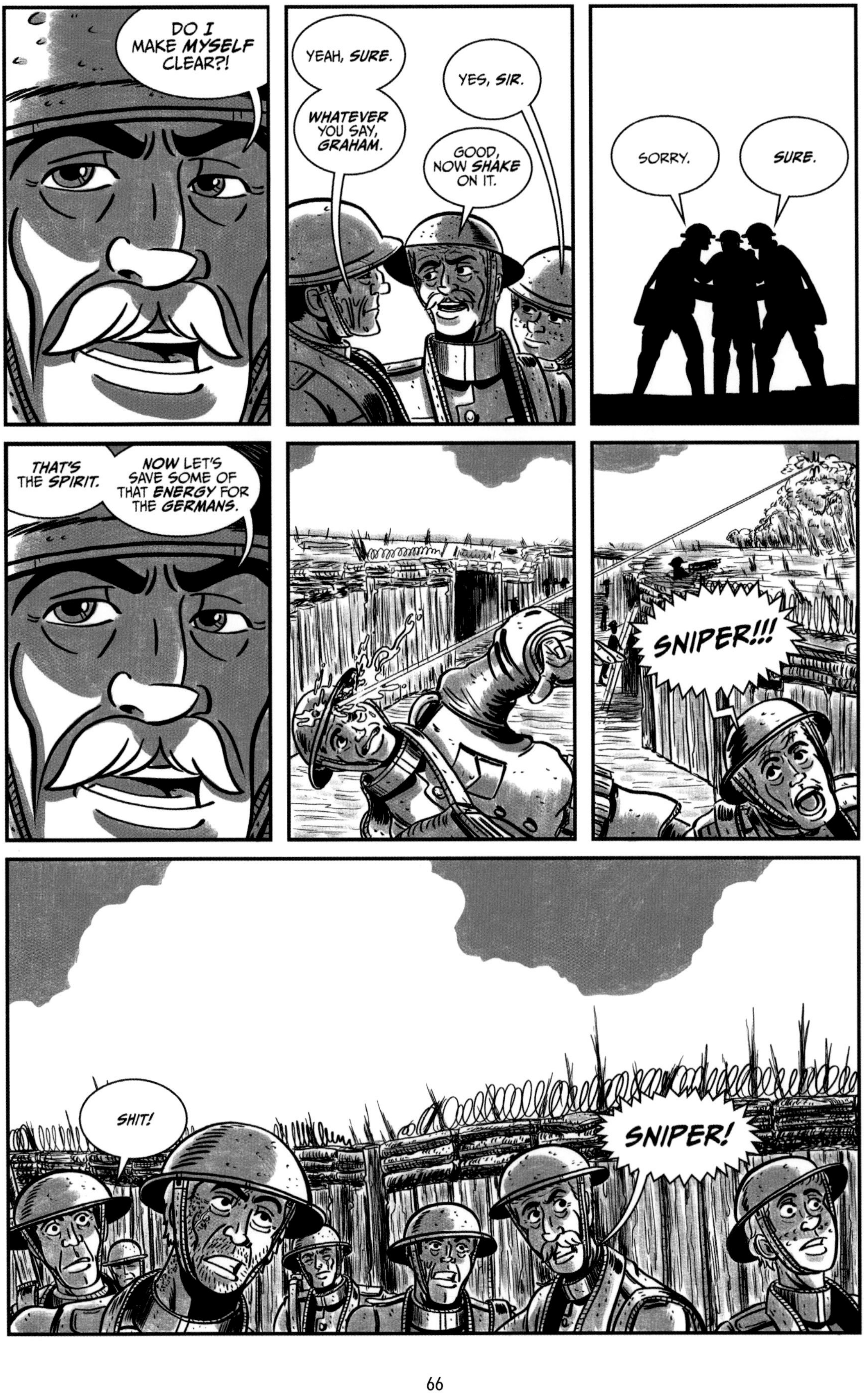
DO I MAKE MYSELF CLEAR?!
YEAH, SURE.
WHATEVER YOU SAY, GRAHAM.
YES, SIR.
GOOD, NOW SHAKE ON IT.
SORRY.
SURE.
THAT'S THE SPIRIT.
NOW LET'S SAVE SOME OF THAT ENERGY FOR THE GERMANS.
SNIPER!!!
SHIT!
SNIPER!

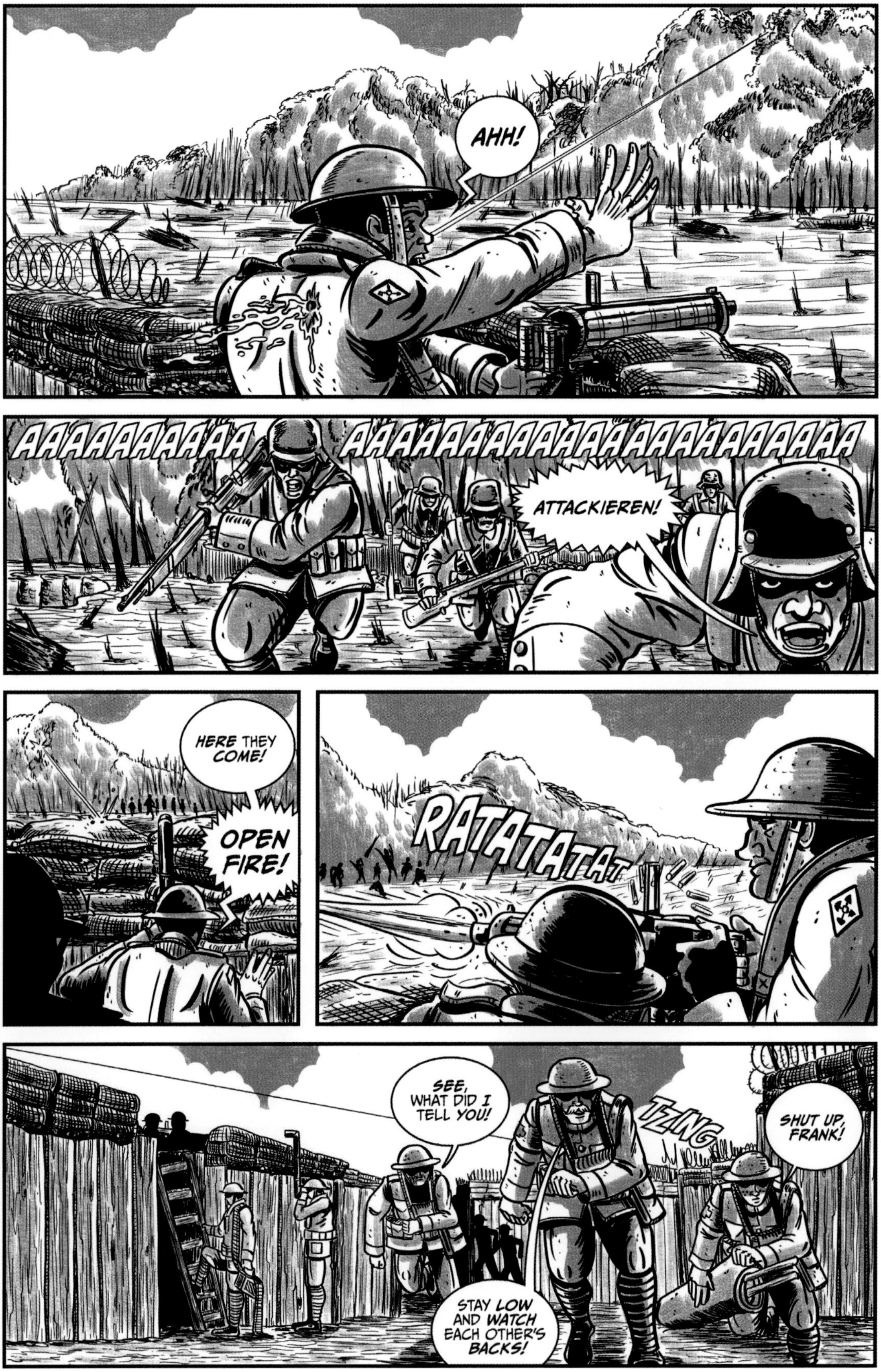
AHH!
AAAAAAAAAA AAAAAAAAAAAAAAAAAAAAA
ATTACKIEREN!
HERE THEY COME!
OPEN FIRE!
RATATATATAT
SEE, WHAT DID I TELL YOU!
TZING
SHUT UP, FRANK!
STAY LOW AND WATCH EACH OTHER'S BACKS!

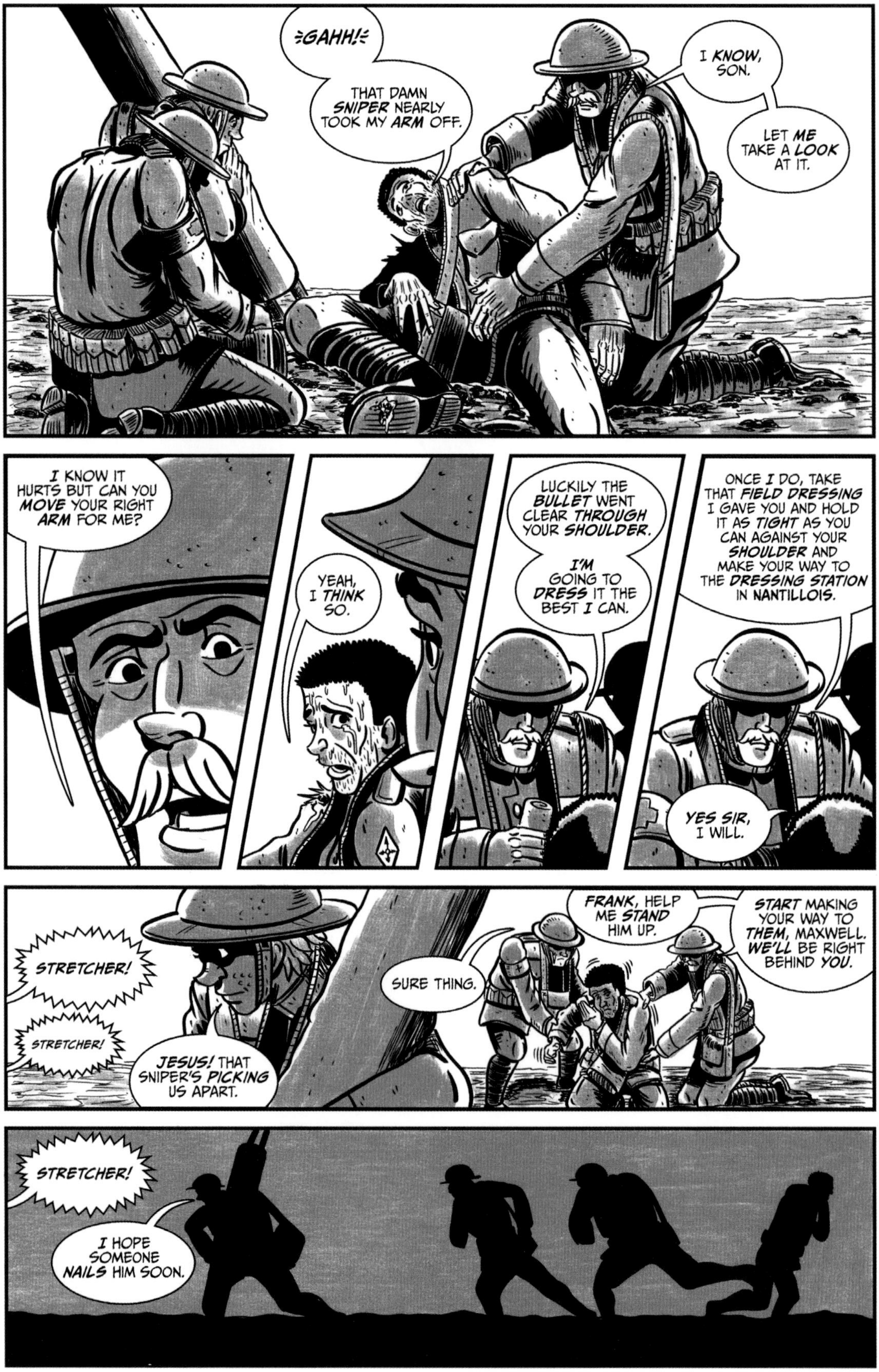
GAHH!
THAT DAMN SNIPER NEARLY TOOK MY ARM OFF.
I KNOW, SON.
LET ME TAKE A LOOK AT IT.
I KNOW IT HURTS BUT CAN YOU MOVE YOUR RIGHT ARM FOR ME?
YEAH, I THINK SO.
LUCKILY THE BULLET WENT CLEAR THROUGH YOUR SHOULDER.
I'M GOING TO DRESS IT THE BEST I CAN.
ONCE I DO, TAKE THAT FIELD DRESSING I GAVE YOU AND HOLD IT AS TIGHT AS YOU CAN AGAINST YOUR SHOULDER AND MAKE YOUR WAY TO THE DRESSING STATION IN NANTILLOIS.
YES SIR, I WILL.
STRETCHER!
STRETCHER!
JESUS! THAT SNIPER'S PICKING US APART.
SURE THING.
FRANK, HELP ME STAND HIM UP.
START MAKING YOUR WAY TO THEM, MAXWELL. WE'LL BE RIGHT BEHIND YOU.
STRETCHER!
I HOPE SOMEONE NAILS HIM SOON.

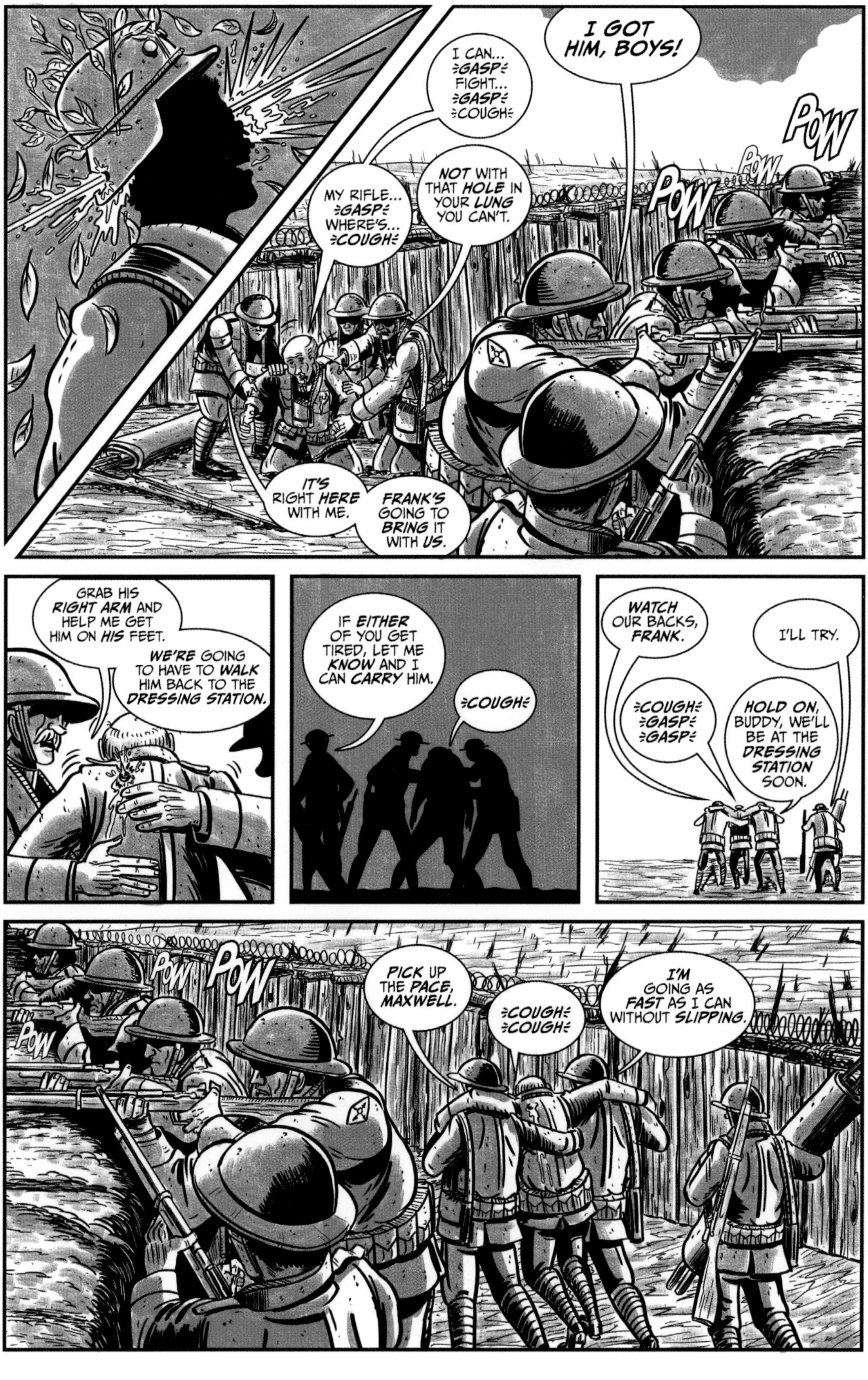
I GOT HIM, BOYS!
I CAN... ≥GASP≤ FIGHT... ≥GASP≤ ≥COUGH≤
POW
POW
POW
MY RIFLE... ≥GASP≤ WHERE'S... ≥COUGH≤
NOT WITH THAT HOLE IN YOUR LUNG YOU CAN'T.
IT'S RIGHT HERE WITH ME.
FRANK'S GOING TO BRING IT WITH US.
GRAB HIS RIGHT ARM AND HELP ME GET HIM ON HIS FEET.
WE'RE GOING TO HAVE TO WALK HIM BACK TO THE DRESSING STATION.
IF EITHER OF YOU GET TIRED, LET ME KNOW AND I CAN CARRY HIM.
≥COUGH≤
WATCH OUR BACKS, FRANK.
I'LL TRY.
≥COUGH≤ ≥GASP≤ ≥GASP≤
HOLD ON, BUDDY, WE'LL BE AT THE DRESSING STATION SOON.
POW
POW
POW
PICK UP THE PACE, MAXWELL.
≥COUGH≤ ≥COUGH≤
I'M GOING AS FAST AS I CAN WITHOUT SLIPPING.

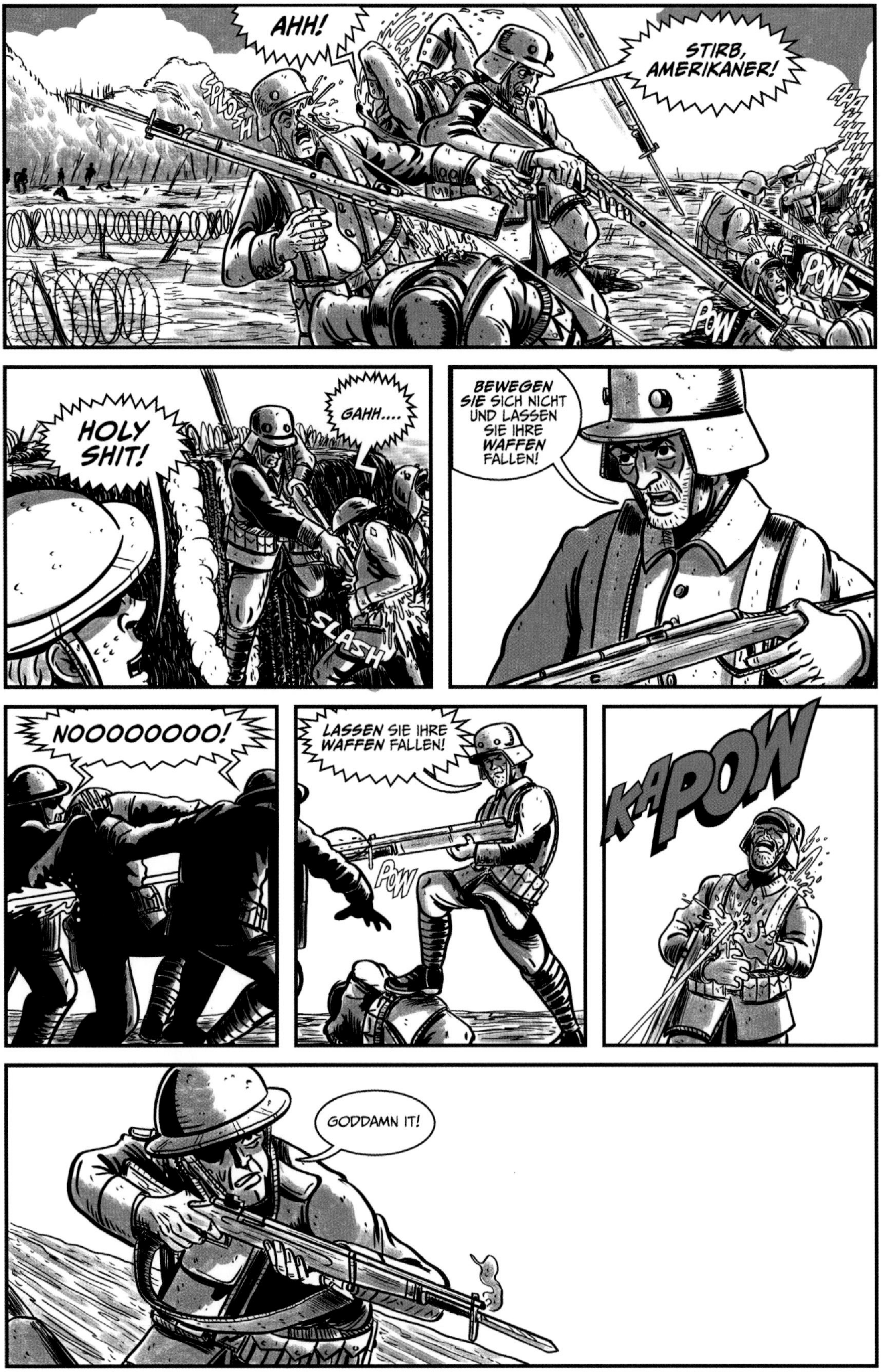
AHH!
STIRB, AMERIKANER!
SPLOOSH
AAAHHHHHH
POW
POW
HOLY SHIT!
GAHH....
SLASH
BEWEGEN SIE SICH NICHT UND LASSEN SIE IHRE WAFFEN FALLEN!
NOOOOOOOO!
LASSEN SIE IHRE WAFFEN FALLEN!
POW
KAPOW
GODDAMN IT!

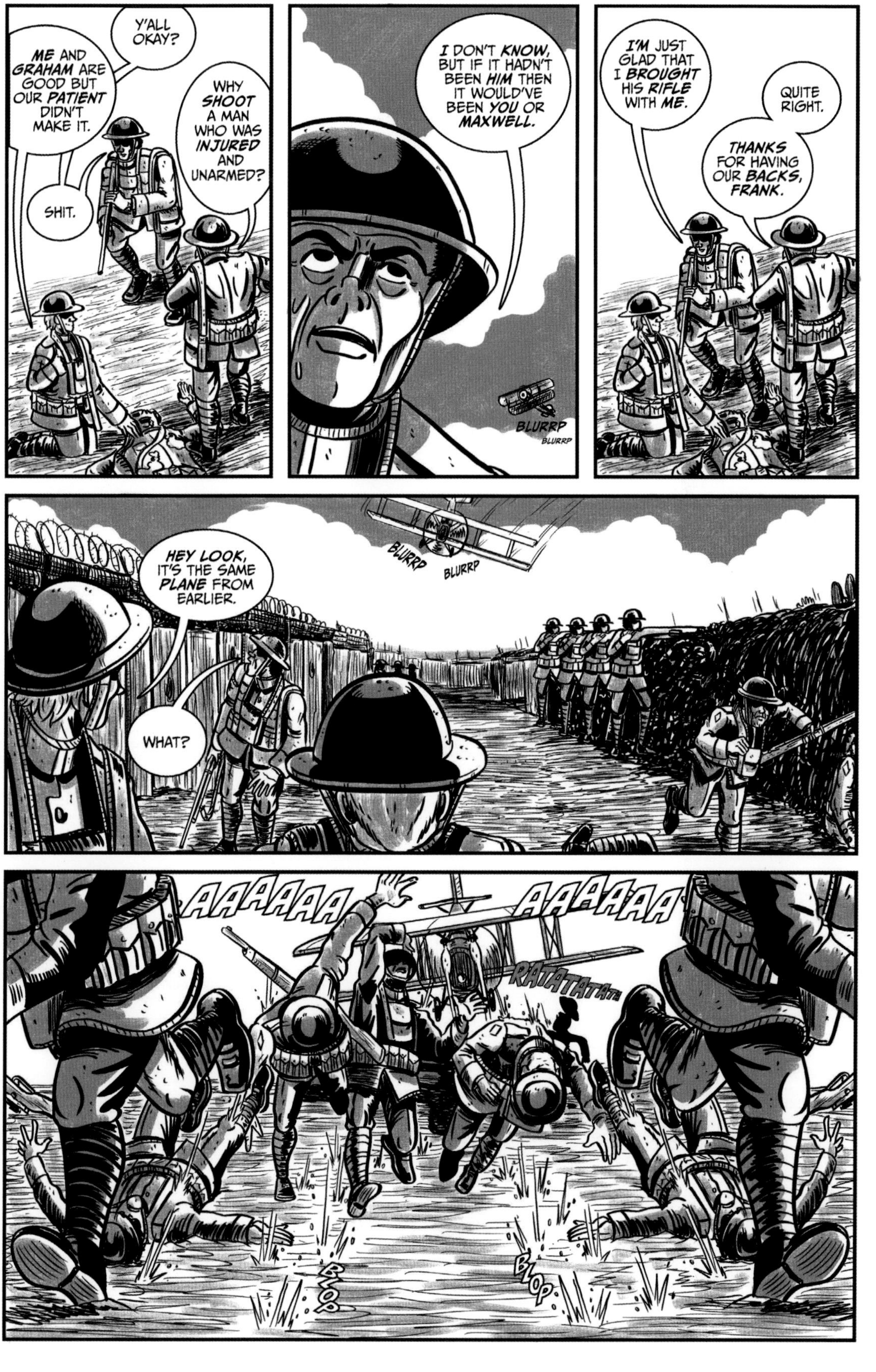
Y'ALL OKAY?
ME AND GRAHAM ARE GOOD BUT OUR PATIENT DIDN'T MAKE IT.
SHIT.
WHY SHOOT A MAN WHO WAS INJURED AND UNARMED?
I DON'T KNOW, BUT IF IT HADN'T BEEN HIM THEN IT WOULD'VE BEEN YOU OR MAXWELL.
BLURRP
BLURRP
I'M JUST GLAD THAT I BROUGHT HIS RIFLE WITH ME.
QUITE RIGHT.
THANKS FOR HAVING OUR BACKS, FRANK.
BLURRP
BLURRP
HEY LOOK, IT'S THE SAME PLANE FROM EARLIER.
WHAT?
AAAAAA
AAAAAA
RATATATATA!
BLOP
BLOP

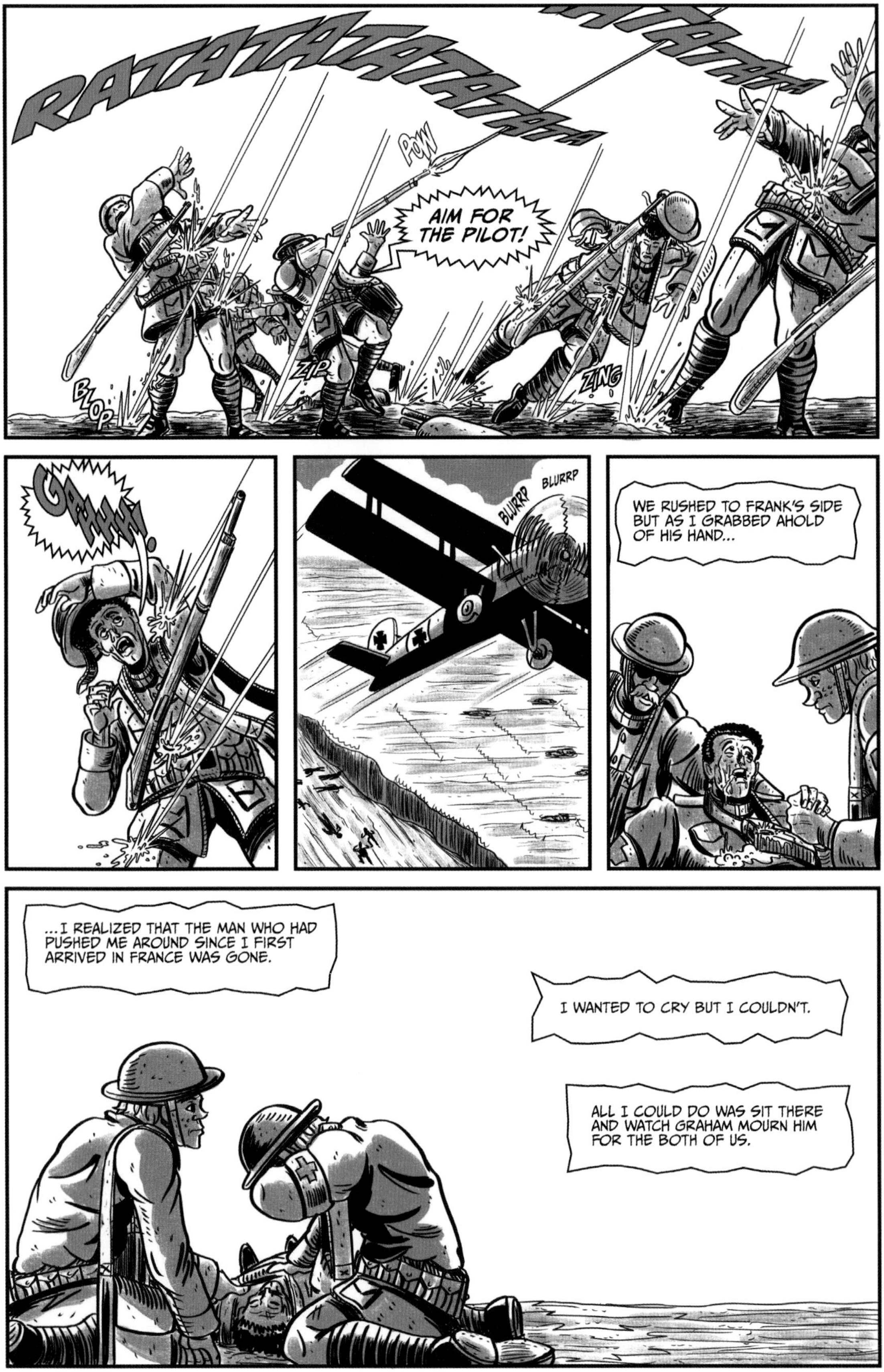
RATATATATATATATATAT!
POW
AIM FOR THE PILOT!
ZIP
BLOP
ZING
GAHHH!
BLURRP
BLURRP
WE RUSHED TO FRANK'S SIDE BUT AS I GRABBED AHOLD OF HIS HAND...
...I REALIZED THAT THE MAN WHO HAD PUSHED ME AROUND SINCE I FIRST ARRIVED IN FRANCE WAS GONE.
I WANTED TO CRY BUT I COULDN'T.
ALL I COULD DO WAS SIT THERE AND WATCH GRAHAM MOURN HIM FOR THE BOTH OF US.

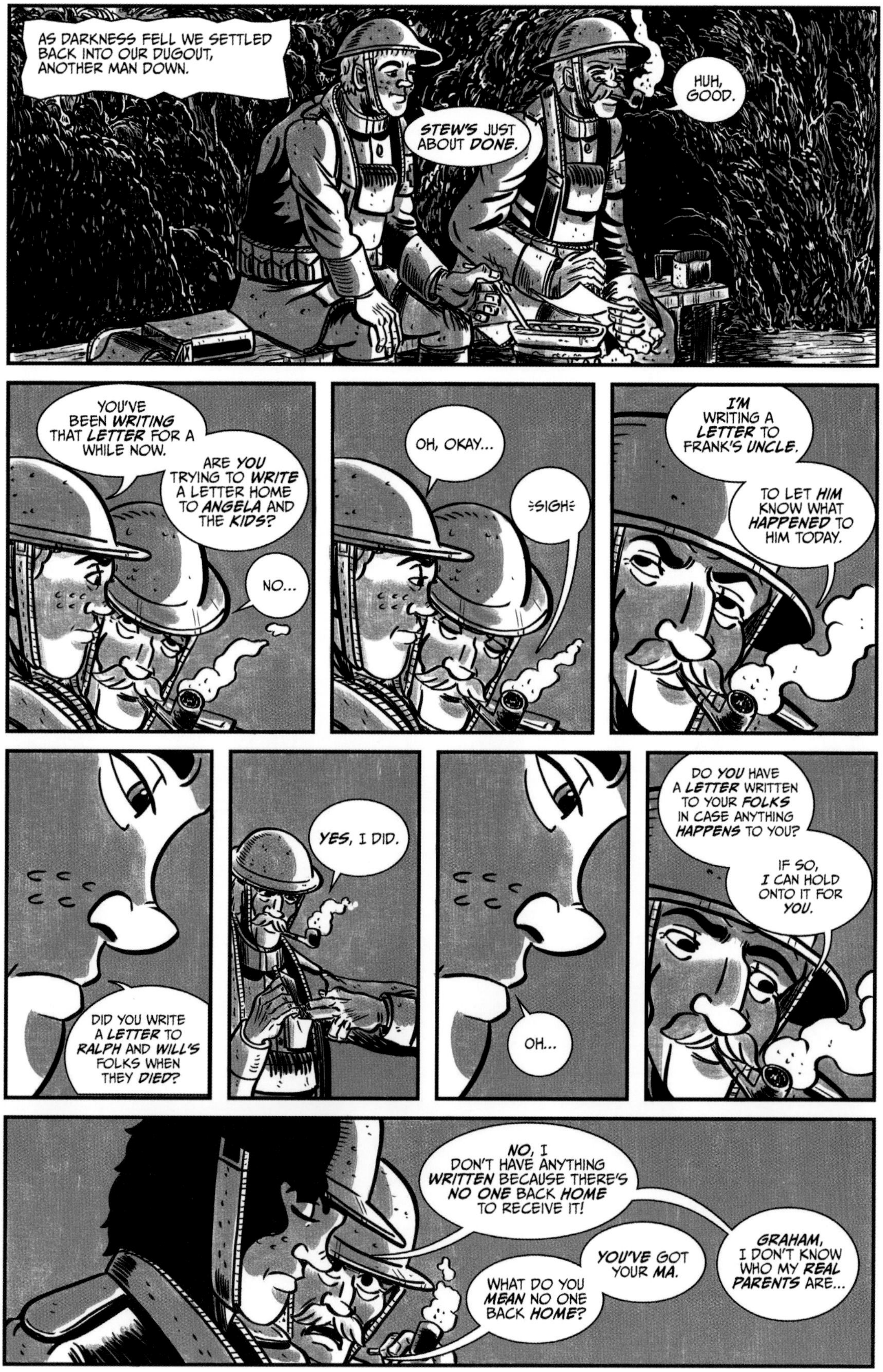
AS DARKNESS FELL WE SETTLED BACK INTO OUR DUGOUT, ANOTHER MAN DOWN.
STEW'S JUST ABOUT DONE.
HUH, GOOD.
YOU'VE BEEN WRITING THAT LETTER FOR A WHILE NOW.
ARE YOU TRYING TO WRITE A LETTER HOME TO ANGELA AND THE KIDS?
NO...
OH, OKAY...
SIGH
I'M WRITING A LETTER TO FRANK'S UNCLE.
TO LET HIM KNOW WHAT HAPPENED TO HIM TODAY.
DID YOU WRITE A LETTER TO RALPH AND WILL'S FOLKS WHEN THEY DIED?
YES, I DID.
OH...
DO YOU HAVE A LETTER WRITTEN TO YOUR FOLKS IN CASE ANYTHING HAPPENS TO YOU?
IF SO, I CAN HOLD ONTO IT FOR YOU.
NO, I DON'T HAVE ANYTHING WRITTEN BECAUSE THERE'S NO ONE BACK HOME TO RECEIVE IT!
WHAT DO YOU MEAN NO ONE BACK HOME?
YOU'VE GOT YOUR MA.
GRAHAM, I DON'T KNOW WHO MY REAL PARENTS ARE...

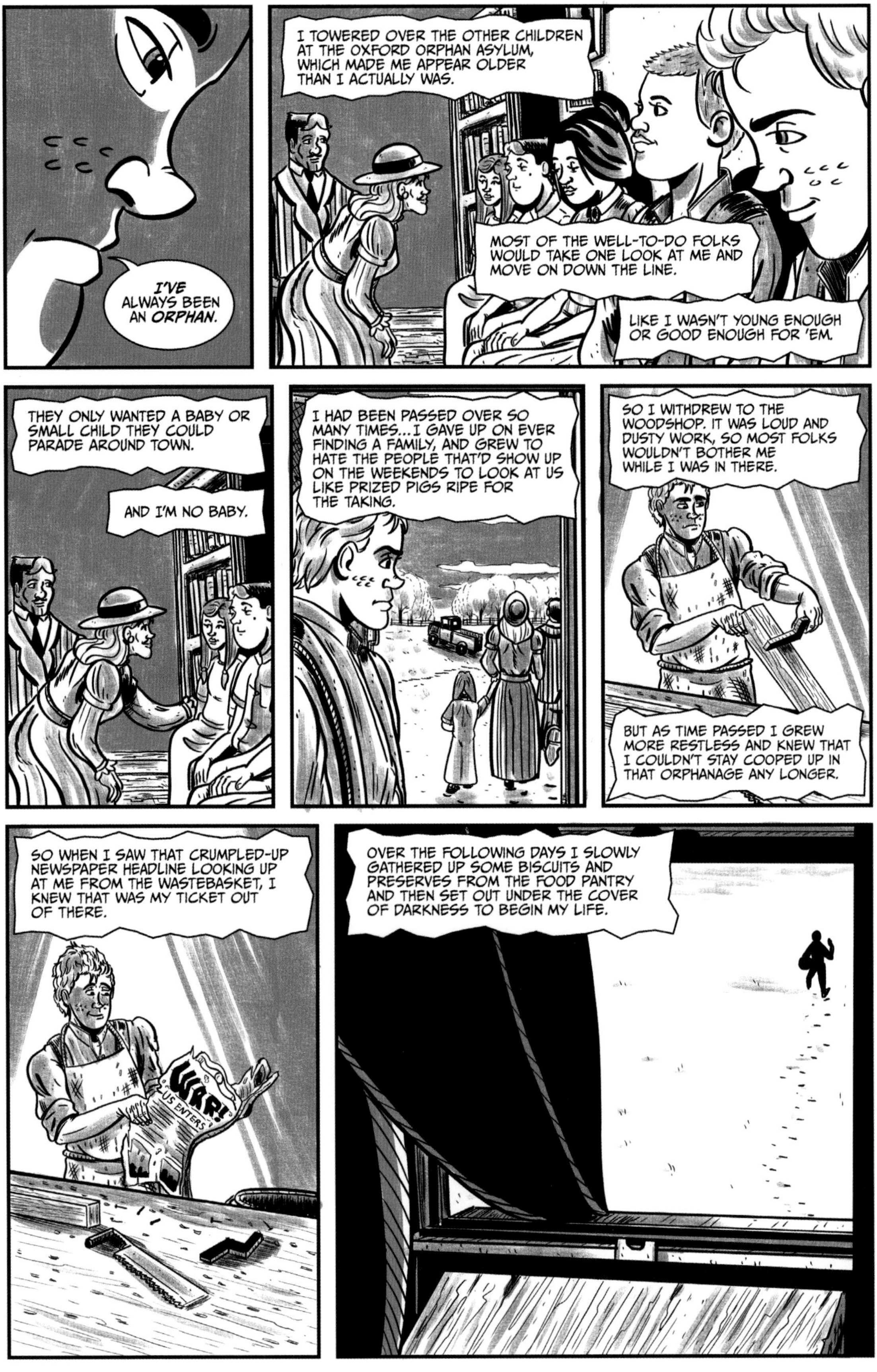
I'VE ALWAYS BEEN AN ORPHAN.
I TOWERED OVER THE OTHER CHILDREN AT THE OXFORD ORPHAN ASYLUM, WHICH MADE ME APPEAR OLDER THAN I ACTUALLY WAS.
MOST OF THE WELL-TO-DO FOLKS WOULD TAKE ONE LOOK AT ME AND MOVE ON DOWN THE LINE.
LIKE I WASN'T YOUNG ENOUGH OR GOOD ENOUGH FOR 'EM.
THEY ONLY WANTED A BABY OR SMALL CHILD THEY COULD PARADE AROUND TOWN.
AND I'M NO BABY.
I HAD BEEN PASSED OVER SO MANY TIMES... I GAVE UP ON EVER FINDING A FAMILY, AND GREW TO HATE THE PEOPLE THAT'D SHOW UP ON THE WEEKENDS TO LOOK AT US LIKE PRIZED PIGS RIPE FOR THE TAKING.
SO I WITHDREW TO THE WOODSHOP. IT WAS LOUD AND DUSTY WORK, SO MOST FOLKS WOULDN'T BOTHER ME WHILE I WAS IN THERE.
BUT AS TIME PASSED I GREW MORE RESTLESS AND KNEW THAT I COULDN'T STAY COOPED UP IN THAT ORPHANAGE ANY LONGER.
SO WHEN I SAW THAT CRUMPLED-UP NEWSPAPER HEADLINE LOOKING UP AT ME FROM THE WASTEBASKET, I KNEW THAT WAS MY TICKET OUT OF THERE.
WAR!
US ENTERS
OVER THE FOLLOWING DAYS I SLOWLY GATHERED UP SOME BISCUITS AND PRESERVES FROM THE FOOD PANTRY AND THEN SET OUT UNDER THE COVER OF DARKNESS TO BEGIN MY LIFE.

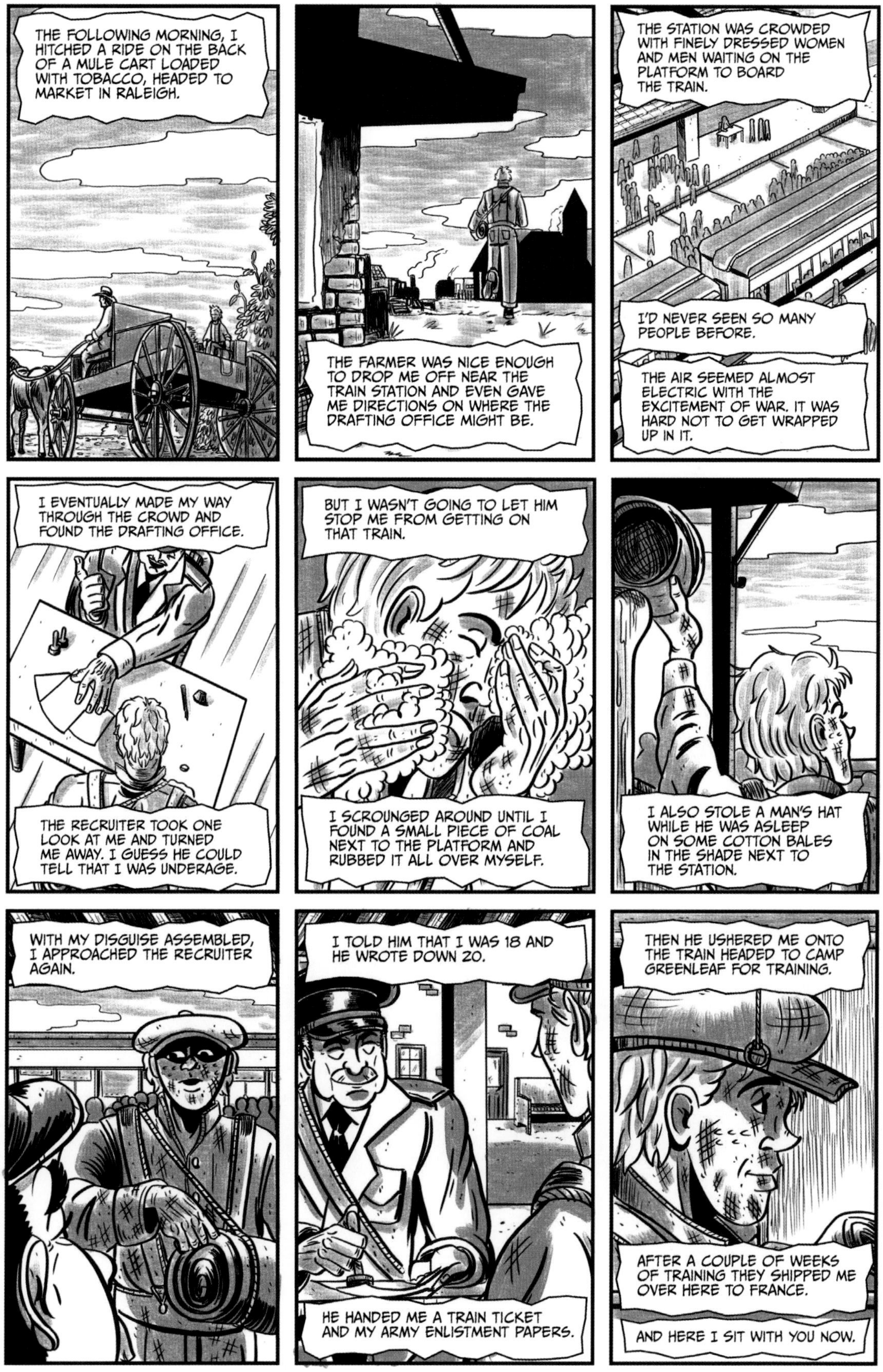
THE FOLLOWING MORNING, I HITCHED A RIDE ON THE BACK OF A MULE CART LOADED WITH TOBACCO, HEADED TO MARKET IN RALEIGH.
THE FARMER WAS NICE ENOUGH TO DROP ME OFF NEAR THE TRAIN STATION AND EVEN GAVE ME DIRECTIONS ON WHERE THE DRAFTING OFFICE MIGHT BE.
THE STATION WAS CROWDED WITH FINELY DRESSED WOMEN AND MEN WAITING ON THE PLATFORM TO BOARD THE TRAIN.
I'D NEVER SEEN SO MANY PEOPLE BEFORE.
THE AIR SEEMED ALMOST ELECTRIC WITH THE EXCITEMENT OF WAR. IT WAS HARD NOT TO GET WRAPPED UP IN IT.
I EVENTUALLY MADE MY WAY THROUGH THE CROWD AND FOUND THE DRAFTING OFFICE.
THE RECRUITER TOOK ONE LOOK AT ME AND TURNED ME AWAY. I GUESS HE COULD TELL THAT I WAS UNDERAGE.
BUT I WASN'T GOING TO LET HIM STOP ME FROM GETTING ON THAT TRAIN.
I SCROUNGED AROUND UNTIL I FOUND A SMALL PIECE OF COAL NEXT TO THE PLATFORM AND RUBBED IT ALL OVER MYSELF.
I ALSO STOLE A MAN'S HAT WHILE HE WAS ASLEEP ON SOME COTTON BALES IN THE SHADE NEXT TO THE STATION.
WITH MY DISGUISE ASSEMBLED, I APPROACHED THE RECRUITER AGAIN.
I TOLD HIM THAT I WAS 18 AND HE WROTE DOWN 20.
HE HANDED ME A TRAIN TICKET AND MY ARMY ENLISTMENT PAPERS.
THEN HE USHERED ME ONTO THE TRAIN HEADED TO CAMP GREENLEAF FOR TRAINING.
AFTER A COUPLE OF WEEKS OF TRAINING THEY SHIPPED ME OVER HERE TO FRANCE.
AND HERE I SIT WITH YOU NOW.

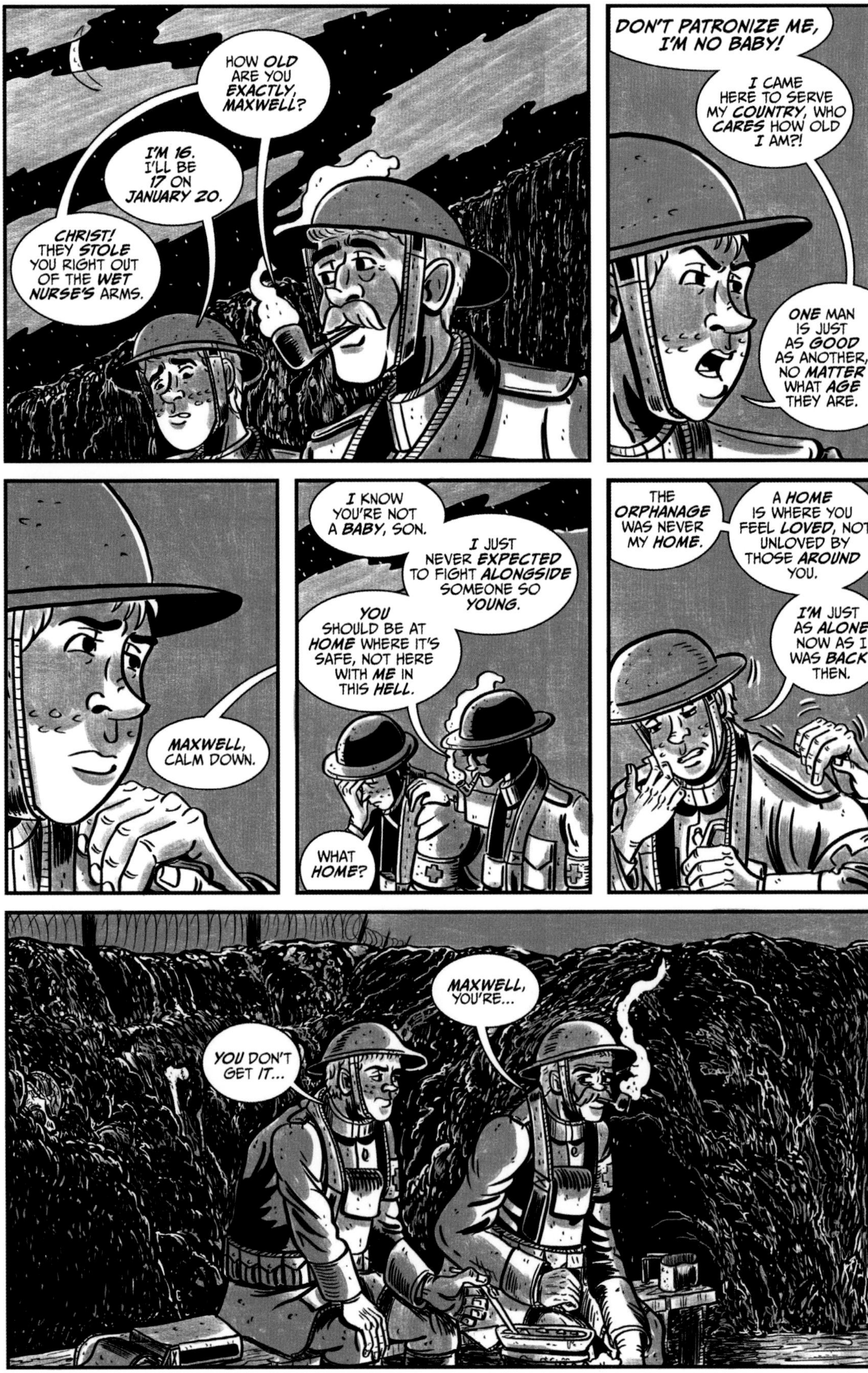
HOW OLD ARE YOU EXACTLY, MAXWELL?
I'M 16. I'LL BE 17 ON JANUARY 20.
CHRIST! THEY STOLE YOU RIGHT OUT OF THE WET NURSE'S ARMS.
DON'T PATRONIZE ME, I'M NO BABY!
I CAME HERE TO SERVE MY COUNTRY, WHO CARES HOW OLD I AM?!
ONE MAN IS JUST AS GOOD AS ANOTHER, NO MATTER WHAT AGE THEY ARE.
MAXWELL, CALM DOWN.
I KNOW YOU'RE NOT A BABY, SON.
I JUST NEVER EXPECTED TO FIGHT ALONGSIDE SOMEONE SO YOUNG.
YOU SHOULD BE AT HOME WHERE IT'S SAFE, NOT HERE WITH ME IN THIS HELL.
WHAT HOME?
THE ORPHANAGE WAS NEVER MY HOME.
A HOME IS WHERE YOU FEEL LOVED, NOT UNLOVED BY THOSE AROUND YOU.
I'M JUST AS ALONE NOW AS I WAS BACK THEN.
MAXWELL, YOU'RE...
YOU DON'T GET IT...

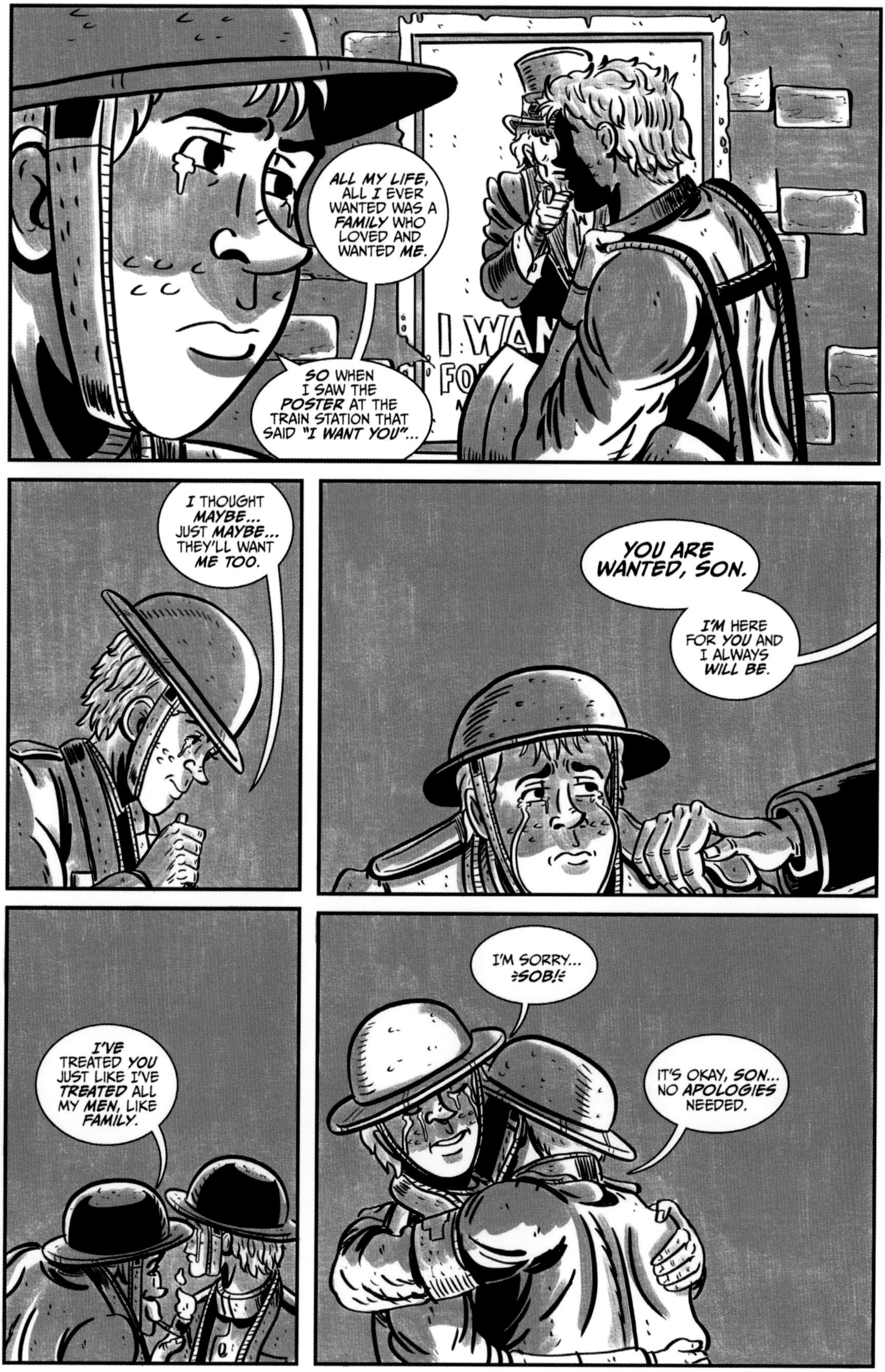
ALL MY LIFE, ALL I EVER WANTED WAS A FAMILY WHO LOVED AND WANTED ME.
SO WHEN I SAW THE POSTER AT THE TRAIN STATION THAT SAID "I WANT YOU"...
I WAN
FO
I THOUGHT MAYBE... JUST MAYBE... THEY'LL WANT ME TOO.
YOU ARE WANTED, SON.
I'M HERE FOR YOU AND I ALWAYS WILL BE.
I'VE TREATED YOU JUST LIKE I'VE TREATED ALL MY MEN, LIKE FAMILY.
I'M SORRY... SOB!
IT'S OKAY, SON... NO APOLOGIES NEEDED.

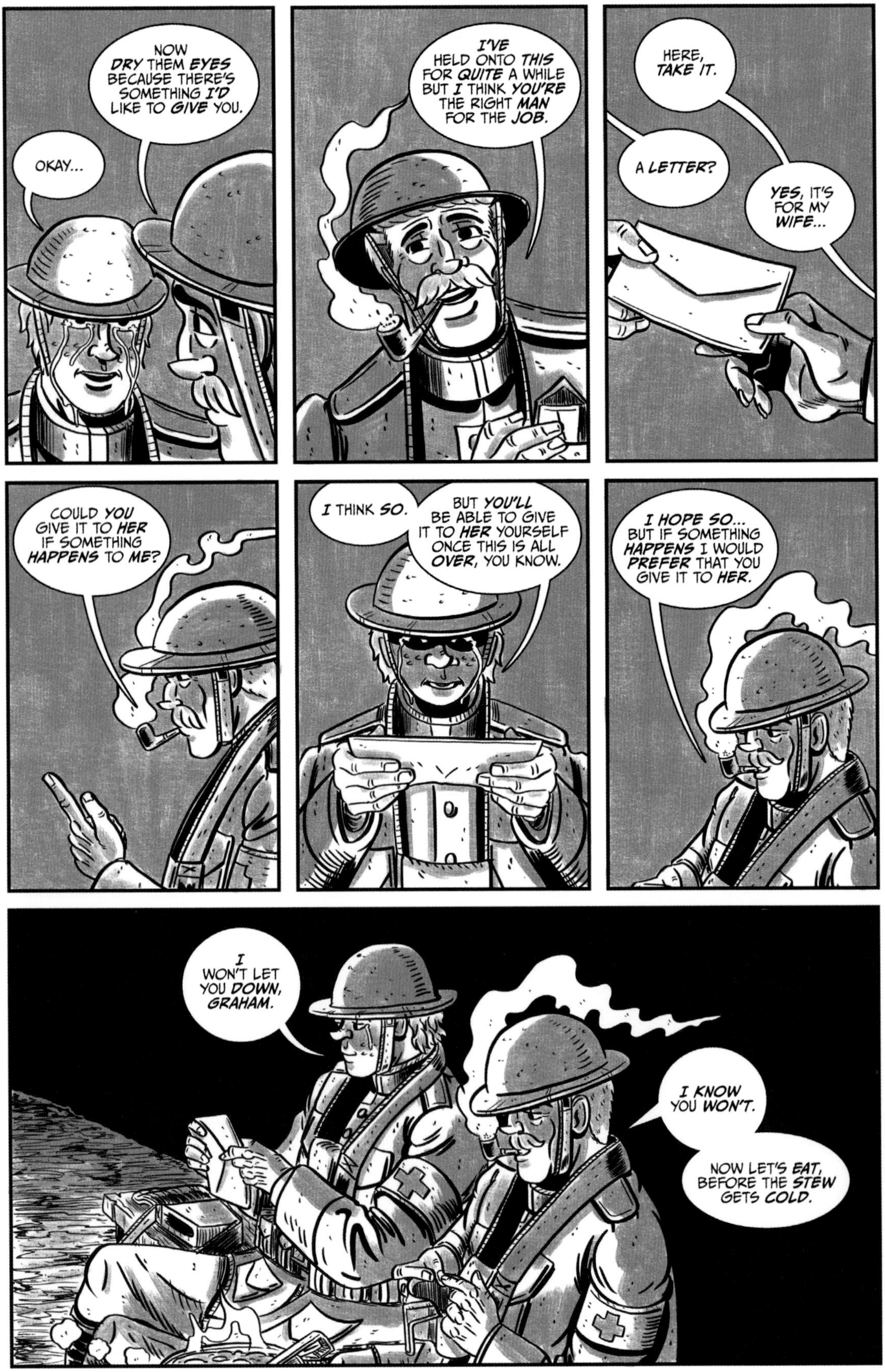
NOW DRY THEM EYES BECAUSE THERE'S SOMETHING I'D LIKE TO GIVE YOU.
OKAY...
I'VE HELD ONTO THIS FOR QUITE A WHILE BUT I THINK YOU'RE THE RIGHT MAN FOR THE JOB.
HERE, TAKE IT.
A LETTER?
YES, IT'S FOR MY WIFE...
COULD YOU GIVE IT TO HER IF SOMETHING HAPPENS TO ME?
I THINK SO.
BUT YOU'LL BE ABLE TO GIVE IT TO HER YOURSELF ONCE THIS IS ALL OVER, YOU KNOW.
I HOPE SO... BUT IF SOMETHING HAPPENS I WOULD PREFER THAT YOU GIVE IT TO HER.
I WON'T LET YOU DOWN, GRAHAM.
I KNOW YOU WON'T.
NOW LET'S EAT, BEFORE THE STEW GETS COLD.

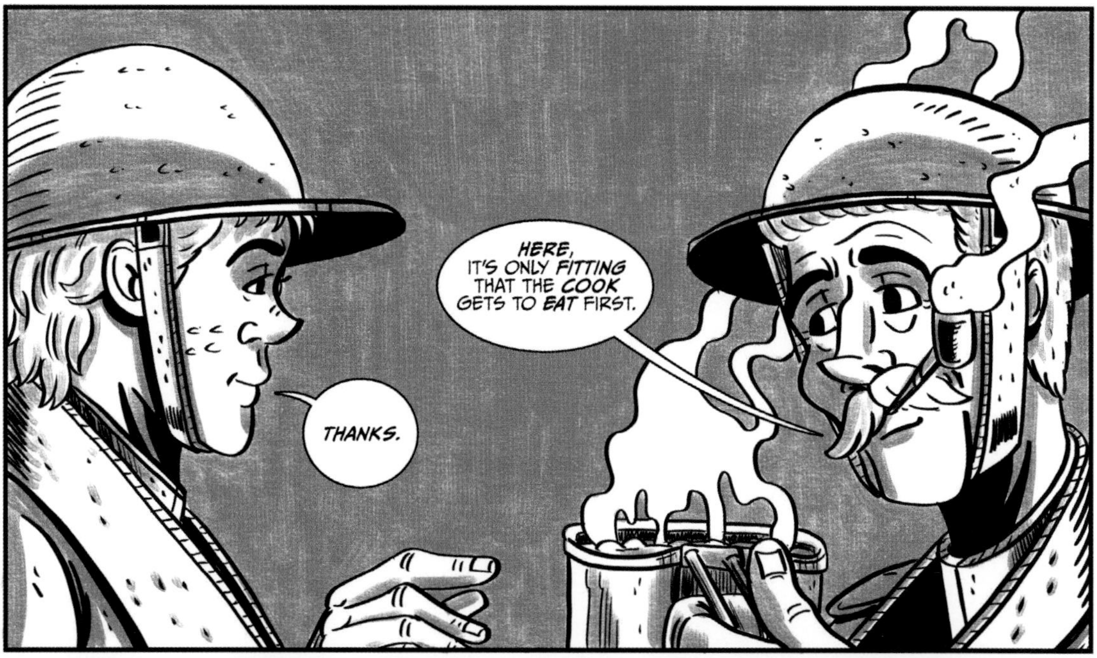
HERE, IT'S ONLY FITTING THAT THE COOK GETS TO EAT FIRST.
THANKS.

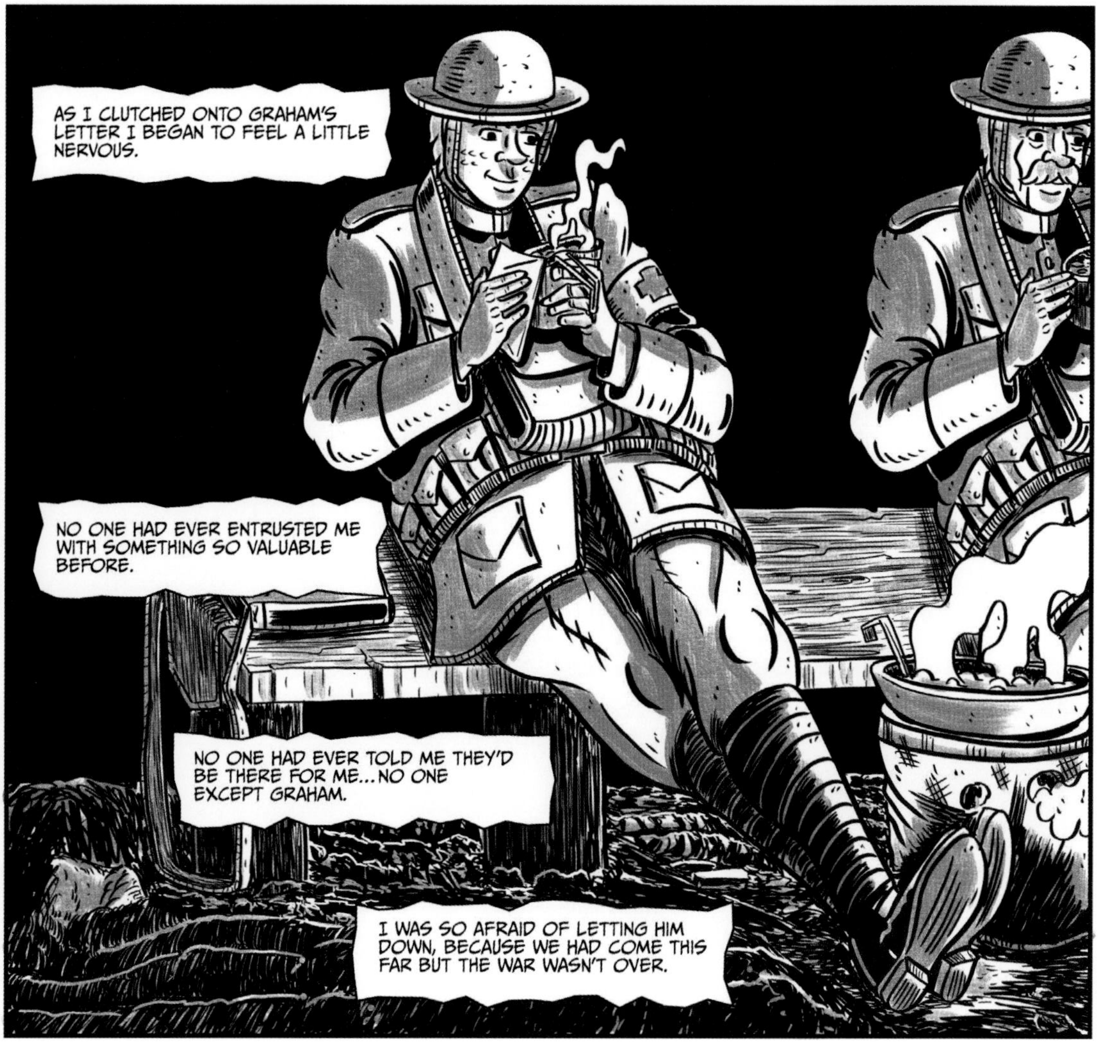
AS I CLUTCHED ONTO GRAHAM'S LETTER I BEGAN TO FEEL A LITTLE NERVOUS.
NO ONE HAD EVER ENTRUSTED ME WITH SOMETHING SO VALUABLE BEFORE.
NO ONE HAD EVER TOLD ME THEY'D BE THERE FOR ME...NO ONE EXCEPT GRAHAM.
I WAS SO AFRAID OF LETTING HIM DOWN, BECAUSE WE HAD COME THIS FAR BUT THE WAR WASN'T OVER.

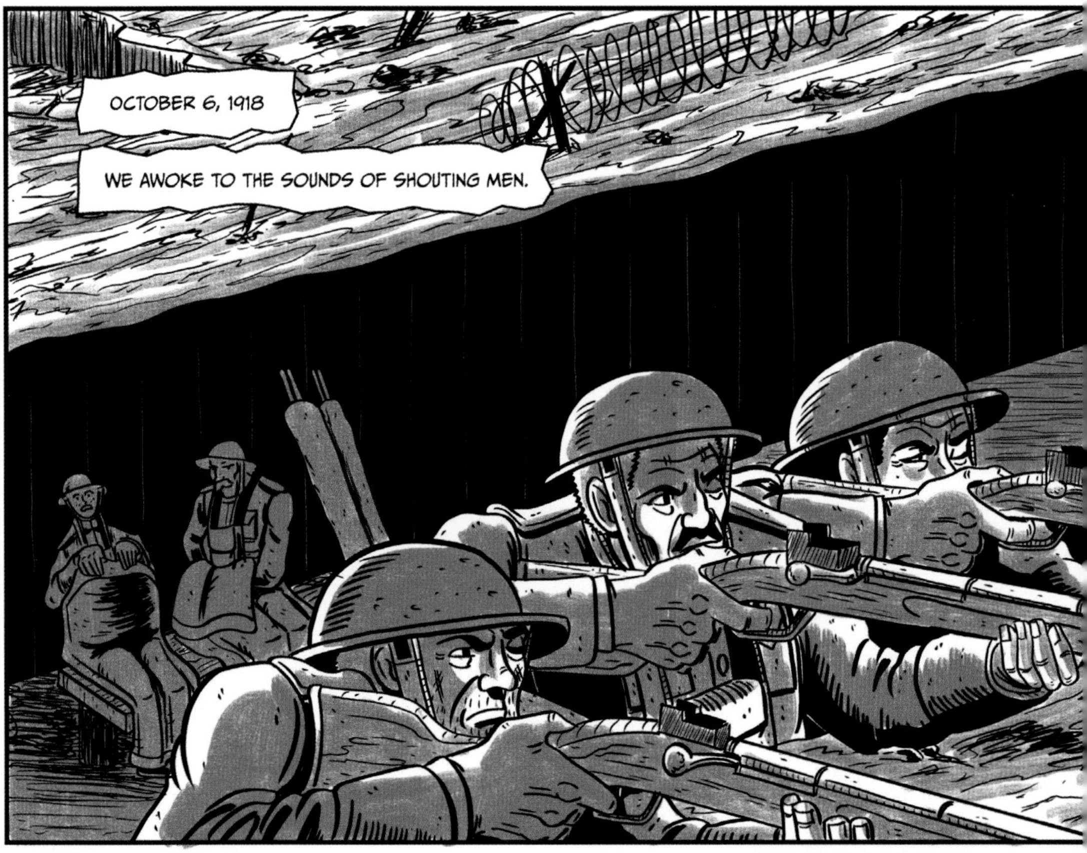
OCTOBER 6, 1918
WE AWOKE TO THE SOUNDS OF SHOUTING MEN.

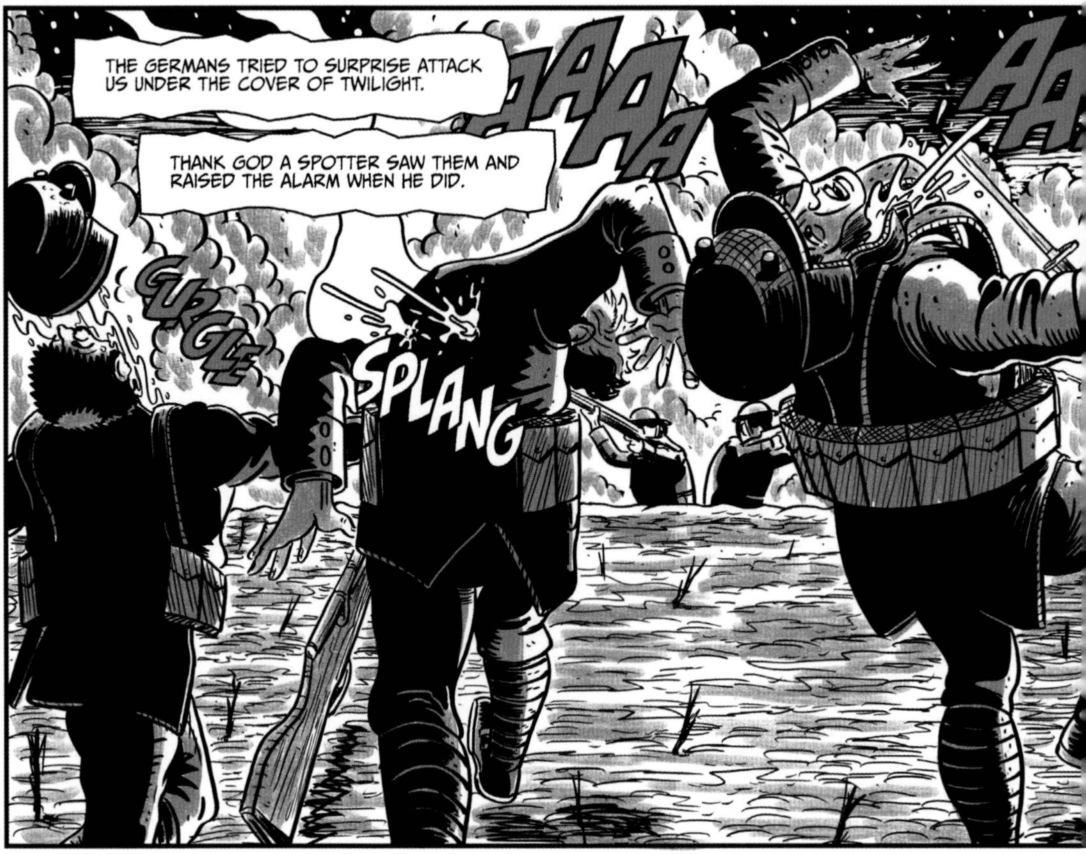
THE GERMANS TRIED TO SURPRISE ATTACK US UNDER THE COVER OF TWILIGHT.
THANK GOD A SPOTTER SAW THEM AND RAISED THE ALARM WHEN HE DID.
AAAAA
AA
GURGLE
SPLANG

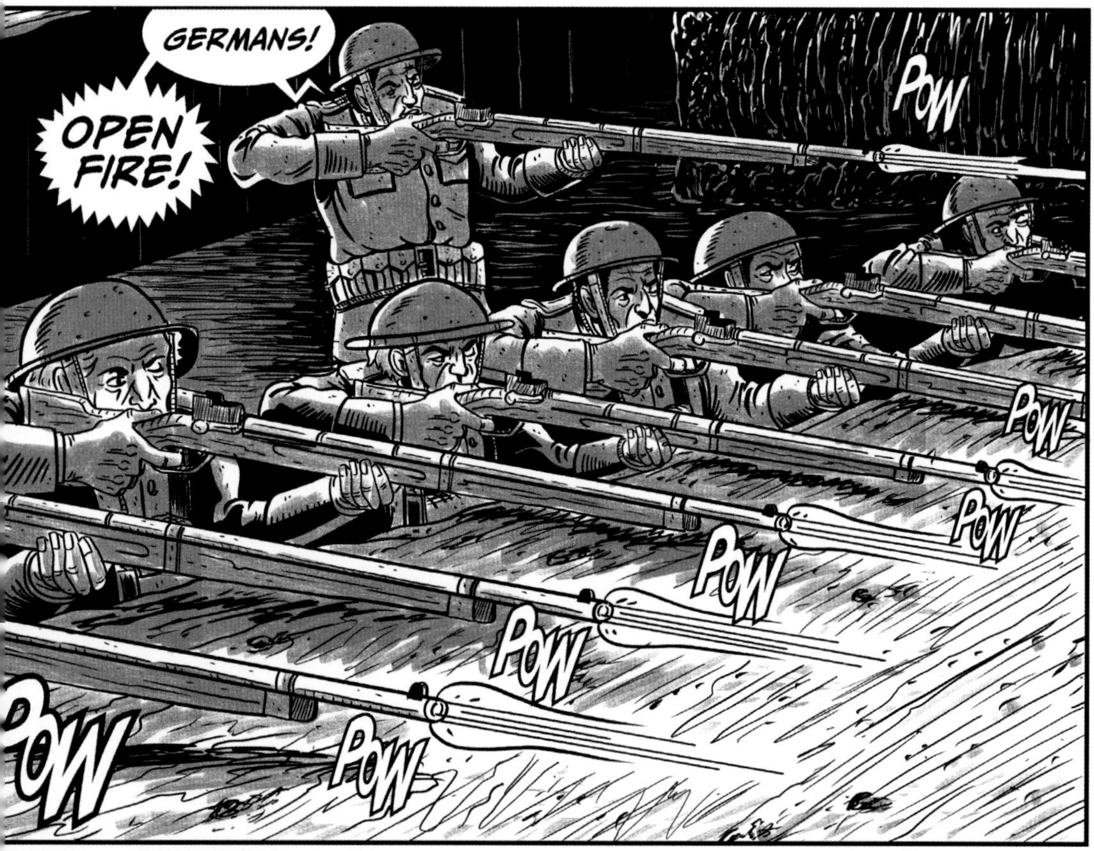
GERMANS!
OPEN FIRE!
POW
POW
POW
POW
POW
POW
POW

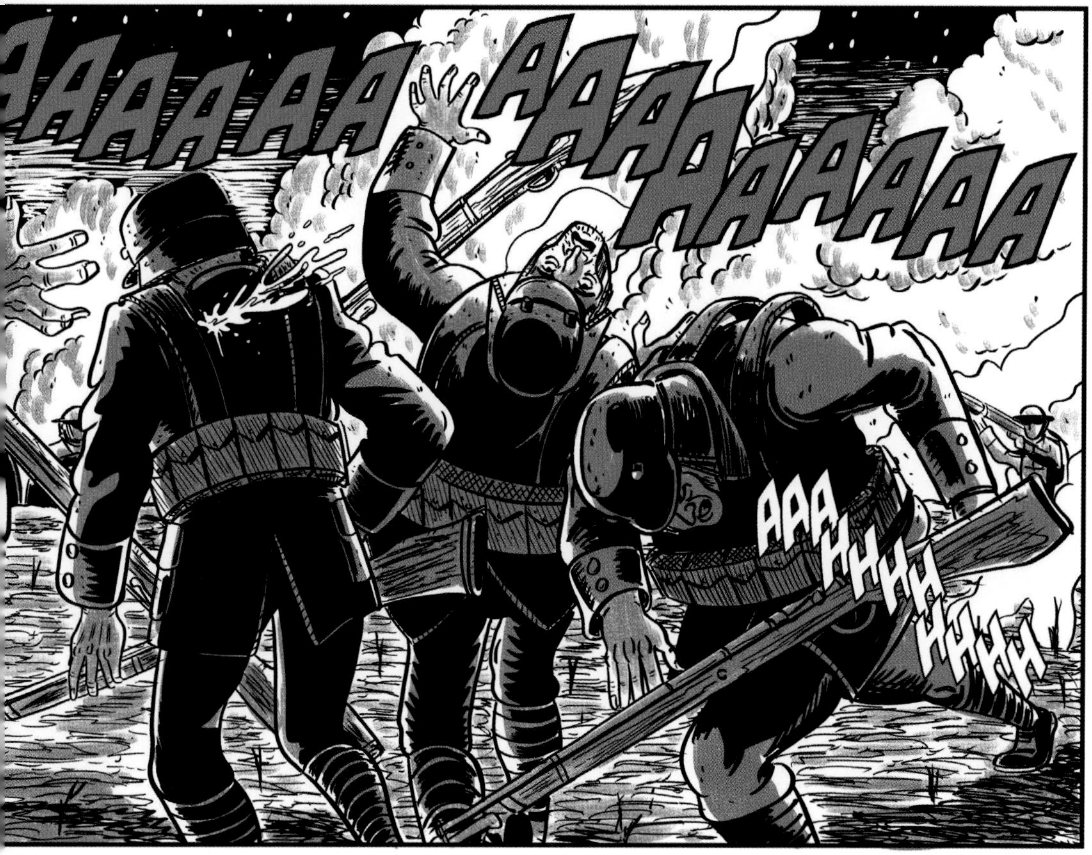
AAAAAAA AAAAAAAAA
AAAHHHHHHHH

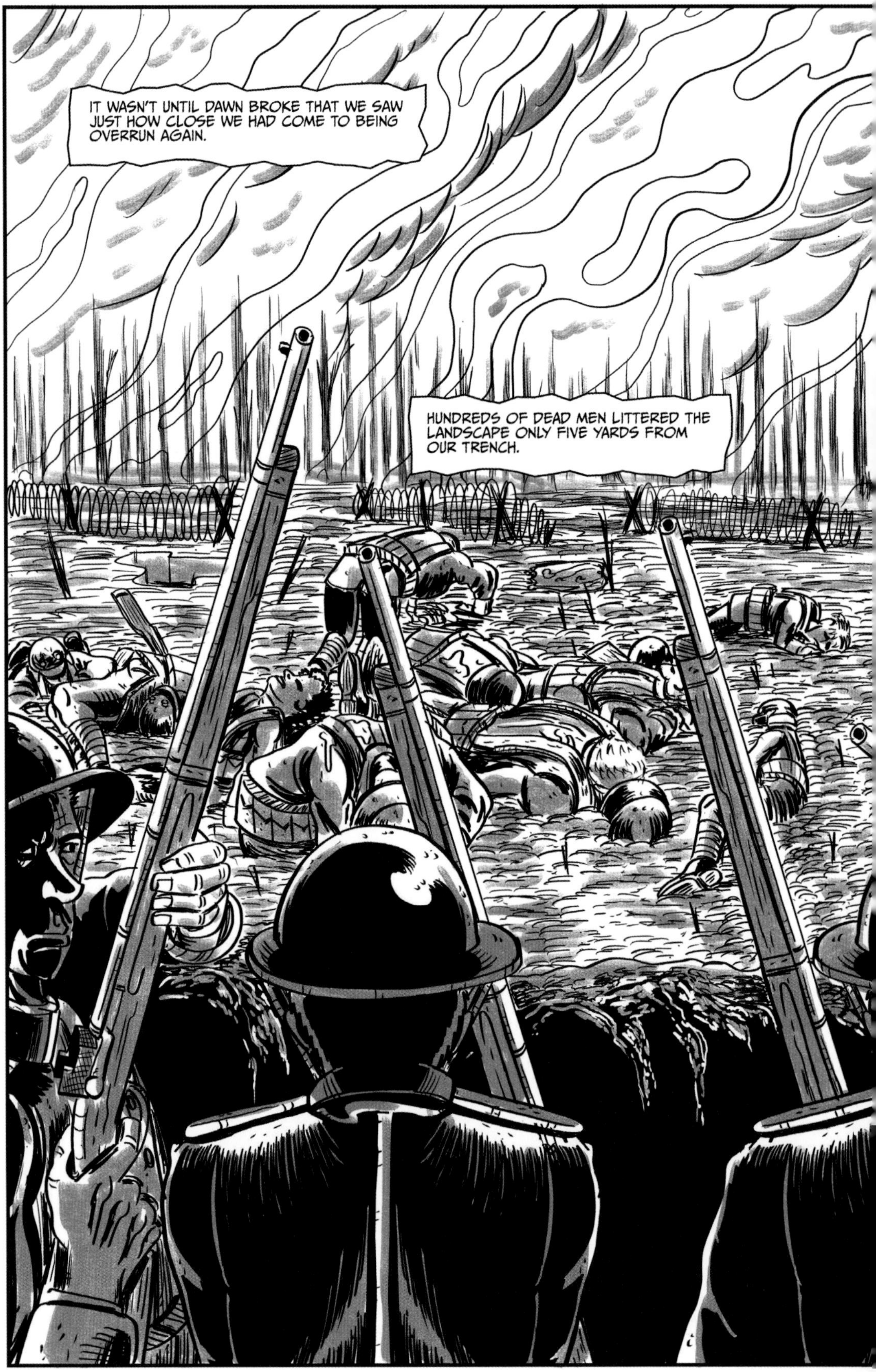
IT WASN'T UNTIL DAWN BROKE THAT WE SAW JUST HOW CLOSE WE HAD COME TO BEING OVERRUN AGAIN.
HUNDREDS OF DEAD MEN LITTERED THE LANDSCAPE ONLY FIVE YARDS FROM OUR TRENCH.

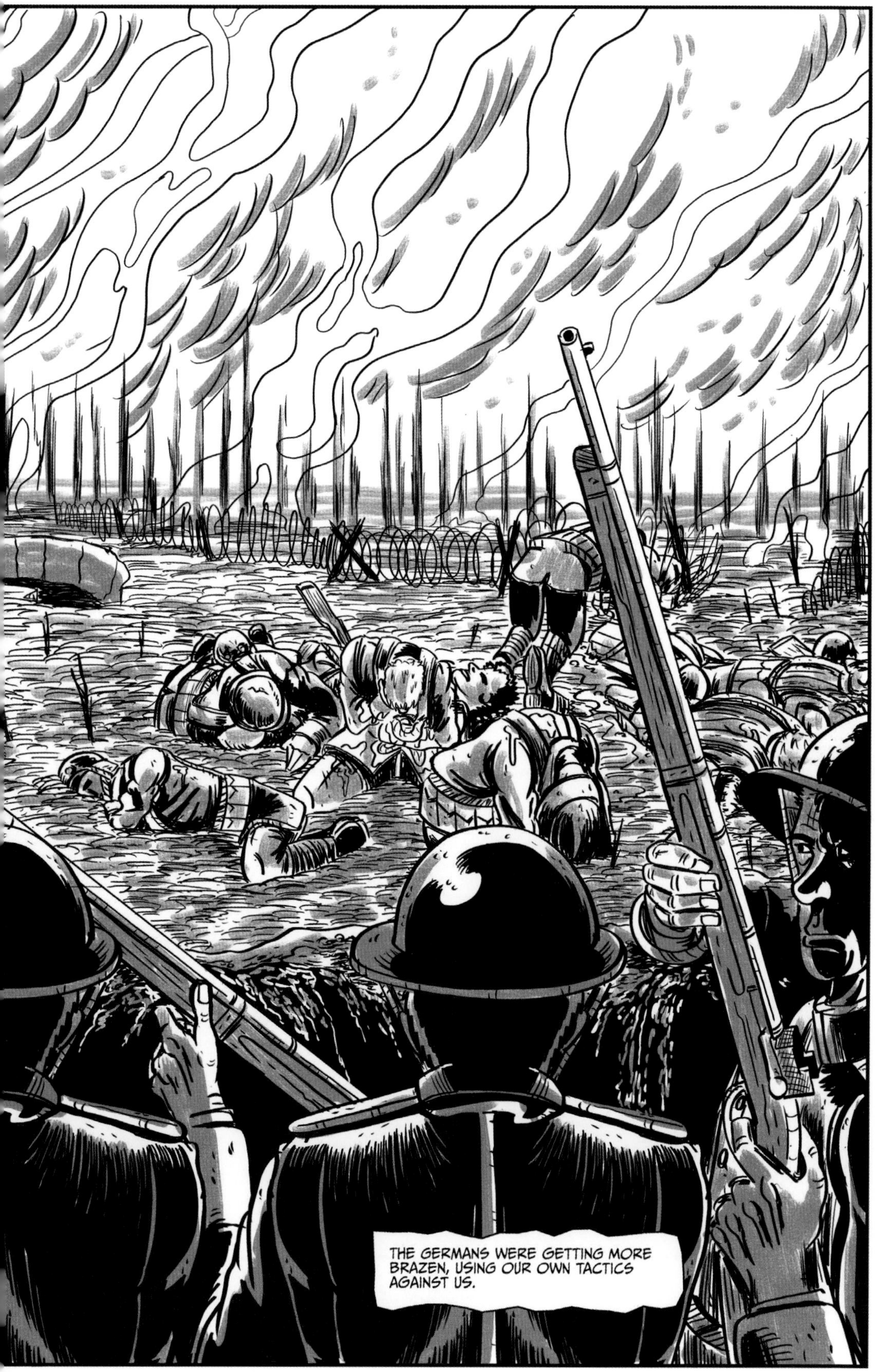
THE GERMANS WERE GETTING MORE BRAZEN, USING OUR OWN TACTICS AGAINST US.

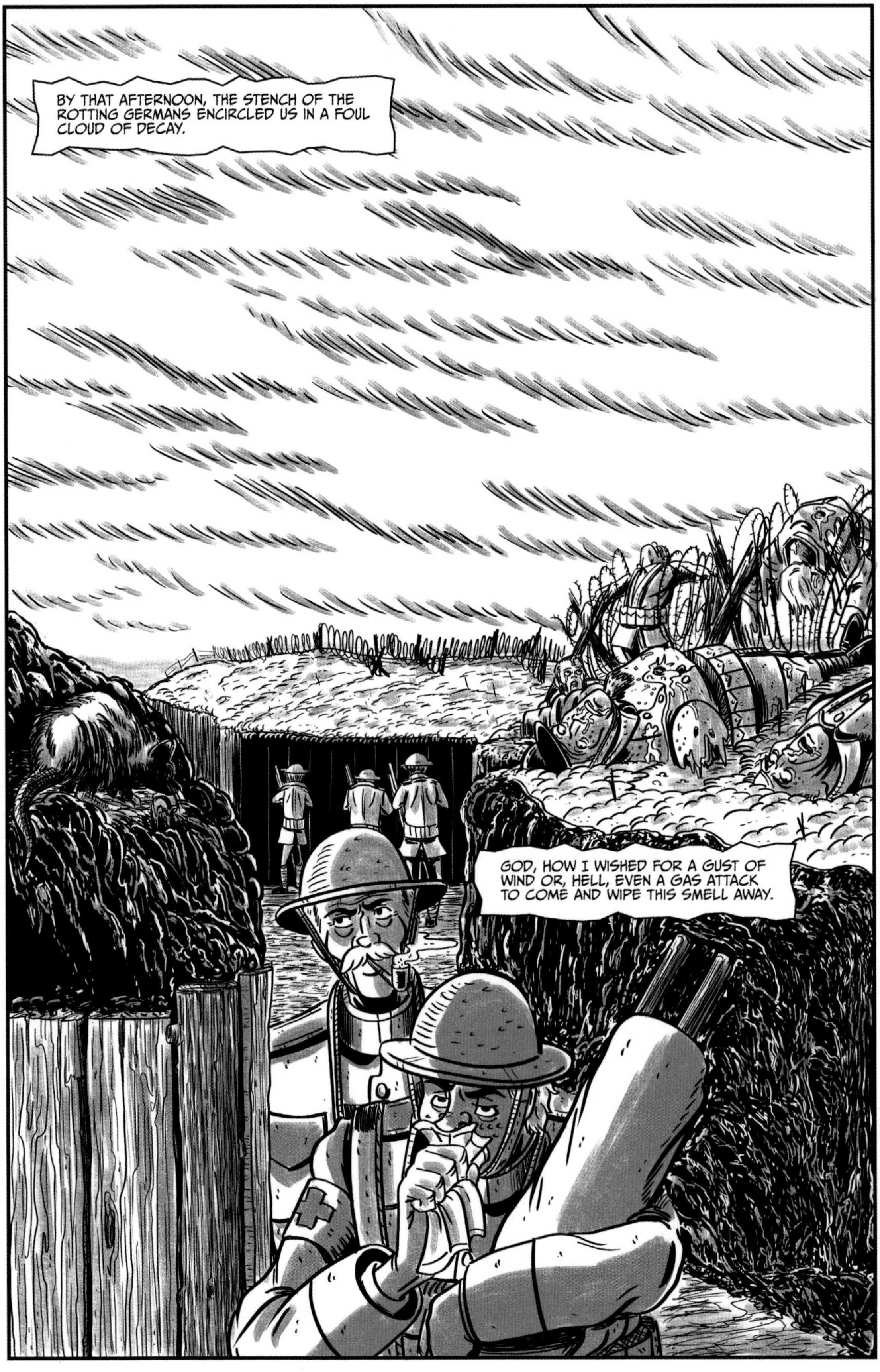
BY THAT AFTERNOON, THE STENCH OF THE ROTTING GERMANS ENCIRCLED US IN A FOUL CLOUD OF DECAY.
GOD, HOW I WISHED FOR A GUST OF WIND OR, HELL, EVEN A GAS ATTACK TO COME AND WIPE THIS SMELL AWAY.

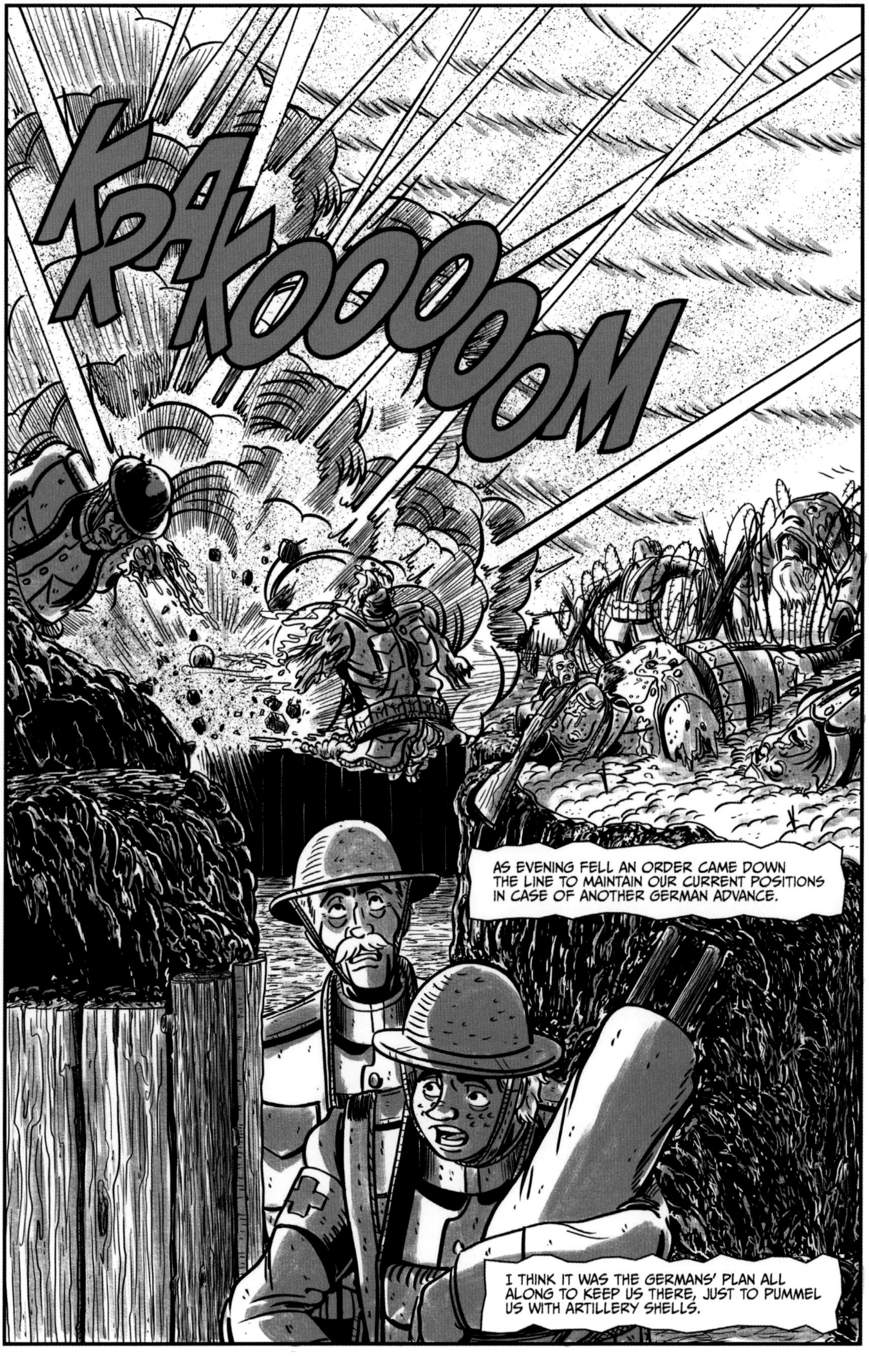
KRAKOOOOOOM
AS EVENING FELL AN ORDER CAME DOWN THE LINE TO MAINTAIN OUR CURRENT POSITIONS IN CASE OF ANOTHER GERMAN ADVANCE.
I THINK IT WAS THE GERMANS' PLAN ALL ALONG TO KEEP US THERE, JUST TO PUMMEL US WITH ARTILLERY SHELLS.

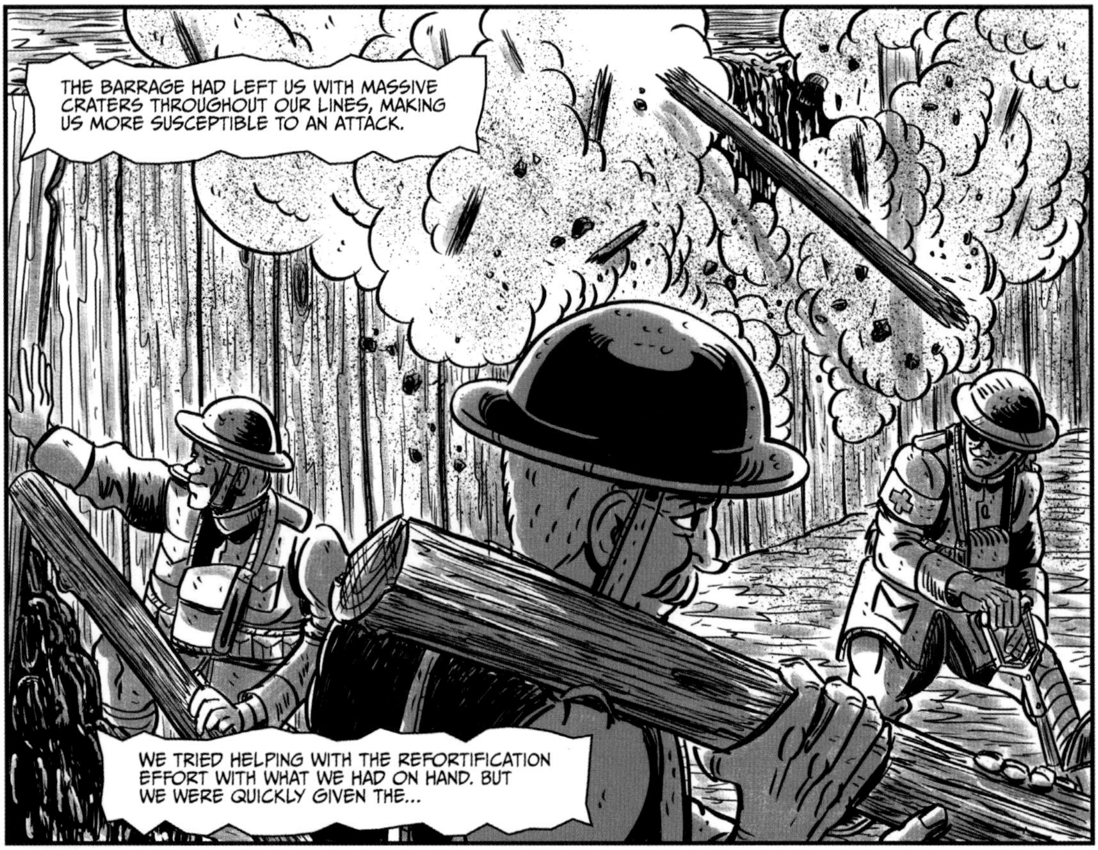
THE BARRAGE HAD LEFT US WITH MASSIVE CRATERS THROUGHOUT OUR LINES, MAKING US MORE SUSCEPTIBLE TO AN ATTACK.
WE TRIED HELPING WITH THE REFORTIFICATION EFFORT WITH WHAT WE HAD ON HAND. BUT WE WERE QUICKLY GIVEN THE...

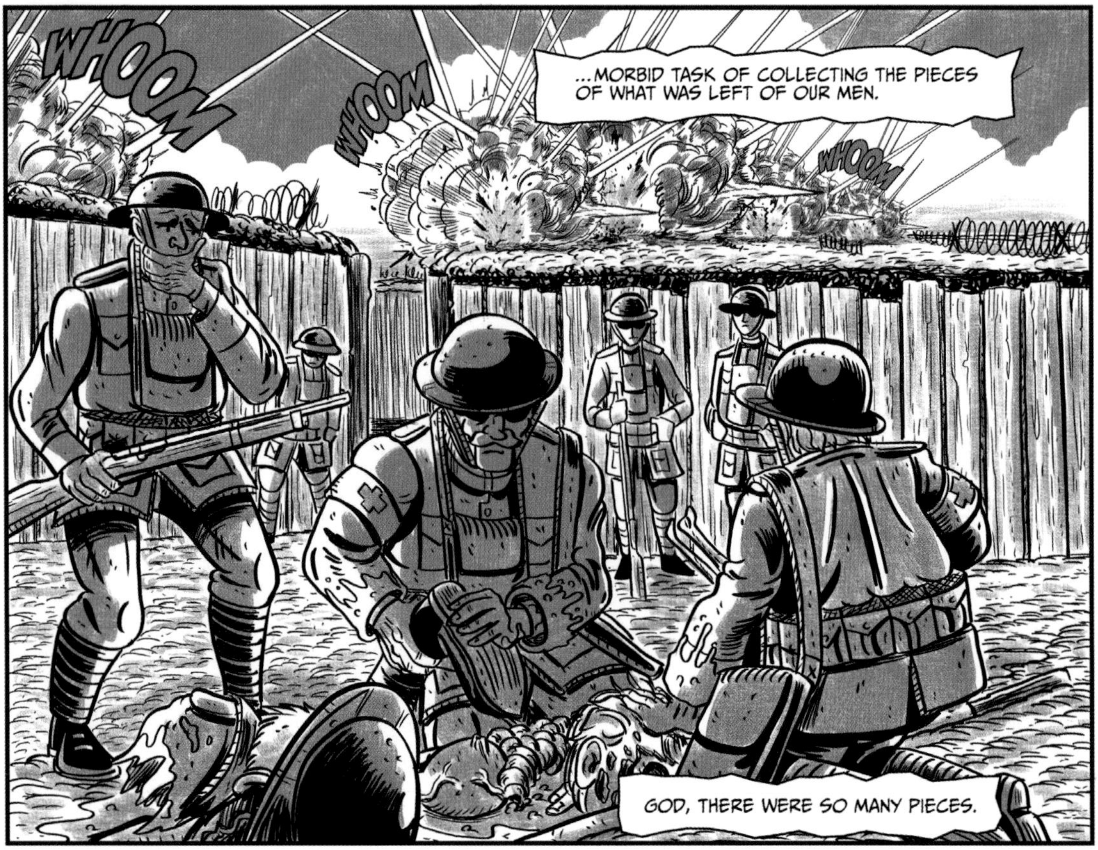
WHOOM
WHOOM
...MORBID TASK OF COLLECTING THE PIECES OF WHAT WAS LEFT OF OUR MEN.
WHOOM
GOD, THERE WERE SO MANY PIECES.

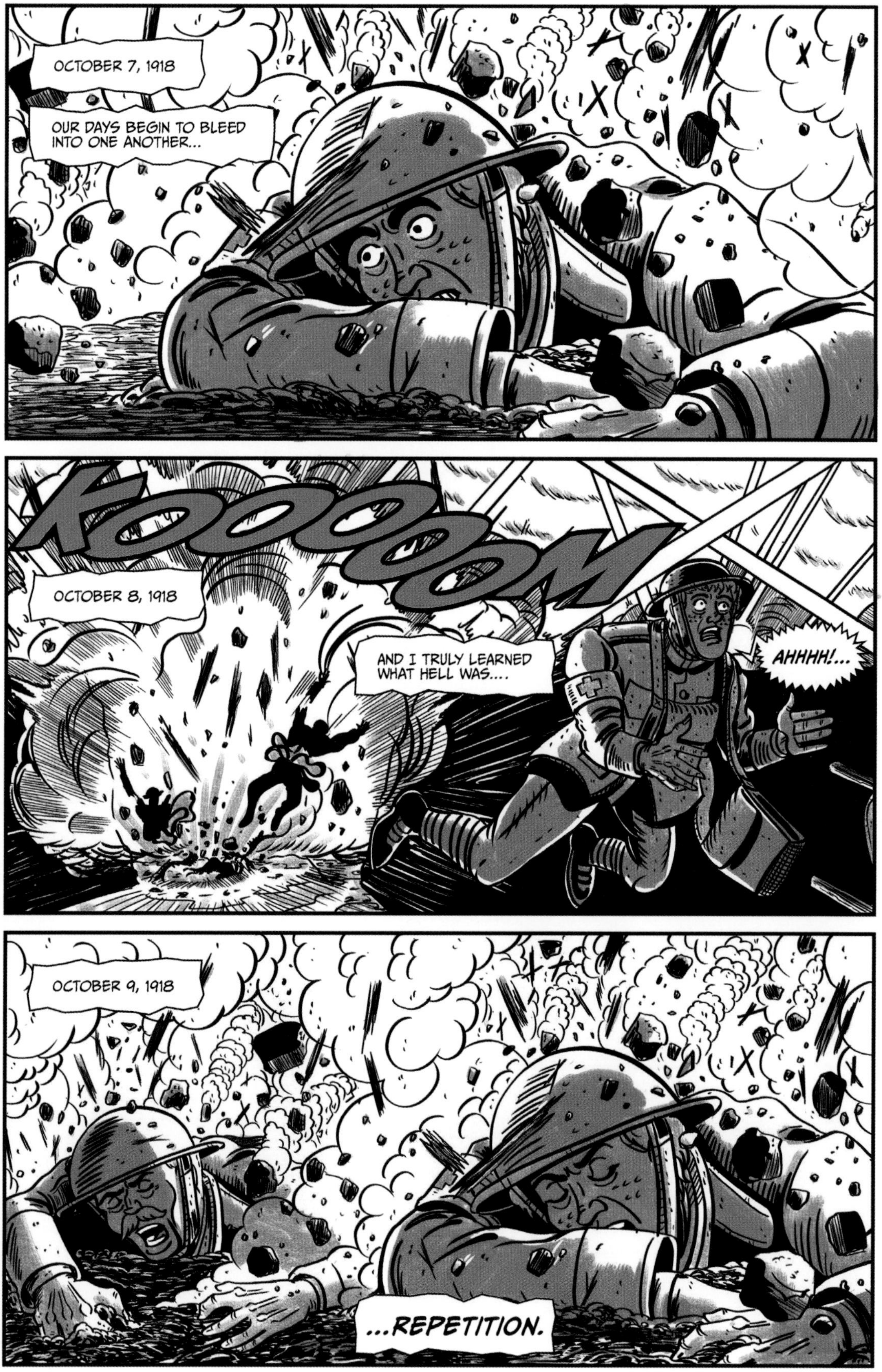
OCTOBER 7, 1918
OUR DAYS BEGIN TO BLEED INTO ONE ANOTHER...
KOOOOOM
OCTOBER 8, 1918
AND I TRULY LEARNED WHAT HELL WAS....
AHHHH!...
OCTOBER 9, 1918
...REPETITION.

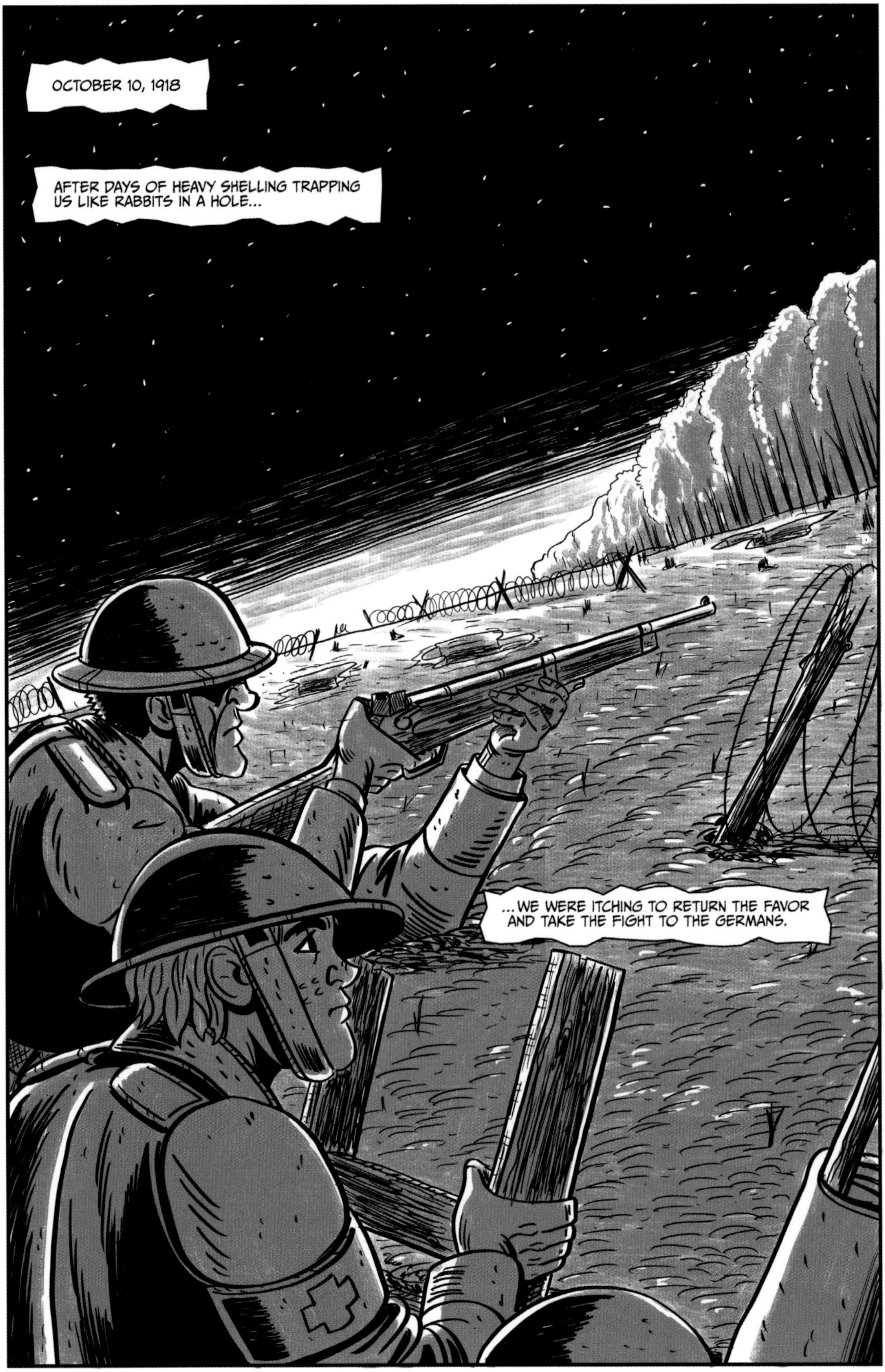
OCTOBER 10, 1918
AFTER DAYS OF HEAVY SHELLING TRAPPING US LIKE RABBITS IN A HOLE...
...WE WERE ITCHING TO RETURN THE FAVOR AND TAKE THE FIGHT TO THE GERMANS.

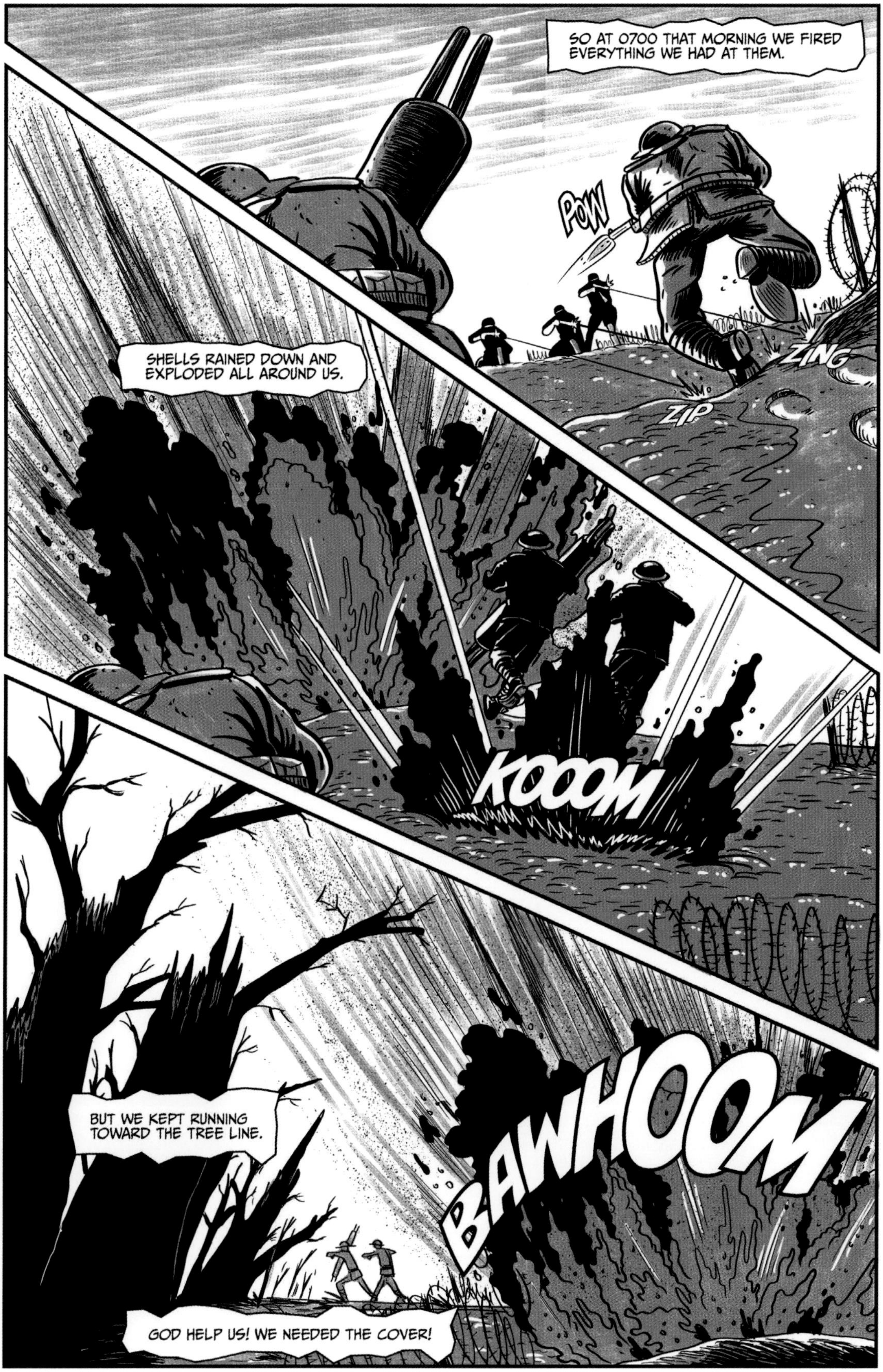
SO AT 0700 THAT MORNING WE FIRED EVERYTHING WE HAD AT THEM.
POW
ZING
ZIP
SHELLS RAINED DOWN AND EXPLODED ALL AROUND US.
KOOOM
BUT WE KEPT RUNNING TOWARD THE TREE LINE.
BAWHOOM
GOD HELP US! WE NEEDED THE COVER!

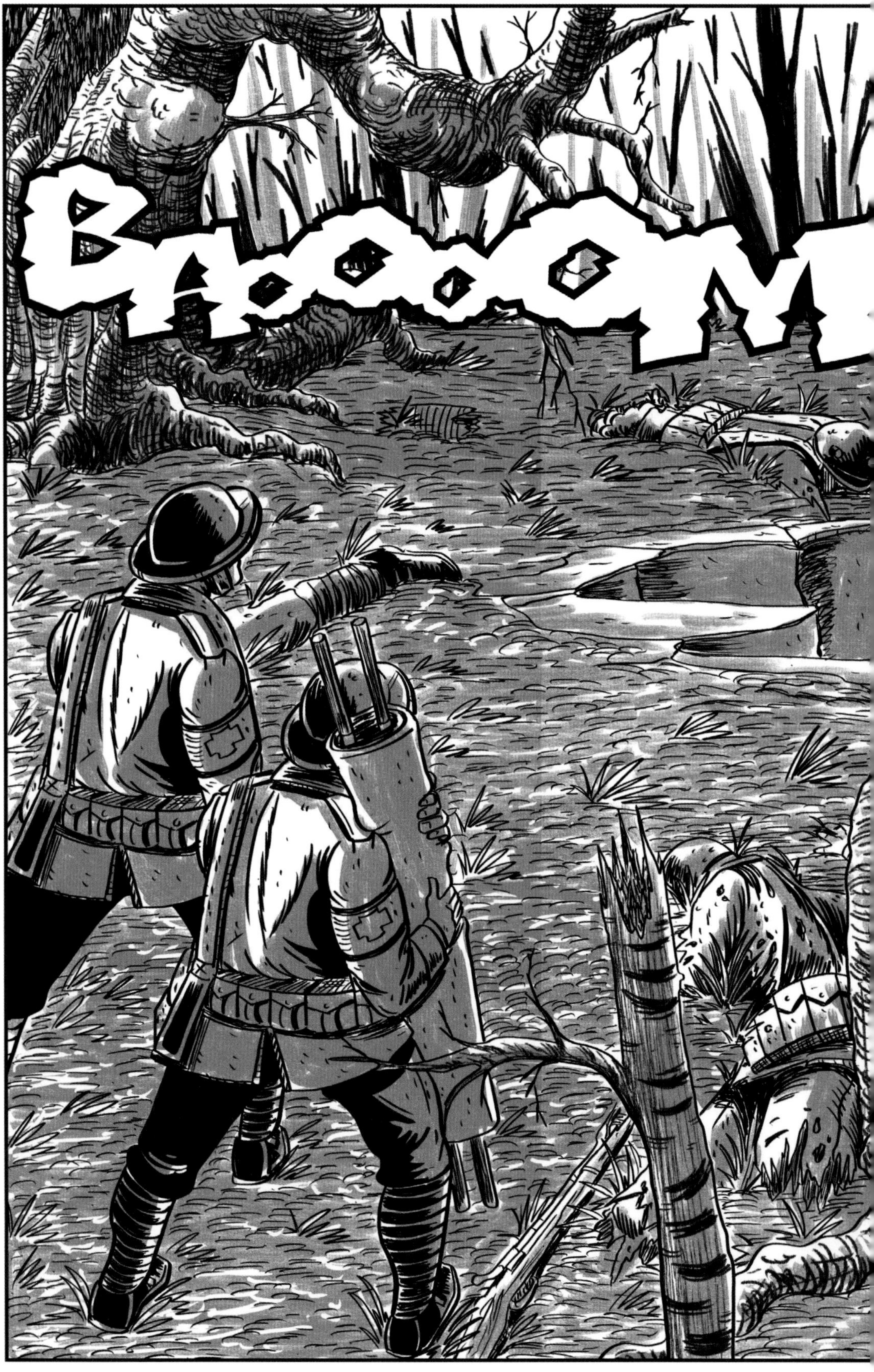
BROOOM

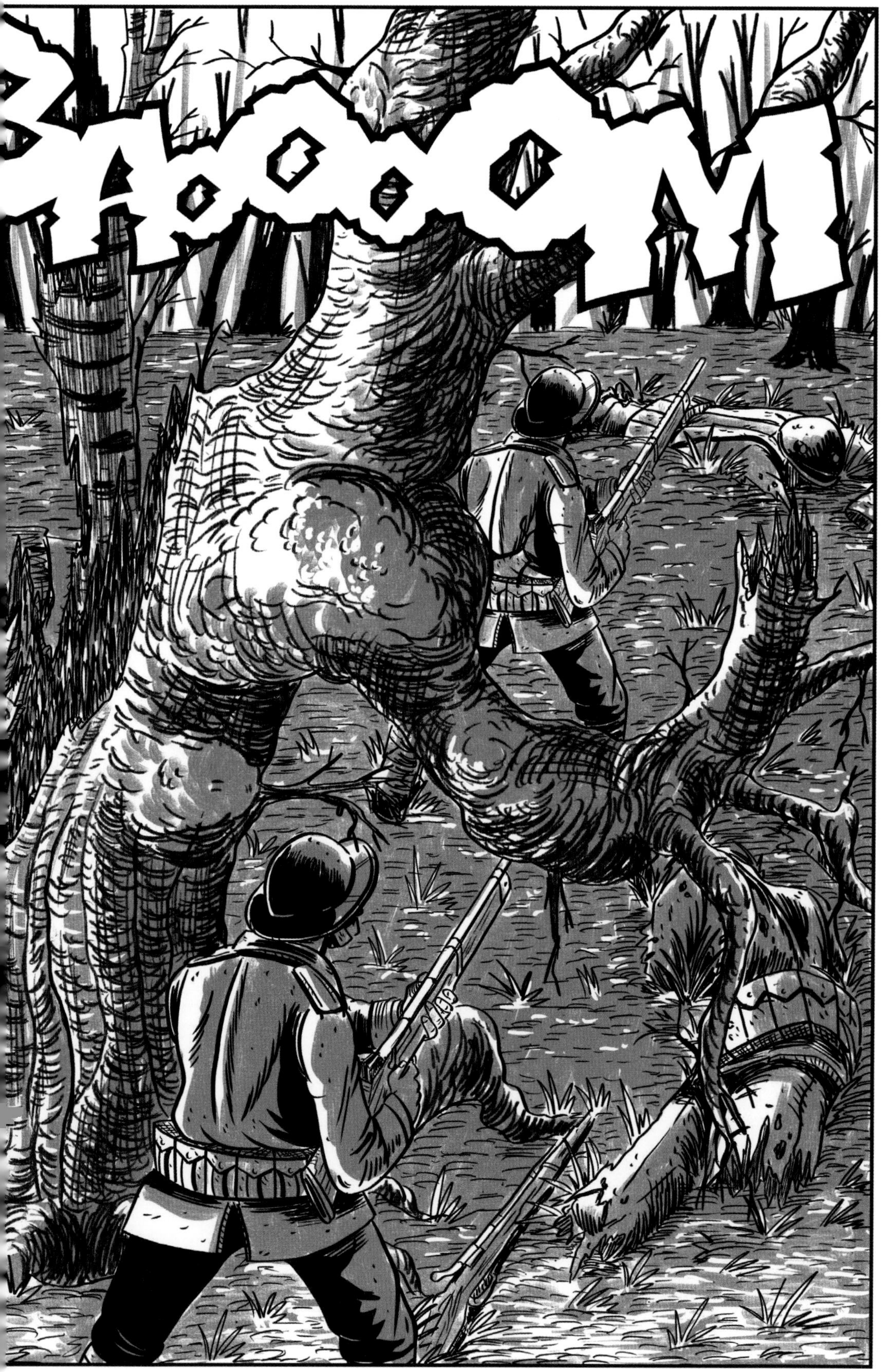
BAOOOOM!

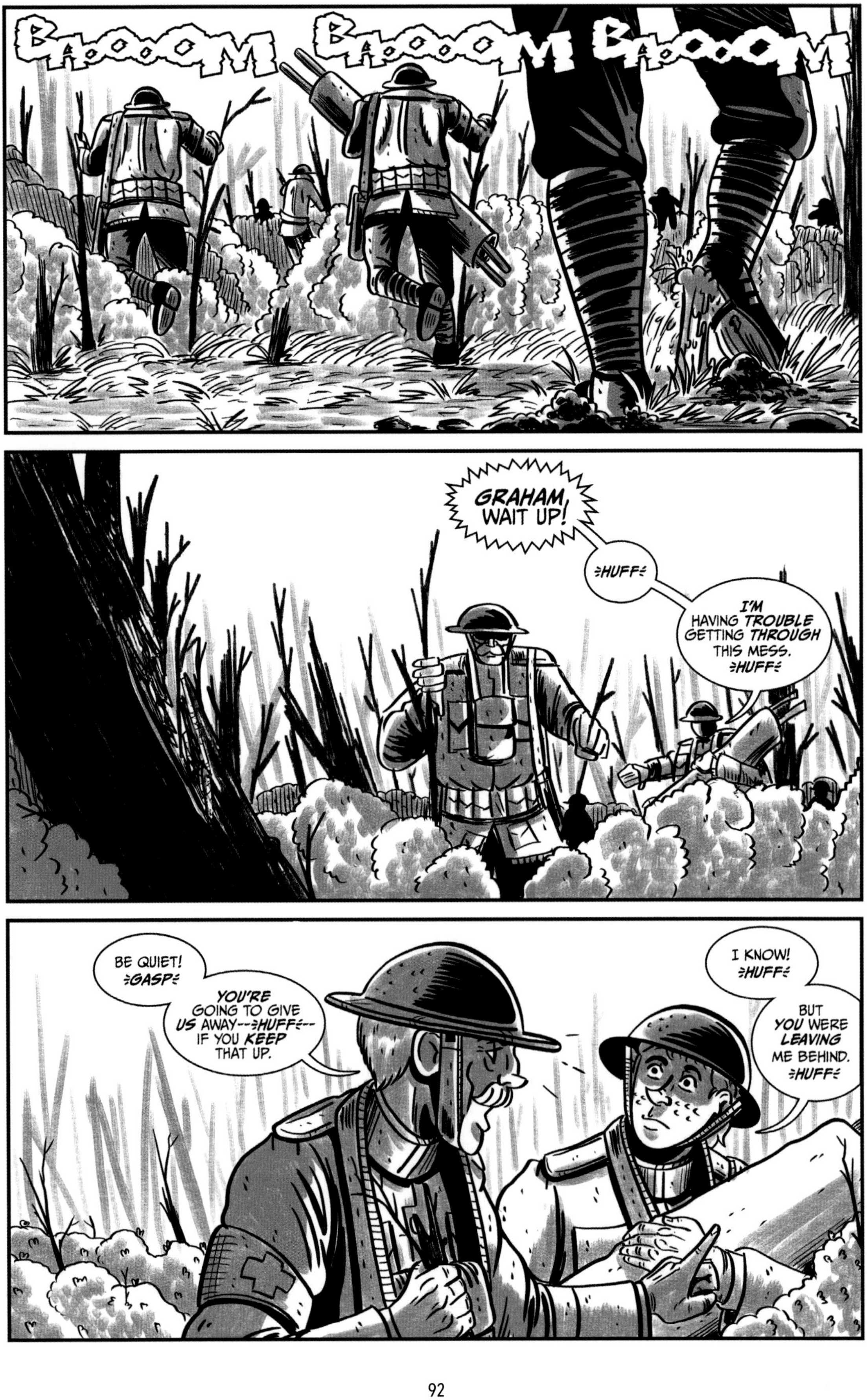
BAOOOM BAOOOM BAOOOM
GRAHAM, WAIT UP!
HUFF
I'M HAVING TROUBLE GETTING THROUGH THIS MESS. HUFF
BE QUIET! GASP
YOU'RE GOING TO GIVE US AWAY--HUFF--IF YOU KEEP THAT UP.
I KNOW! HUFF
BUT YOU WERE LEAVING ME BEHIND. HUFF

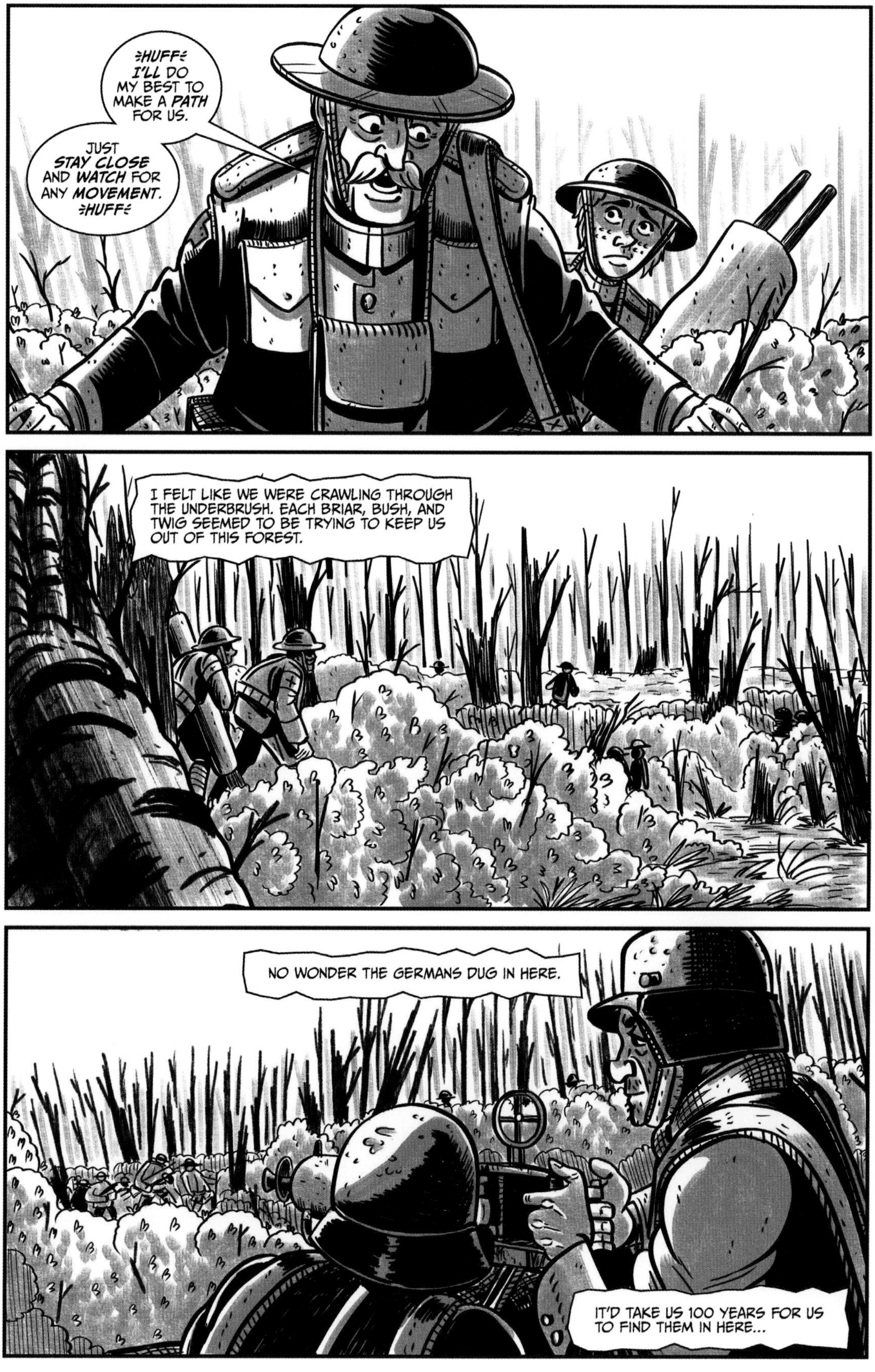

⪢HUFF⪡ I'LL DO MY BEST TO MAKE A PATH FOR US.
JUST STAY CLOSE AND WATCH FOR ANY MOVEMENT. ⪢HUFF⪡
I FELT LIKE WE WERE CRAWLING THROUGH THE UNDERBRUSH. EACH BRIAR, BUSH, AND TWIG SEEMED TO BE TRYING TO KEEP US OUT OF THIS FOREST.
NO WONDER THE GERMANS DUG IN HERE.
IT'D TAKE US 100 YEARS FOR US TO FIND THEM IN HERE...

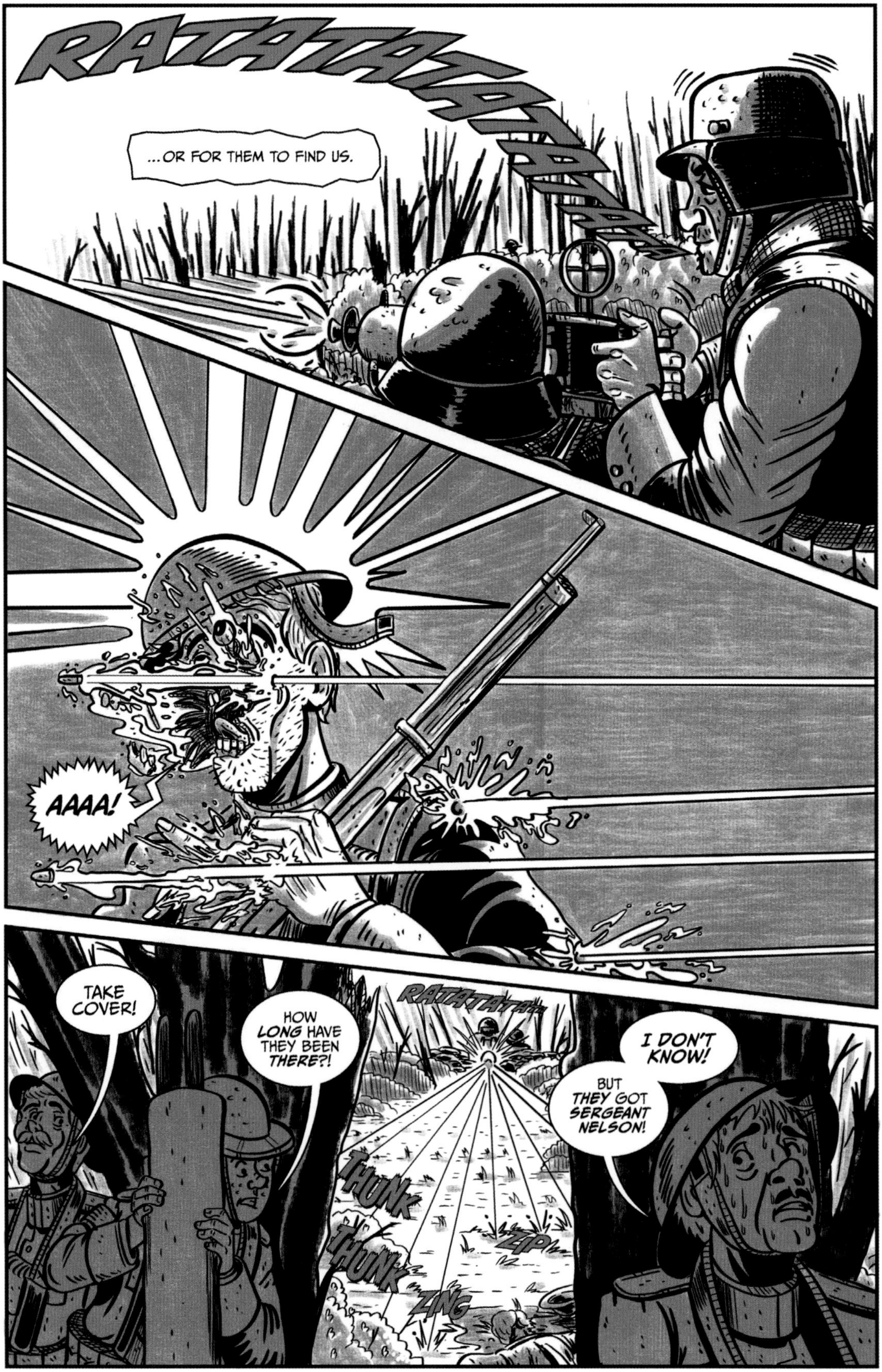
RATATATATATATA
...OR FOR THEM TO FIND US.
AAAA!
TAKE COVER!
HOW LONG HAVE THEY BEEN THERE?!
RATATATATA...
I DON'T KNOW!
BUT THEY GOT SERGEANT NELSON!
THUNK
THUNK
ZIP
ZING

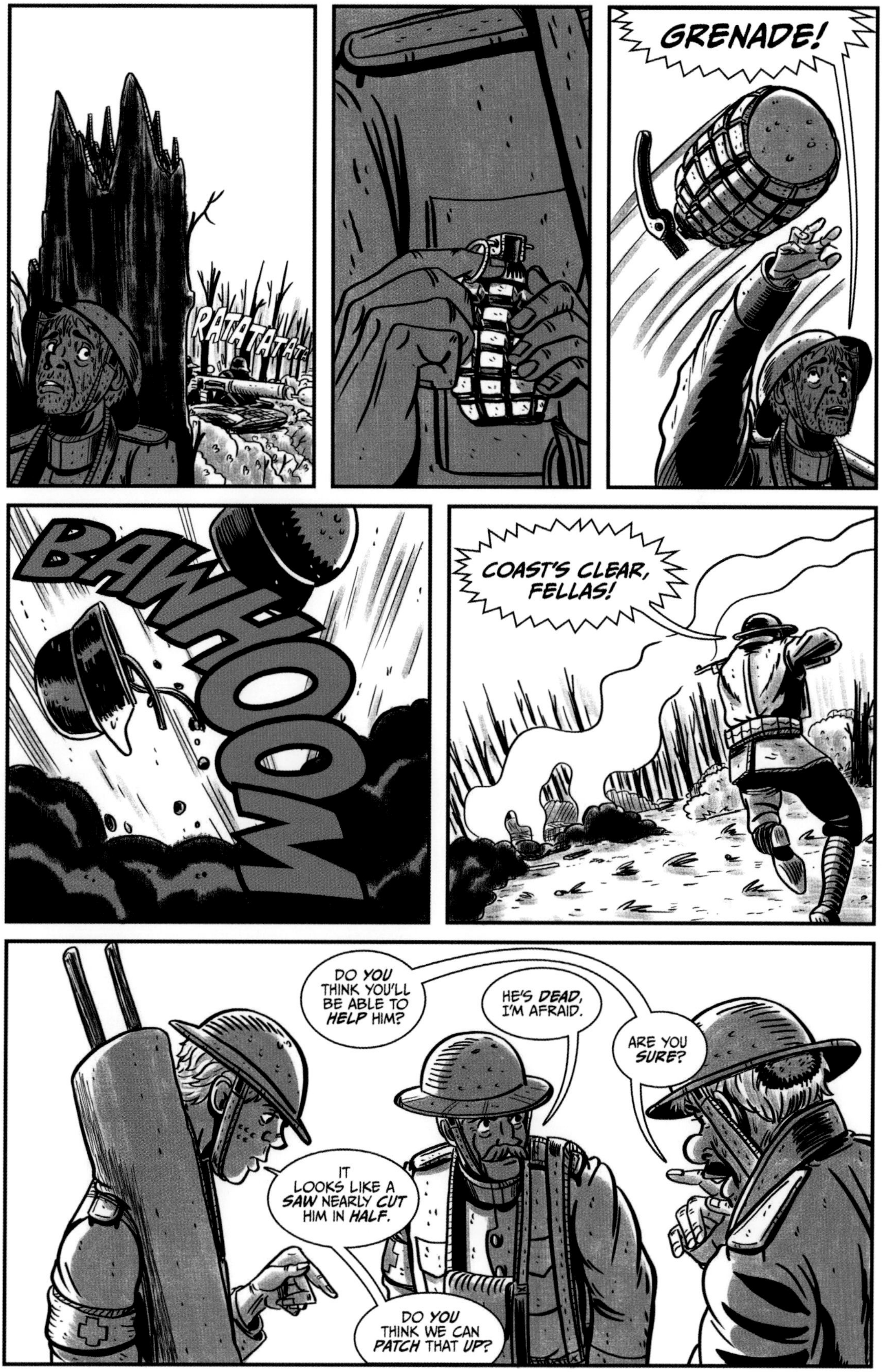
RATATATATAT!
GRENADE!
BAWHOOM
COAST'S CLEAR, FELLAS!
DO YOU THINK YOU'LL BE ABLE TO HELP HIM?
HE'S DEAD, I'M AFRAID.
ARE YOU SURE?
IT LOOKS LIKE A SAW NEARLY CUT HIM IN HALF.
DO YOU THINK WE CAN PATCH THAT UP?

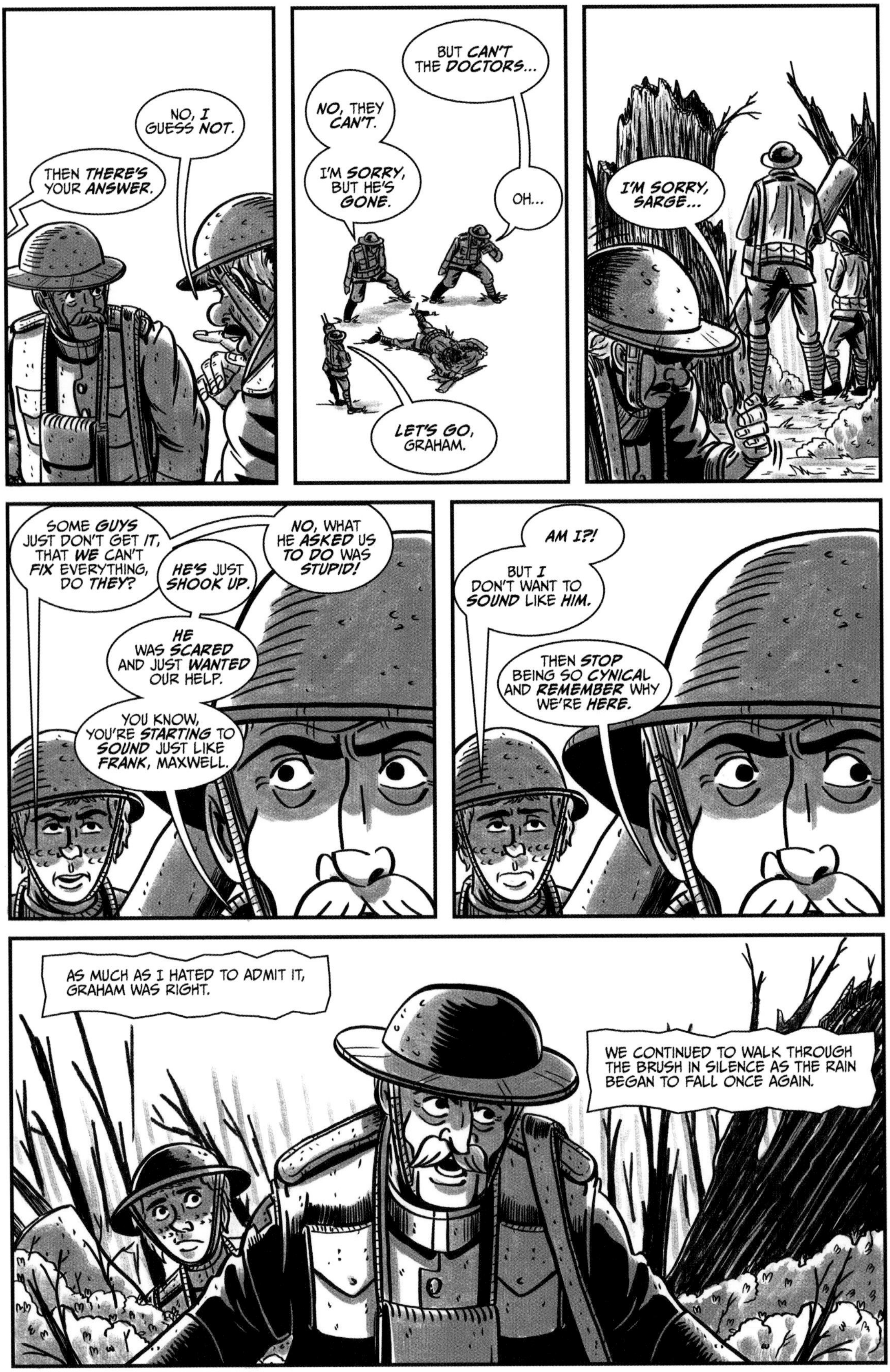
THEN THERE'S YOUR ANSWER.
NO, I GUESS NOT.
NO, THEY CAN'T.
I'M SORRY, BUT HE'S GONE.
BUT CAN'T THE DOCTORS...
OH...
LET'S GO, GRAHAM.
I'M SORRY, SARGE...
SOME GUYS JUST DON'T GET IT, THAT WE CAN'T FIX EVERYTHING, DO THEY?
HE'S JUST SHOOK UP.
NO, WHAT HE ASKED US TO DO WAS STUPID!
HE WAS SCARED AND JUST WANTED OUR HELP.
YOU KNOW, YOU'RE STARTING TO SOUND JUST LIKE FRANK, MAXWELL.
AM I?!
BUT I DON'T WANT TO SOUND LIKE HIM.
THEN STOP BEING SO CYNICAL AND REMEMBER WHY WE'RE HERE.
AS MUCH AS I HATED TO ADMIT IT, GRAHAM WAS RIGHT.
WE CONTINUED TO WALK THROUGH THE BRUSH IN SILENCE AS THE RAIN BEGAN TO FALL ONCE AGAIN.

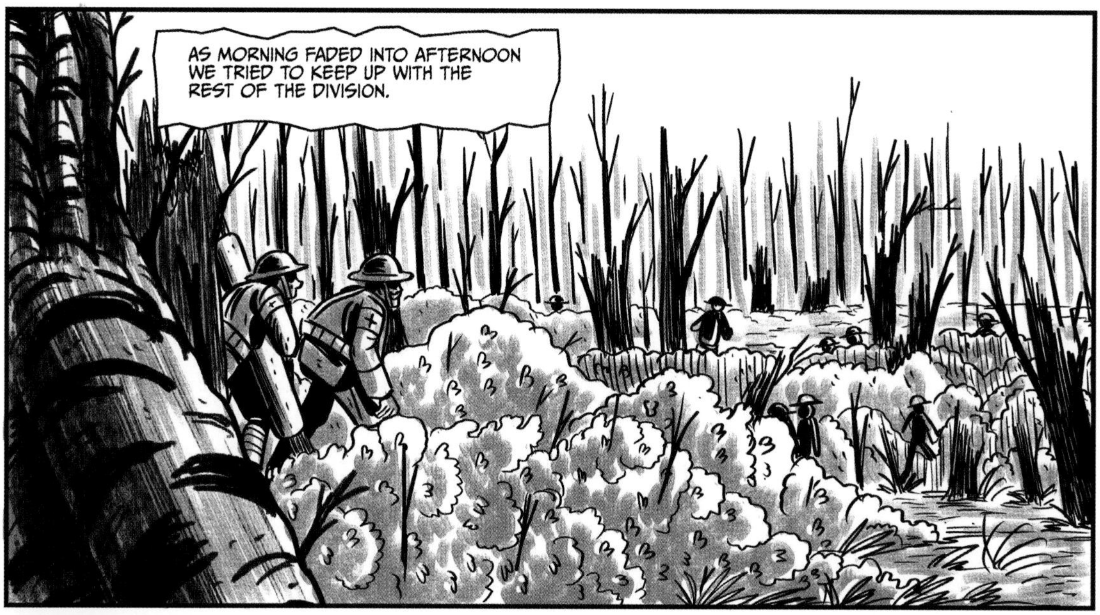
AS MORNING FADED INTO AFTERNOON WE TRIED TO KEEP UP WITH THE REST OF THE DIVISION.

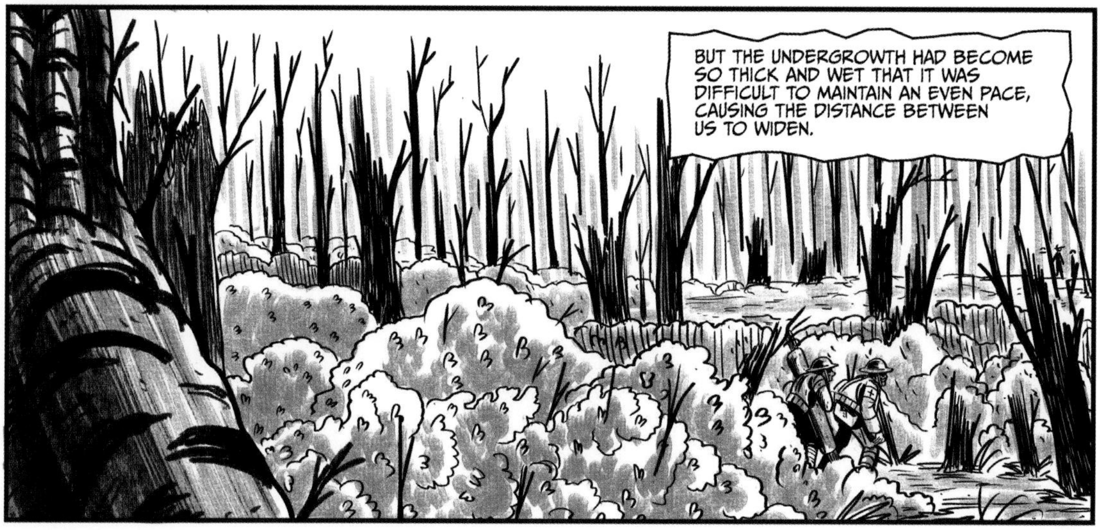
BUT THE UNDERGROWTH HAD BECOME SO THICK AND WET THAT IT WAS DIFFICULT TO MAINTAIN AN EVEN PACE, CAUSING THE DISTANCE BETWEEN US TO WIDEN.

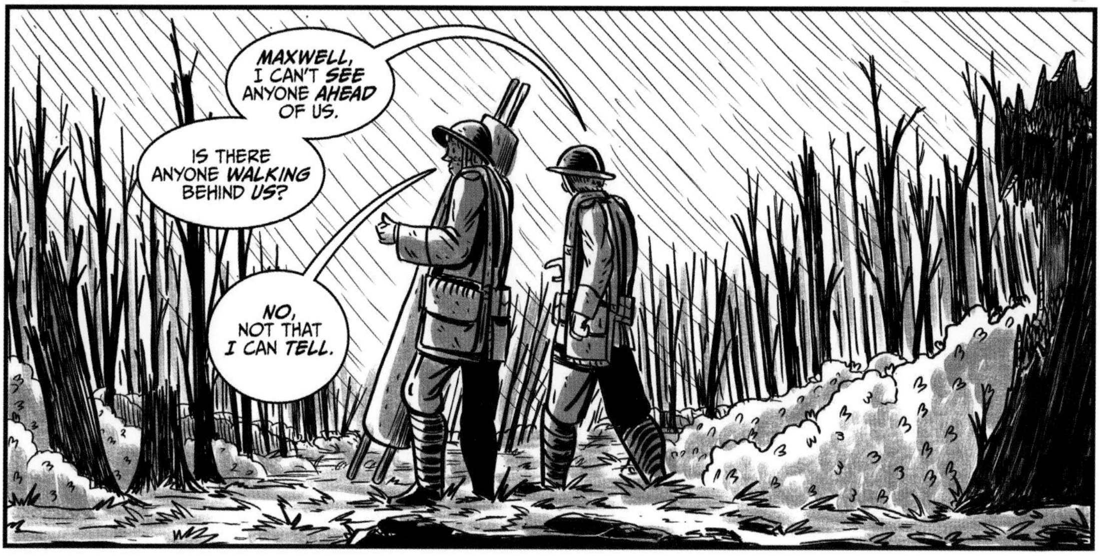
MAXWELL, I CAN'T SEE ANYONE AHEAD OF US.
IS THERE ANYONE WALKING BEHIND US?
NO, NOT THAT I CAN TELL.

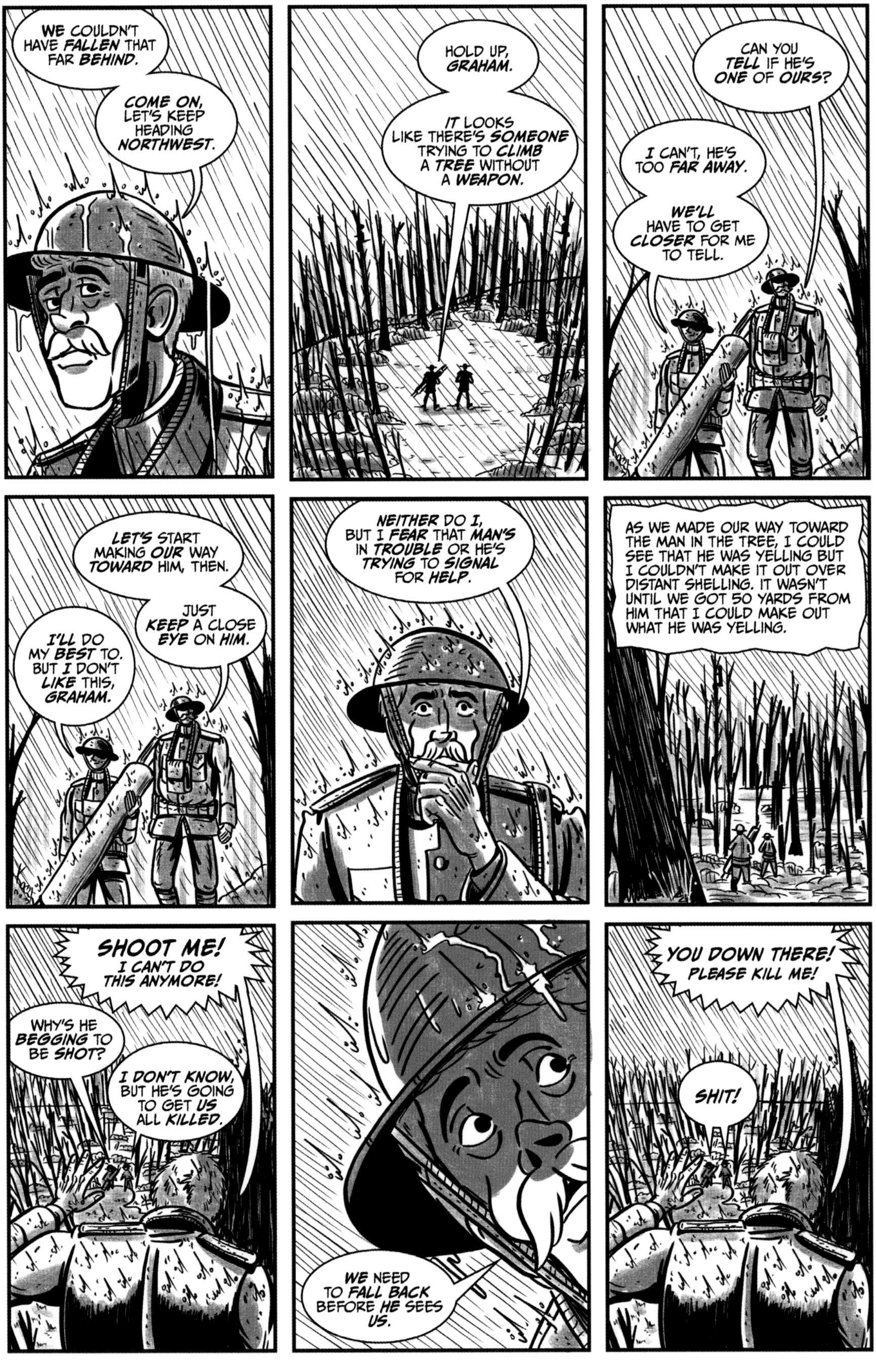
WE COULDN'T HAVE FALLEN THAT FAR BEHIND.
COME ON, LET'S KEEP HEADING NORTHWEST.
HOLD UP, GRAHAM.
IT LOOKS LIKE THERE'S SOMEONE TRYING TO CLIMB A TREE WITHOUT A WEAPON.
CAN YOU TELL IF HE'S ONE OF OURS?
I CAN'T, HE'S TOO FAR AWAY.
WE'LL HAVE TO GET CLOSER FOR ME TO TELL.
LET'S START MAKING OUR WAY TOWARD HIM, THEN.
JUST KEEP A CLOSE EYE ON HIM.
I'LL DO MY BEST TO. BUT I DON'T LIKE THIS, GRAHAM.
NEITHER DO I, BUT I FEAR THAT MAN'S IN TROUBLE OR HE'S TRYING TO SIGNAL FOR HELP.
AS WE MADE OUR WAY TOWARD THE MAN IN THE TREE, I COULD SEE THAT HE WAS YELLING BUT I COULDN'T MAKE IT OUT OVER DISTANT SHELLING. IT WASN'T UNTIL WE GOT 50 YARDS FROM HIM THAT I COULD MAKE OUT WHAT HE WAS YELLING.
SHOOT ME! I CAN'T DO THIS ANYMORE!
WHY'S HE BEGGING TO BE SHOT?
I DON'T KNOW, BUT HE'S GOING TO GET US ALL KILLED.
WE NEED TO FALL BACK BEFORE HE SEES US.
YOU DOWN THERE! PLEASE KILL ME!
SHIT!

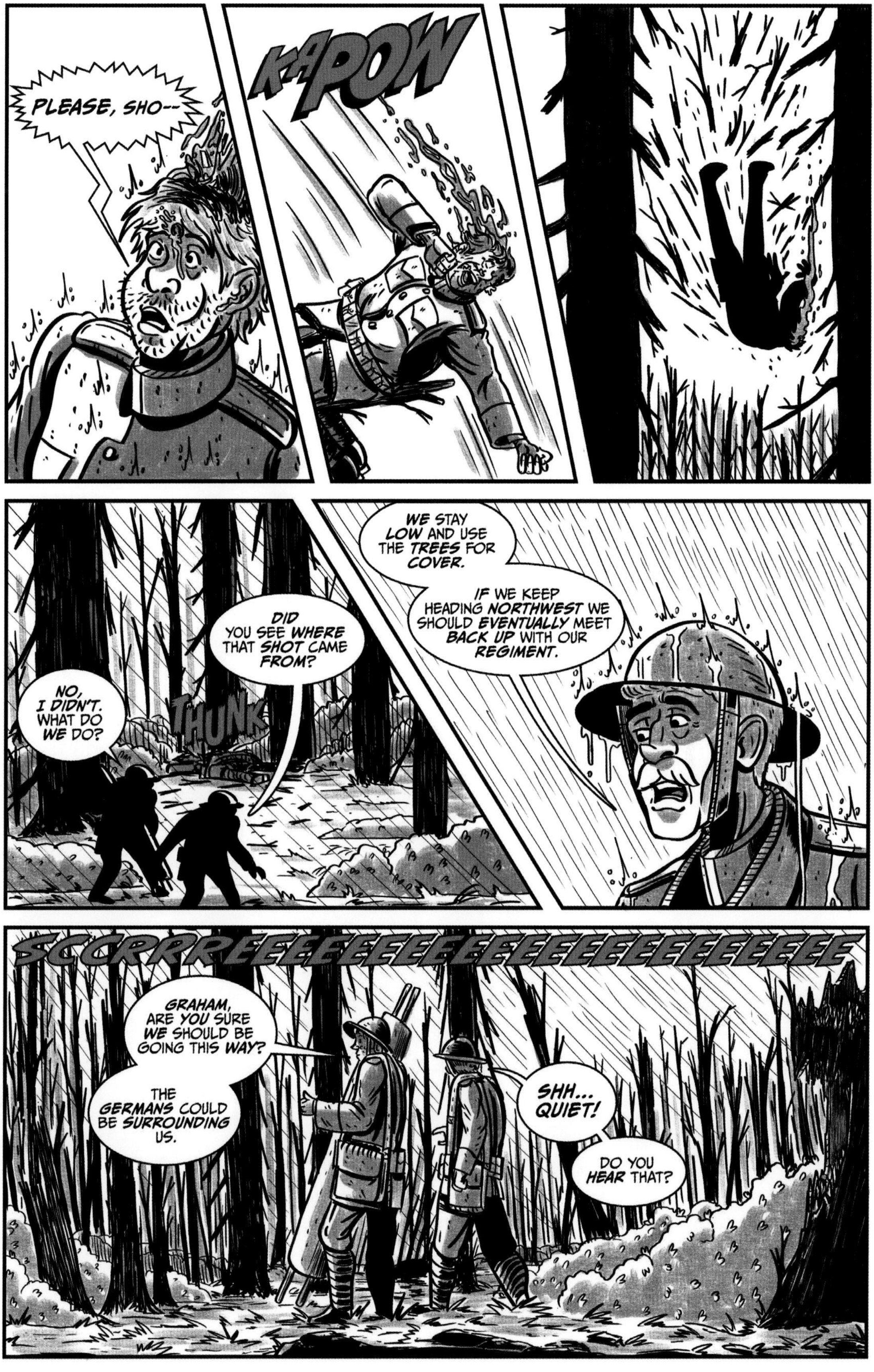
PLEASE, SHO--
KAPOW
NO, I DIDN'T. WHAT DO WE DO?
THUNK
DID YOU SEE WHERE THAT SHOT CAME FROM?
WE STAY LOW AND USE THE TREES FOR COVER.
IF WE KEEP HEADING NORTHWEST WE SHOULD EVENTUALLY MEET BACK UP WITH OUR REGIMENT.
SCCRRREEEEEEEEEEEEEEEEEEEEEEEE
GRAHAM, ARE YOU SURE WE SHOULD BE GOING THIS WAY?
THE GERMANS COULD BE SURROUNDING US.
SHH... QUIET!
DO YOU HEAR THAT?

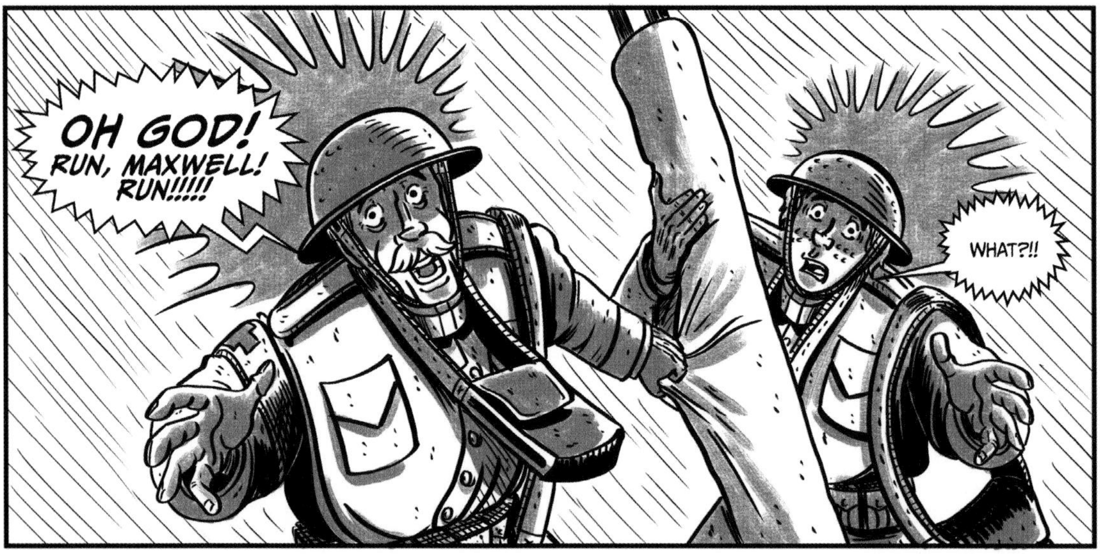
OH GOD!
RUN, MAXWELL!
RUN!!!!!
WHAT?!!

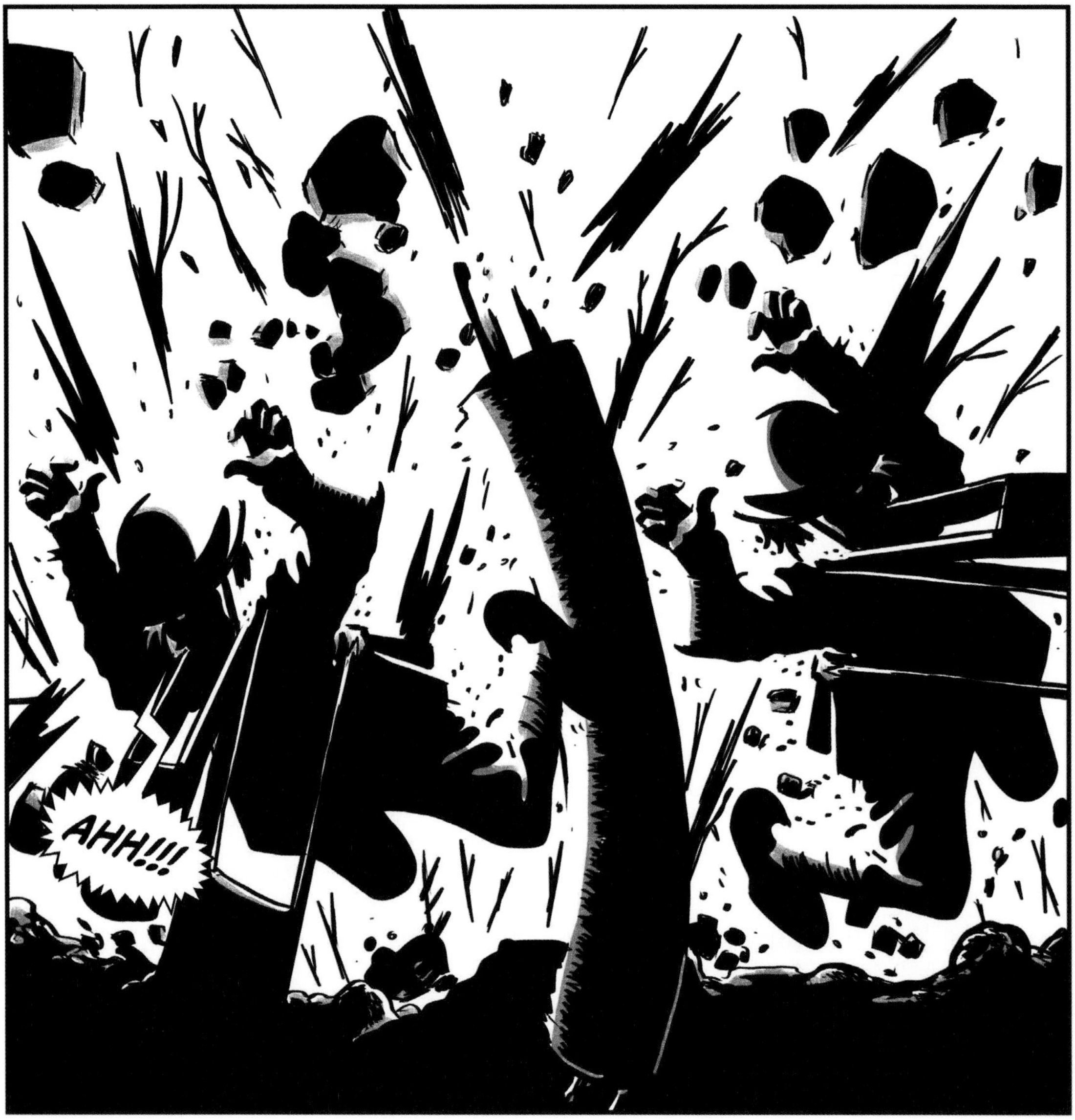
AHH!!!

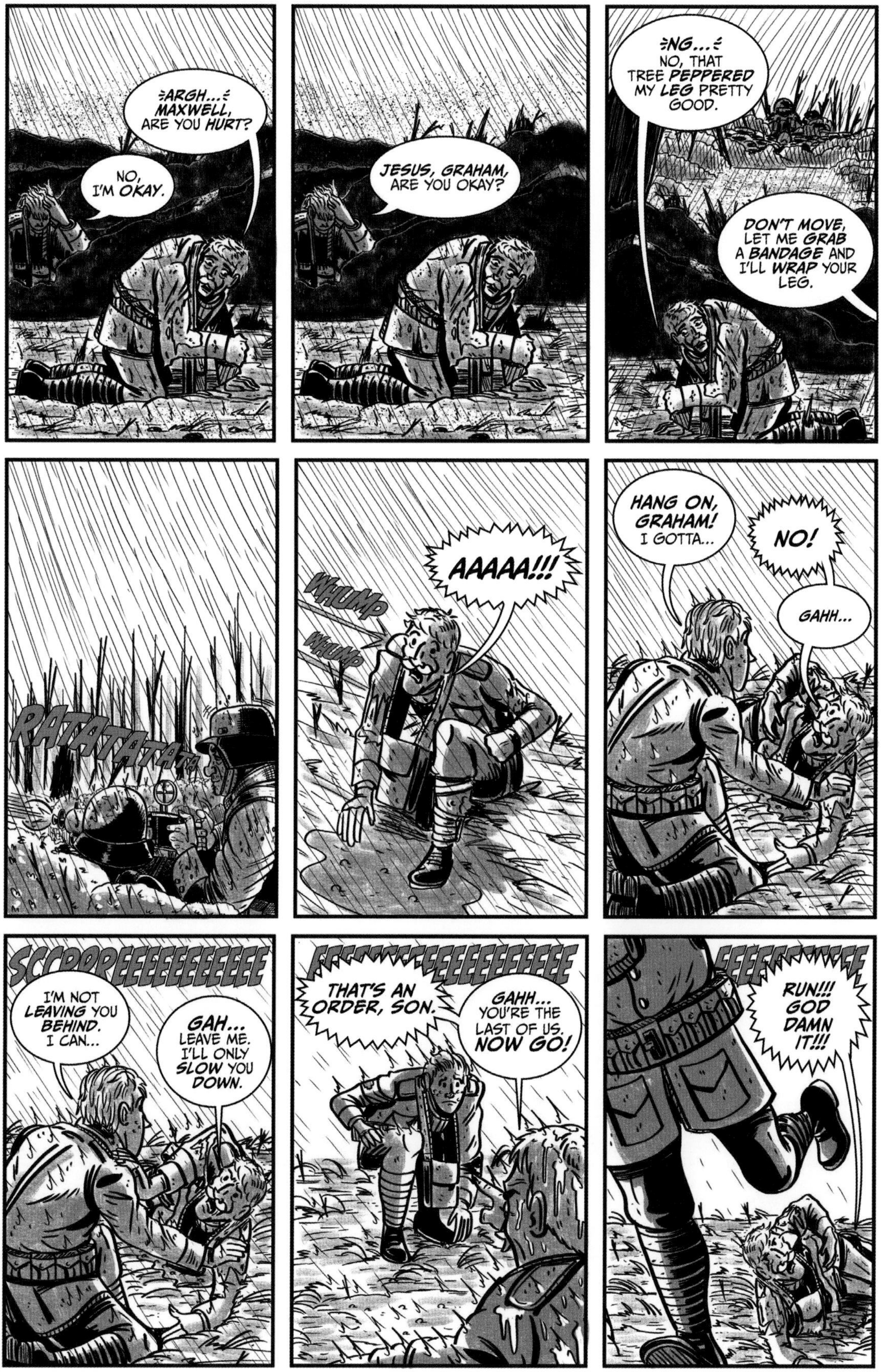
ARGH... MAXWELL, ARE YOU HURT?
NO, I'M OKAY.
JESUS, GRAHAM, ARE YOU OKAY?
NG... NO, THAT TREE PEPPERED MY LEG PRETTY GOOD.
DON'T MOVE, LET ME GRAB A BANDAGE AND I'LL WRAP YOUR LEG.
RATATATATA
WHUMP
WHUMP
AAAAA!!!
HANG ON, GRAHAM! I GOTTA...
NO!
GAHH...
SCCPPREEEEEEEEEEEE
I'M NOT LEAVING YOU BEHIND. I CAN...
GAH... LEAVE ME. I'LL ONLY SLOW YOU DOWN.
THAT'S AN ORDER, SON.
GAHH... YOU'RE THE LAST OF US. NOW GO!
RUN!!! GOD DAMN IT!!!

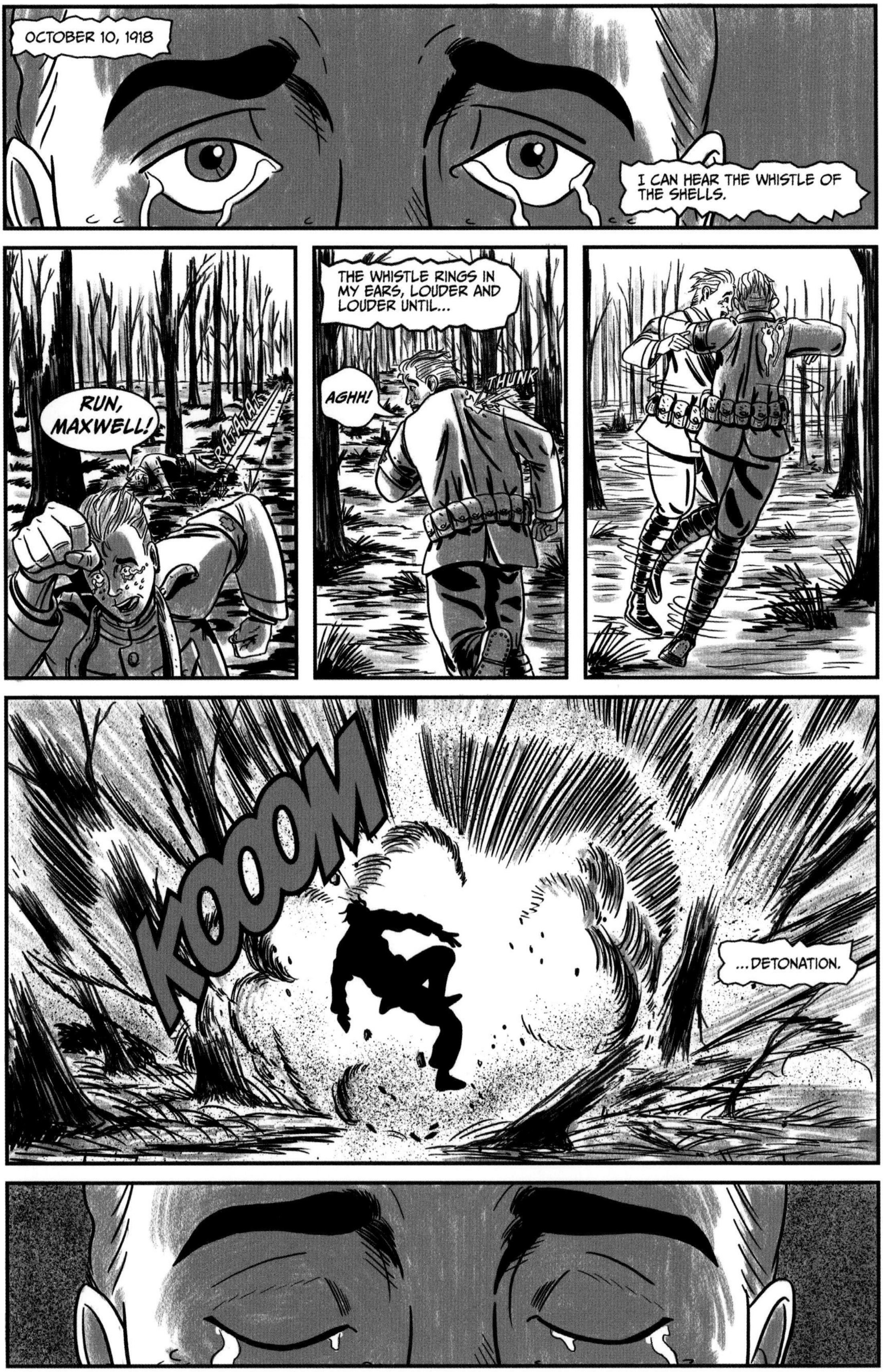
OCTOBER 10, 1918
I CAN HEAR THE WHISTLE OF THE SHELLS.
RUN, MAXWELL!
THE WHISTLE RINGS IN MY EARS, LOUDER AND LOUDER UNTIL...
AGHH!
THUNK
KOOOM
...DETONATION.

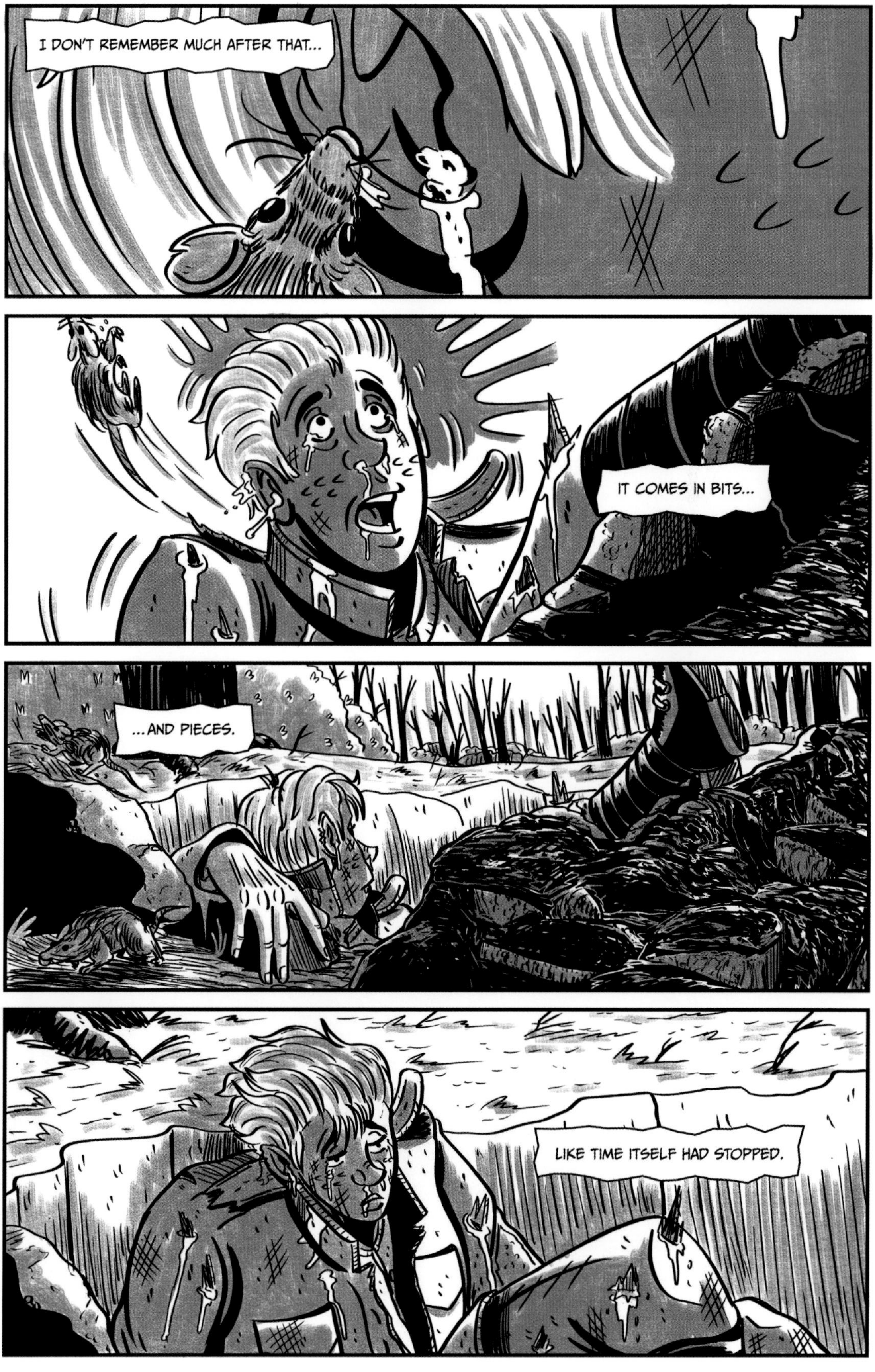
I DON'T REMEMBER MUCH AFTER THAT...
IT COMES IN BITS...
...AND PIECES.
LIKE TIME ITSELF HAD STOPPED.

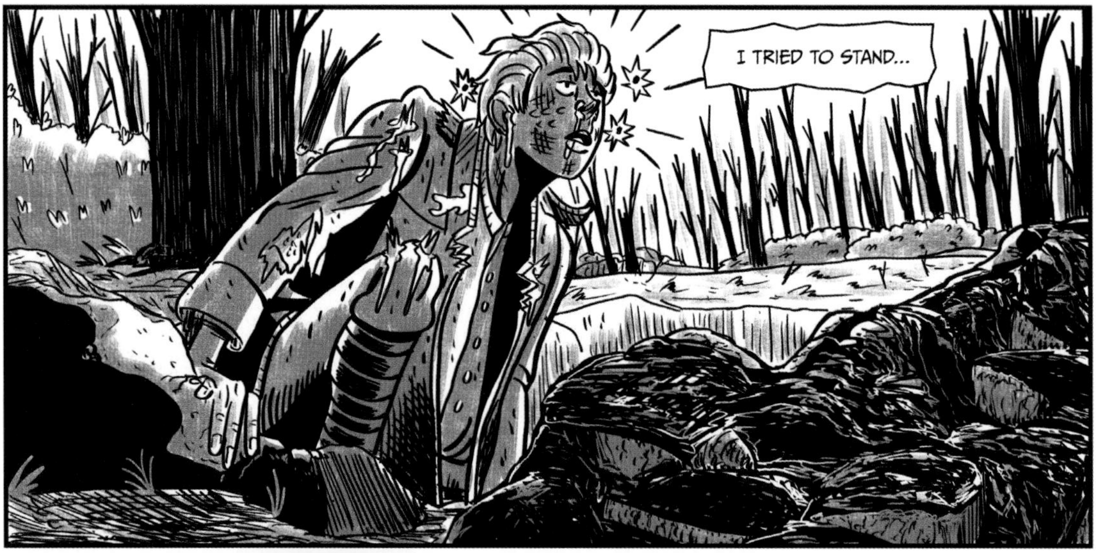
I TRIED TO STAND...
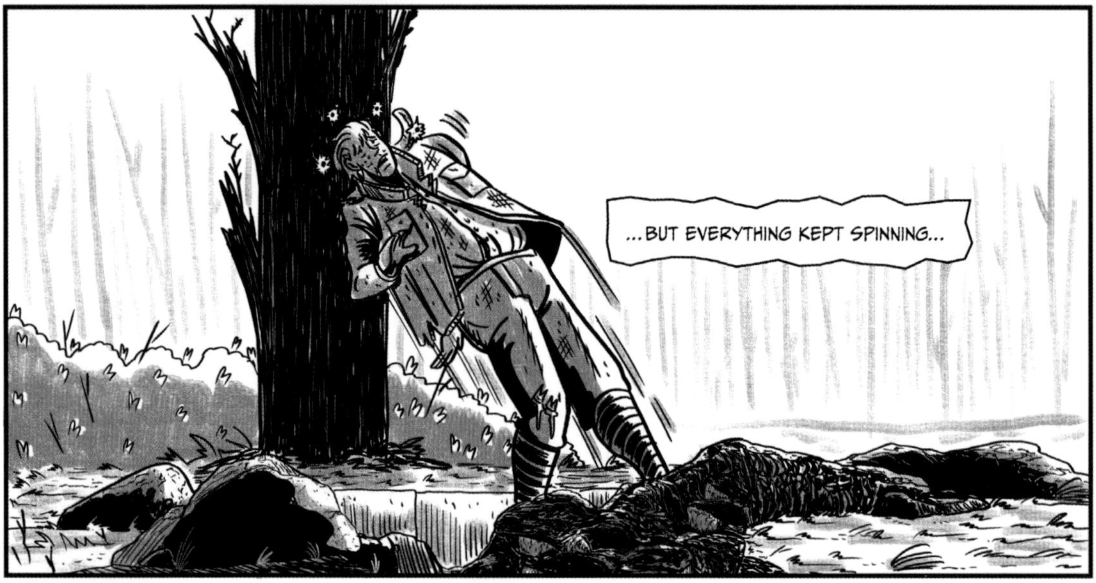
...BUT EVERYTHING KEPT SPINNING...
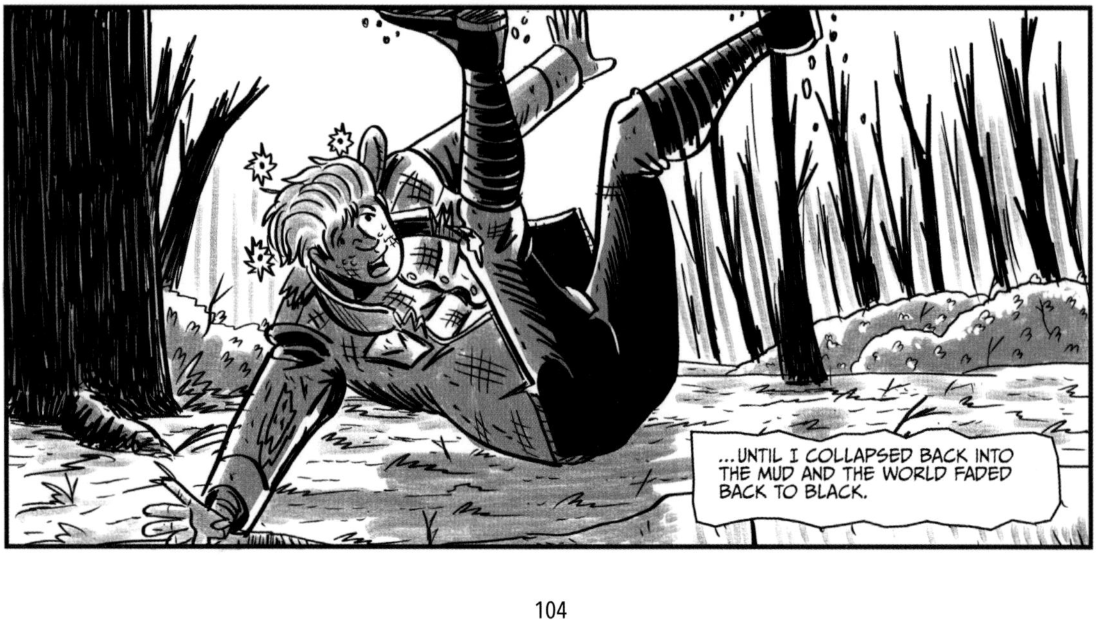
...UNTIL I COLLAPSED BACK INTO THE MUD AND THE WORLD FADED BACK TO BLACK.

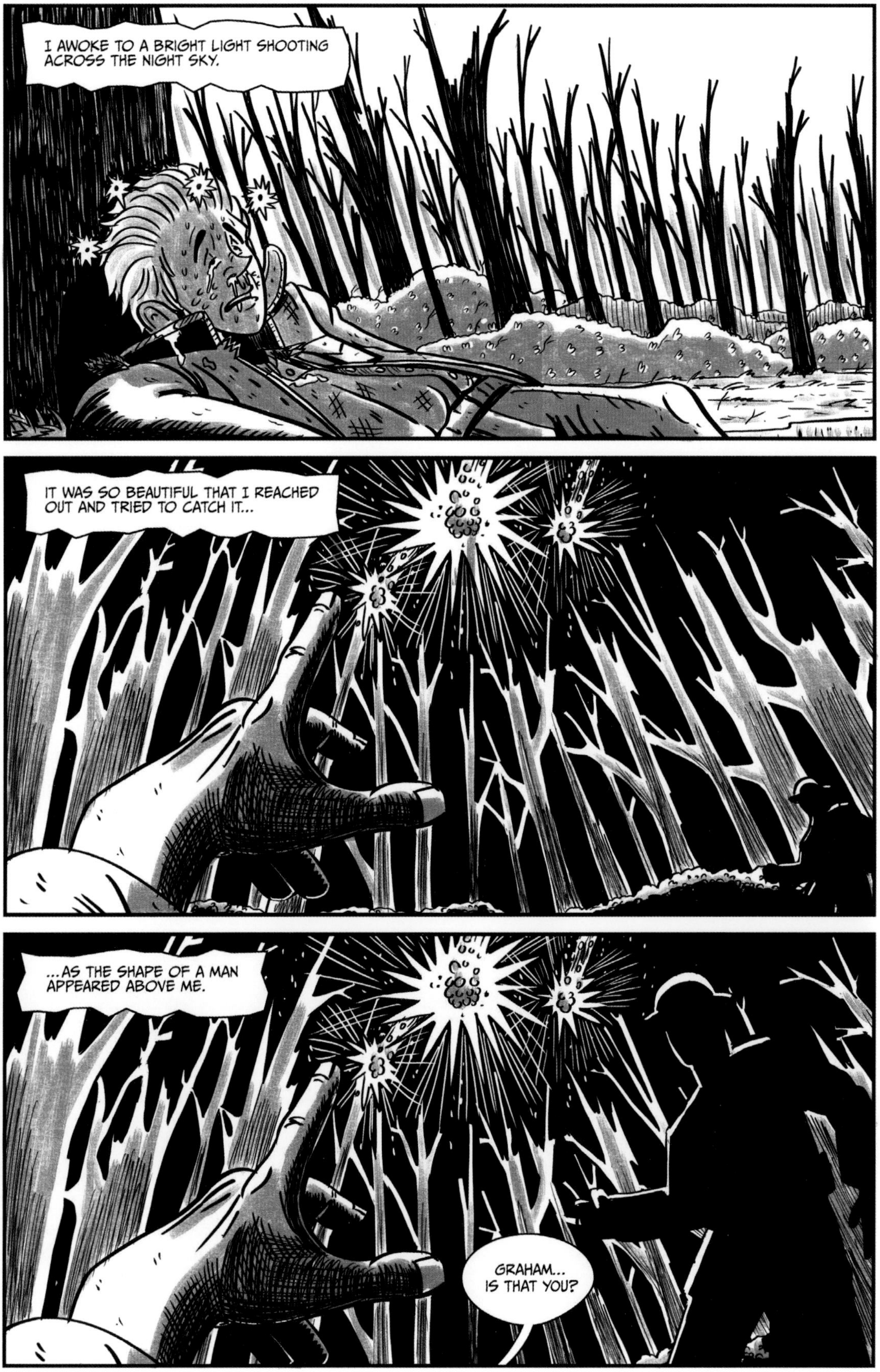
I AWOKE TO A BRIGHT LIGHT SHOOTING ACROSS THE NIGHT SKY.
IT WAS SO BEAUTIFUL THAT I REACHED OUT AND TRIED TO CATCH IT...
...AS THE SHAPE OF A MAN APPEARED ABOVE ME.
GRAHAM... IS THAT YOU?

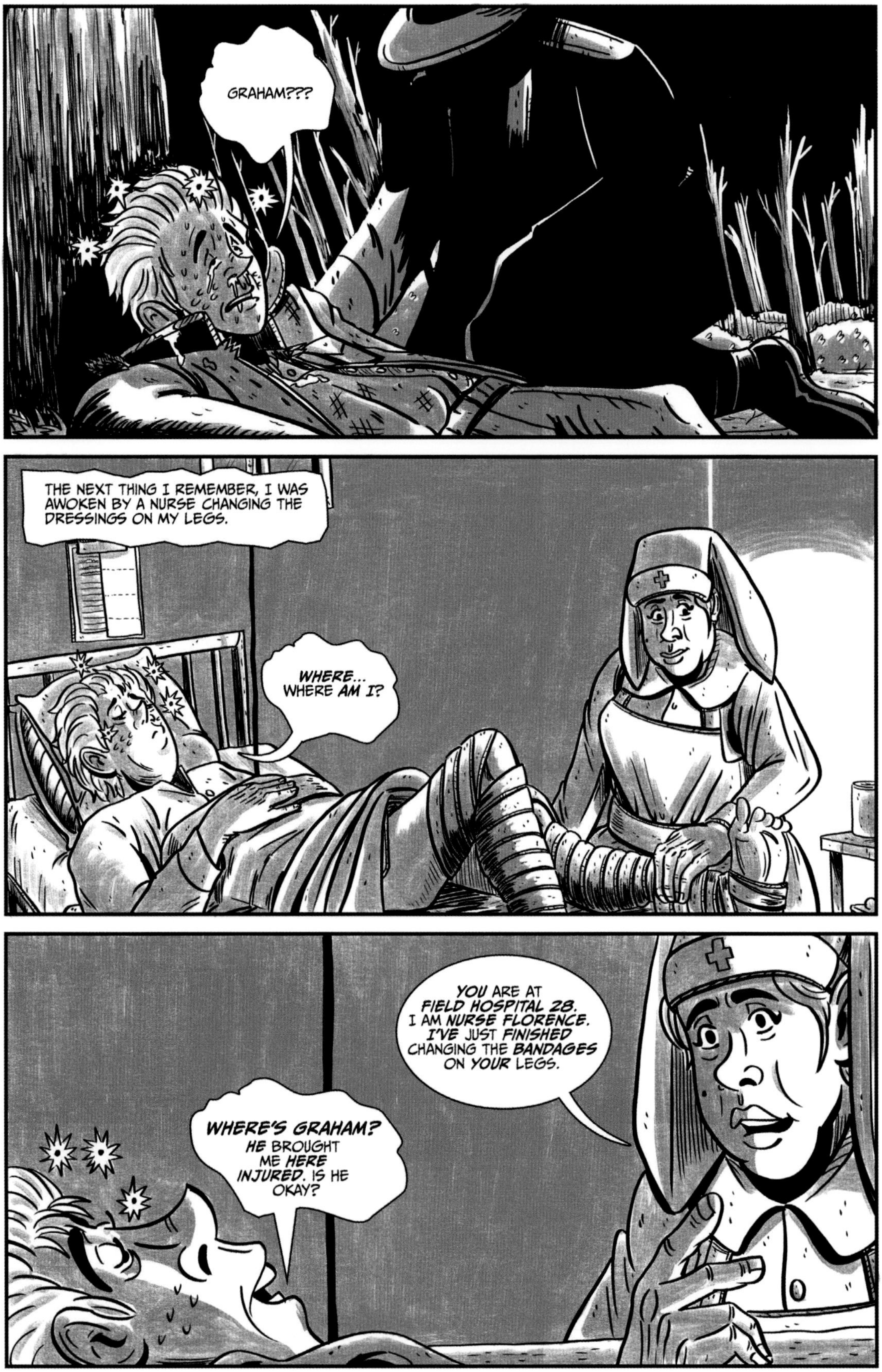
GRAHAM???
THE NEXT THING I REMEMBER, I WAS AWOKEN BY A NURSE CHANGING THE DRESSINGS ON MY LEGS.
WHERE... WHERE AM I?
YOU ARE AT FIELD HOSPITAL 28. I AM NURSE FLORENCE. I'VE JUST FINISHED CHANGING THE BANDAGES ON YOUR LEGS.
WHERE'S GRAHAM? HE BROUGHT ME HERE INJURED. IS HE OKAY?

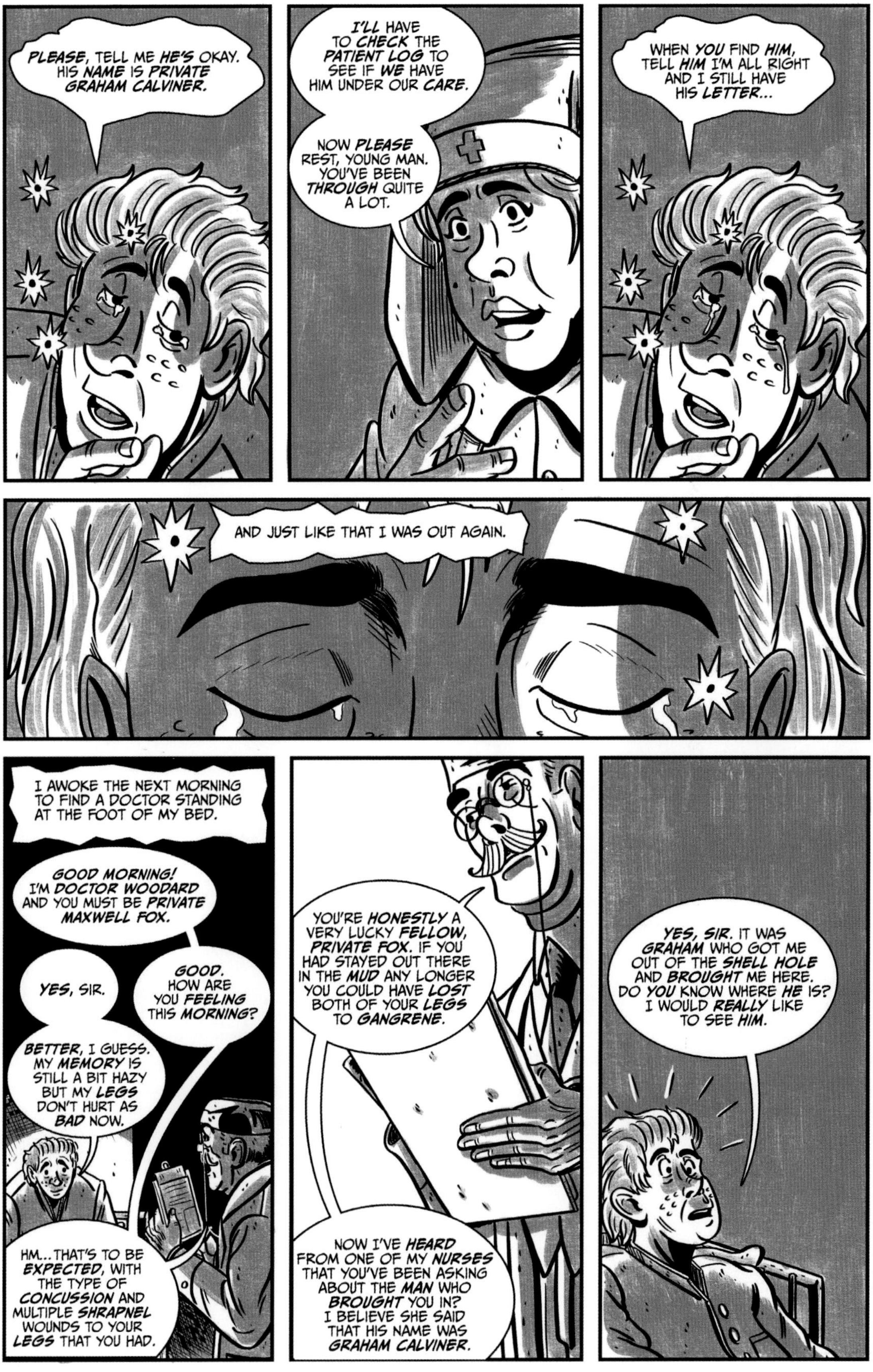
PLEASE, TELL ME HE'S OKAY. HIS NAME IS PRIVATE GRAHAM CALVINER.
I'LL HAVE TO CHECK THE PATIENT LOG TO SEE IF WE HAVE HIM UNDER OUR CARE.
NOW PLEASE REST, YOUNG MAN. YOU'VE BEEN THROUGH QUITE A LOT.
WHEN YOU FIND HIM, TELL HIM I'M ALL RIGHT AND I STILL HAVE HIS LETTER...
AND JUST LIKE THAT I WAS OUT AGAIN.
I AWOKE THE NEXT MORNING TO FIND A DOCTOR STANDING AT THE FOOT OF MY BED.
GOOD MORNING! I'M DOCTOR WOODARD AND YOU MUST BE PRIVATE MAXWELL FOX.
YES, SIR.
GOOD. HOW ARE YOU FEELING THIS MORNING?
BETTER, I GUESS. MY MEMORY IS STILL A BIT HAZY BUT MY LEGS DON'T HURT AS BAD NOW.
HM...THAT'S TO BE EXPECTED, WITH THE TYPE OF CONCUSSION AND MULTIPLE SHRAPNEL WOUNDS TO YOUR LEGS THAT YOU HAD.
YOU'RE HONESTLY A VERY LUCKY FELLOW, PRIVATE FOX. IF YOU HAD STAYED OUT THERE IN THE MUD ANY LONGER YOU COULD HAVE LOST BOTH OF YOUR LEGS TO GANGRENE.
NOW I'VE HEARD FROM ONE OF MY NURSES THAT YOU'VE BEEN ASKING ABOUT THE MAN WHO BROUGHT YOU IN? I BELIEVE SHE SAID THAT HIS NAME WAS GRAHAM CALVINER.
YES, SIR. IT WAS GRAHAM WHO GOT ME OUT OF THE SHELL HOLE AND BROUGHT ME HERE. DO YOU KNOW WHERE HE IS? I WOULD REALLY LIKE TO SEE HIM.

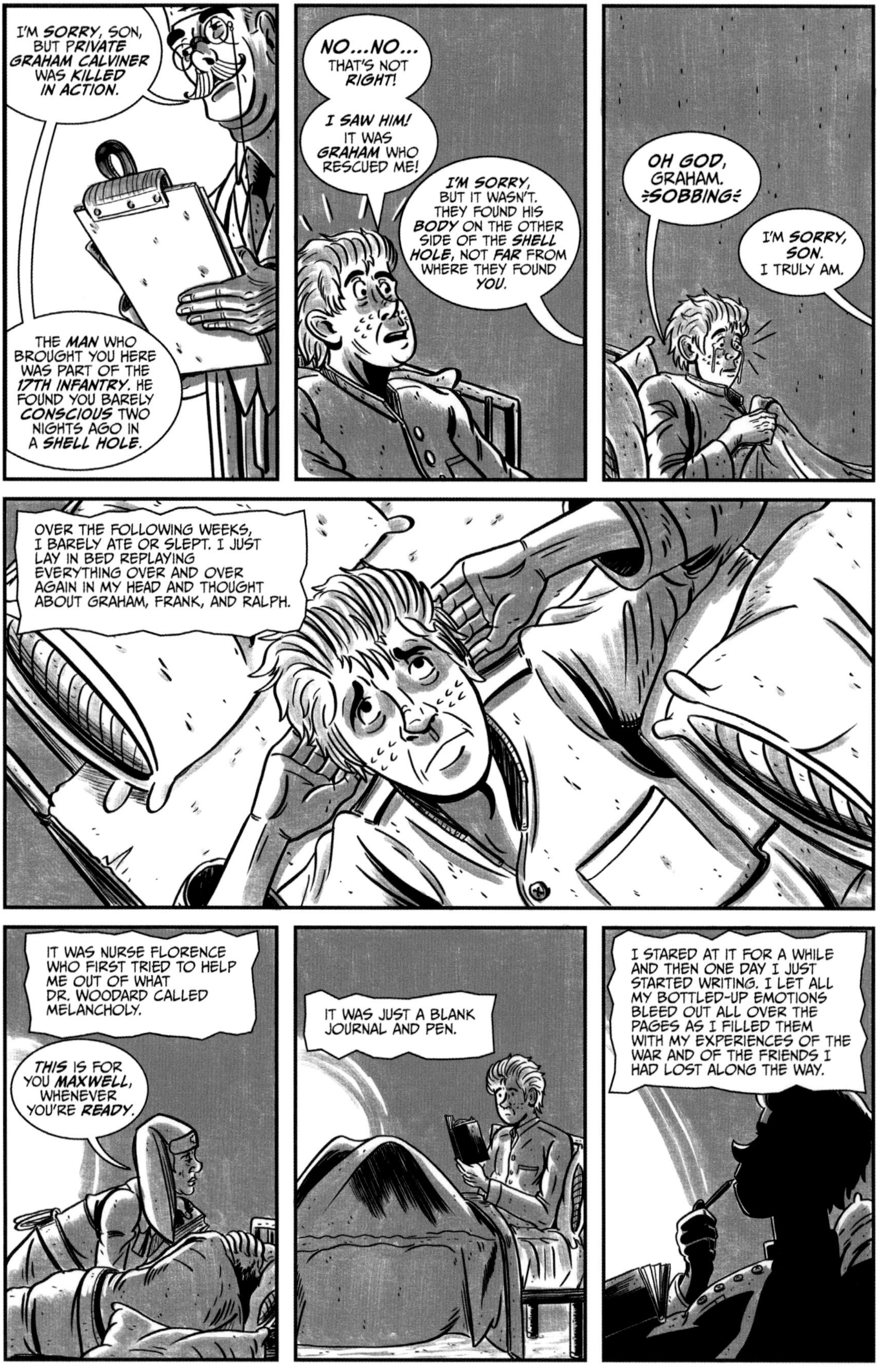
I'M SORRY, SON, BUT PRIVATE GRAHAM CALVINER WAS KILLED IN ACTION.
THE MAN WHO BROUGHT YOU HERE WAS PART OF THE 17TH INFANTRY. HE FOUND YOU BARELY CONSCIOUS TWO NIGHTS AGO IN A SHELL HOLE.
NO...NO... THAT'S NOT RIGHT!
I SAW HIM! IT WAS GRAHAM WHO RESCUED ME!
I'M SORRY, BUT IT WASN'T. THEY FOUND HIS BODY ON THE OTHER SIDE OF THE SHELL HOLE, NOT FAR FROM WHERE THEY FOUND YOU.
OH GOD, GRAHAM. SOBBING
I'M SORRY, SON. I TRULY AM.
OVER THE FOLLOWING WEEKS, I BARELY ATE OR SLEPT. I JUST LAY IN BED REPLAYING EVERYTHING OVER AND OVER AGAIN IN MY HEAD AND THOUGHT ABOUT GRAHAM, FRANK, AND RALPH.
IT WAS NURSE FLORENCE WHO FIRST TRIED TO HELP ME OUT OF WHAT DR. WOODARD CALLED MELANCHOLY.
THIS IS FOR YOU MAXWELL, WHENEVER YOU'RE READY.
IT WAS JUST A BLANK JOURNAL AND PEN.
I STARED AT IT FOR A WHILE AND THEN ONE DAY I JUST STARTED WRITING. I LET ALL MY BOTTLED-UP EMOTIONS BLEED OUT ALL OVER THE PAGES AS I FILLED THEM WITH MY EXPERIENCES OF THE WAR AND OF THE FRIENDS I HAD LOST ALONG THE WAY.

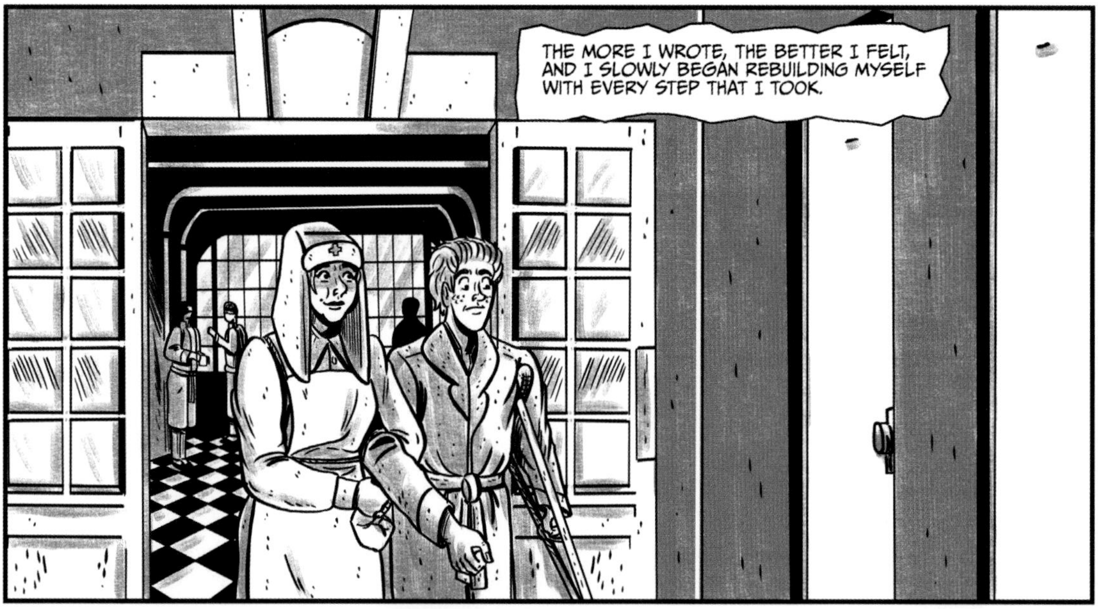
THE MORE I WROTE, THE BETTER I FELT, AND I SLOWLY BEGAN REBUILDING MYSELF WITH EVERY STEP THAT I TOOK.

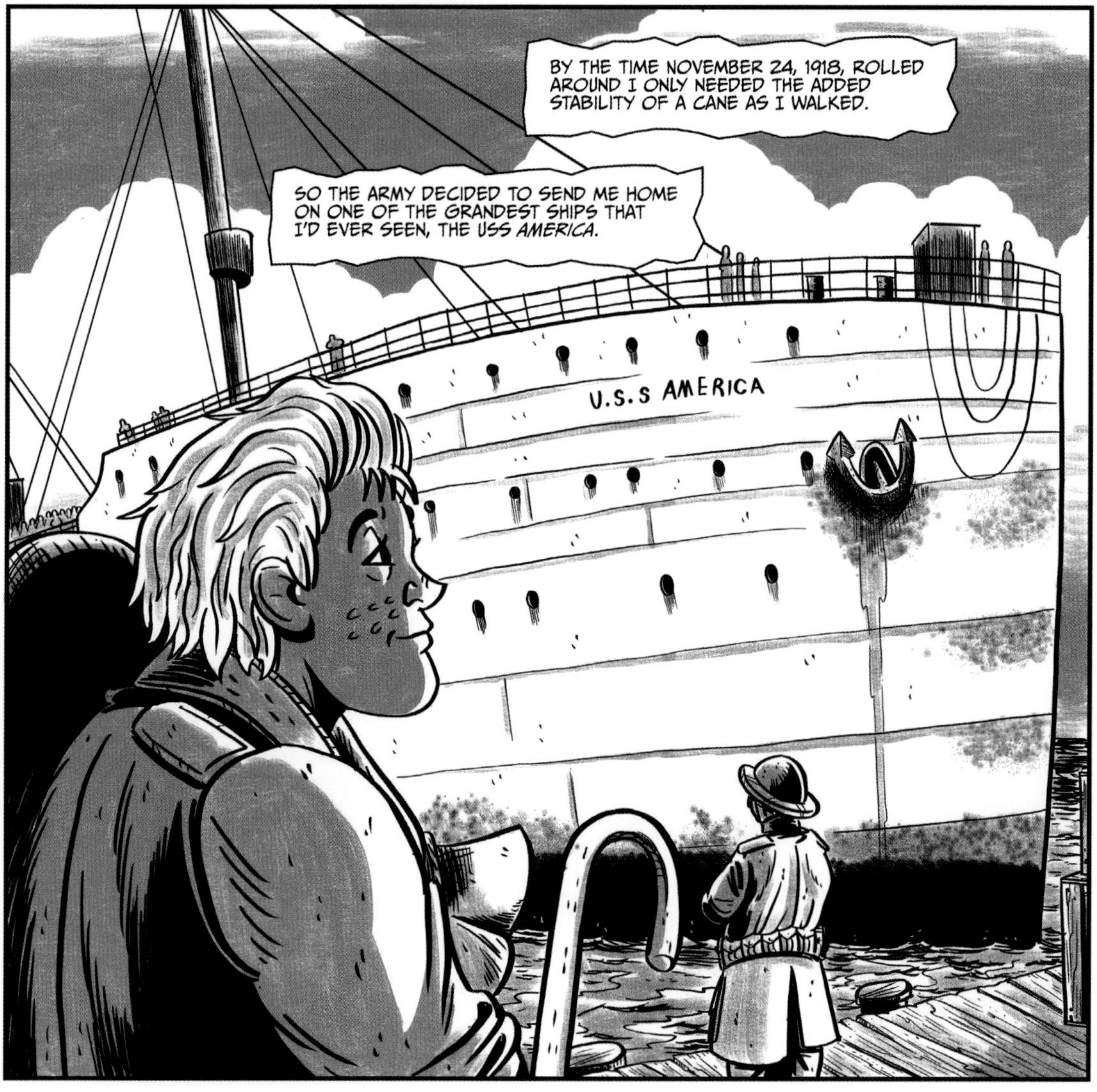
BY THE TIME NOVEMBER 24, 1918, ROLLED AROUND I ONLY NEEDED THE ADDED STABILITY OF A CANE AS I WALKED.
SO THE ARMY DECIDED TO SEND ME HOME ON ONE OF THE GRANDEST SHIPS THAT I'D EVER SEEN, THE USS *AMERICA*.
U.S.S AMERICA

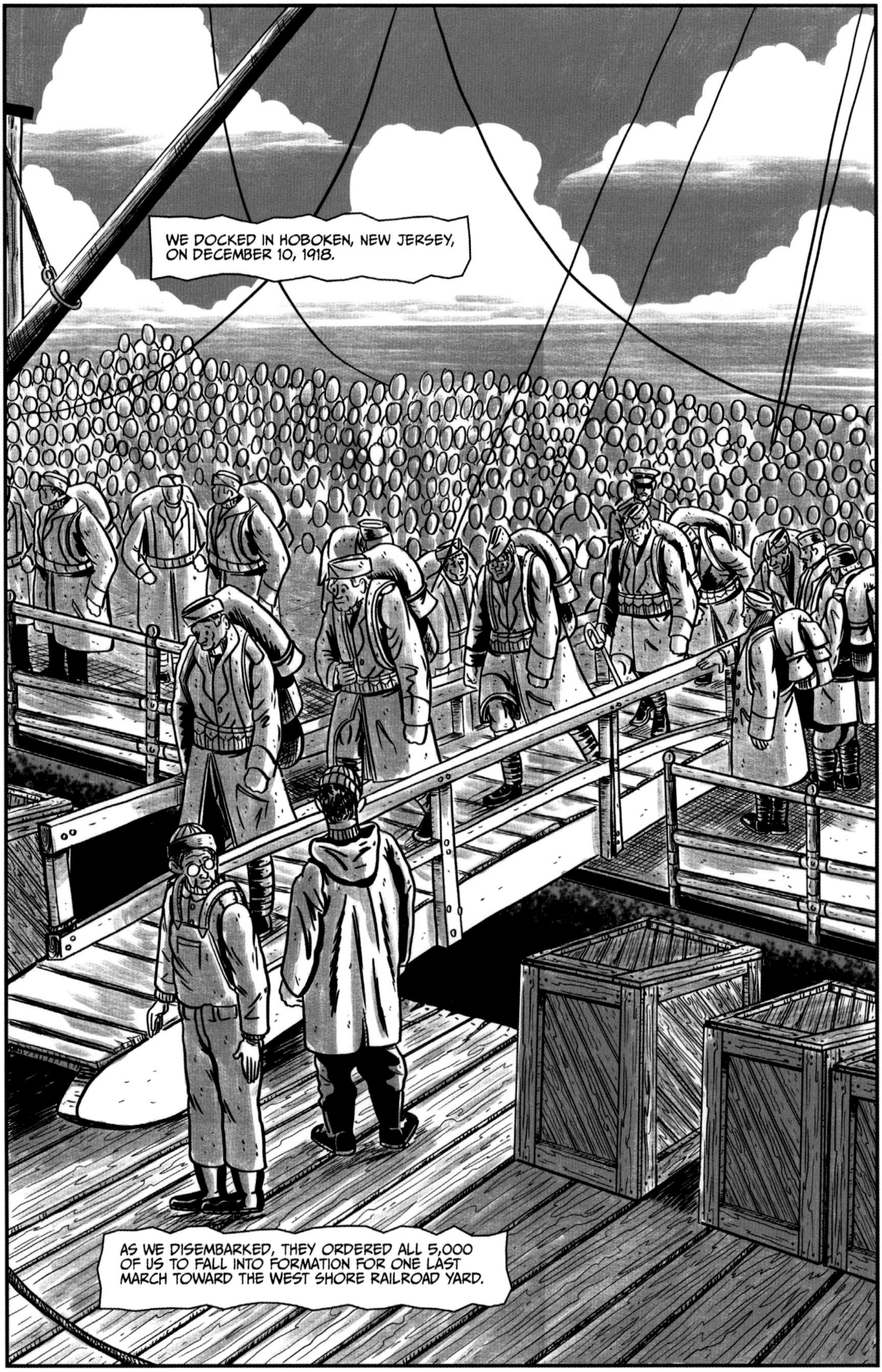
WE DOCKED IN HOBOKEN, NEW JERSEY, ON DECEMBER 10, 1918.
AS WE DISEMBARKED, THEY ORDERED ALL 5,000 OF US TO FALL INTO FORMATION FOR ONE LAST MARCH TOWARD THE WEST SHORE RAILROAD YARD.

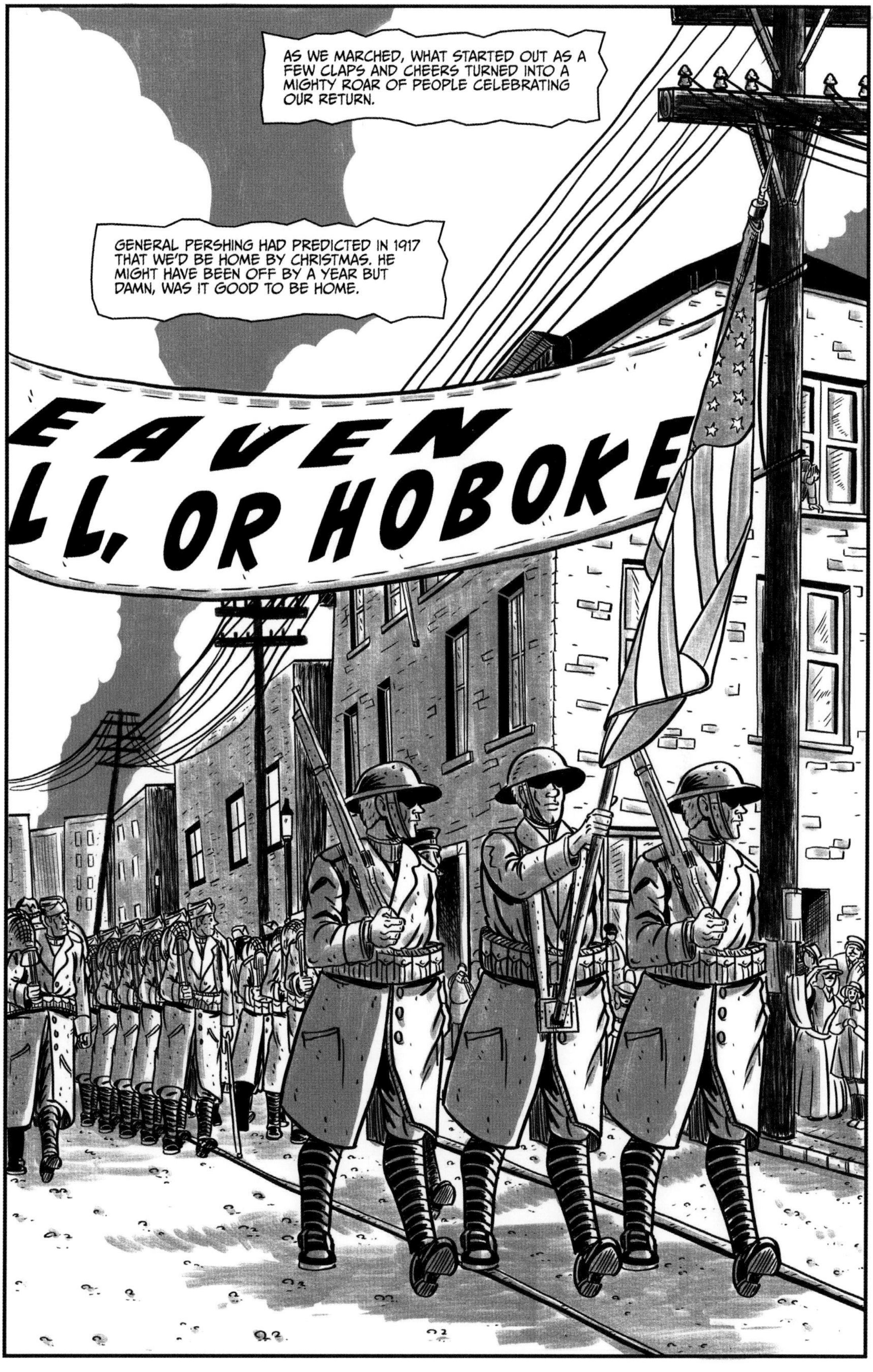
AS WE MARCHED, WHAT STARTED OUT AS A FEW CLAPS AND CHEERS TURNED INTO A MIGHTY ROAR OF PEOPLE CELEBRATING OUR RETURN.
GENERAL PERSHING HAD PREDICTED IN 1917 THAT WE'D BE HOME BY CHRISTMAS. HE MIGHT HAVE BEEN OFF BY A YEAR BUT DAMN, WAS IT GOOD TO BE HOME.
EAVEN
LL, OR HOBOKE

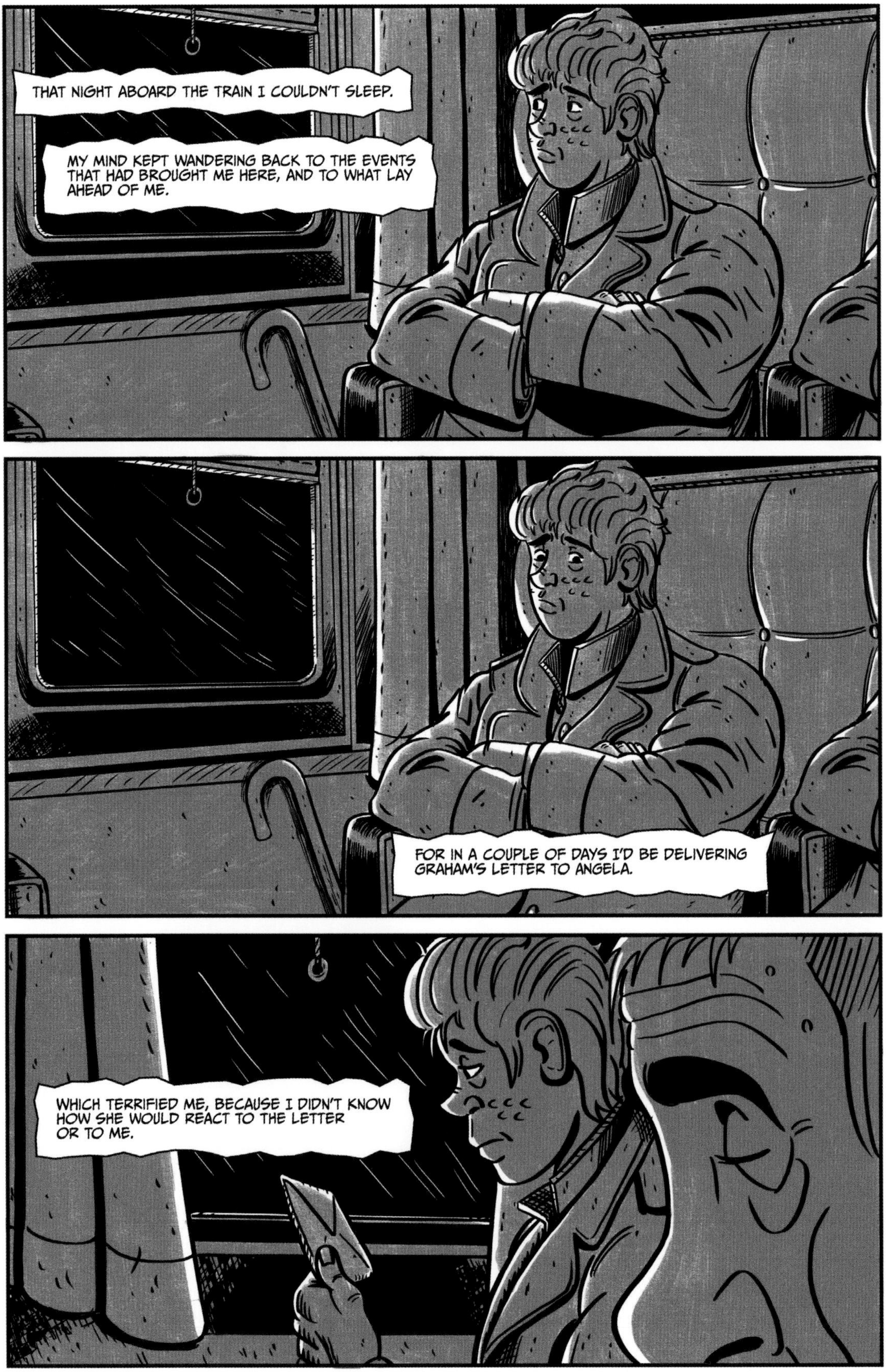
THAT NIGHT ABOARD THE TRAIN I COULDN'T SLEEP.
MY MIND KEPT WANDERING BACK TO THE EVENTS THAT HAD BROUGHT ME HERE, AND TO WHAT LAY AHEAD OF ME.
FOR IN A COUPLE OF DAYS I'D BE DELIVERING GRAHAM'S LETTER TO ANGELA.
WHICH TERRIFIED ME, BECAUSE I DIDN'T KNOW HOW SHE WOULD REACT TO THE LETTER OR TO ME.

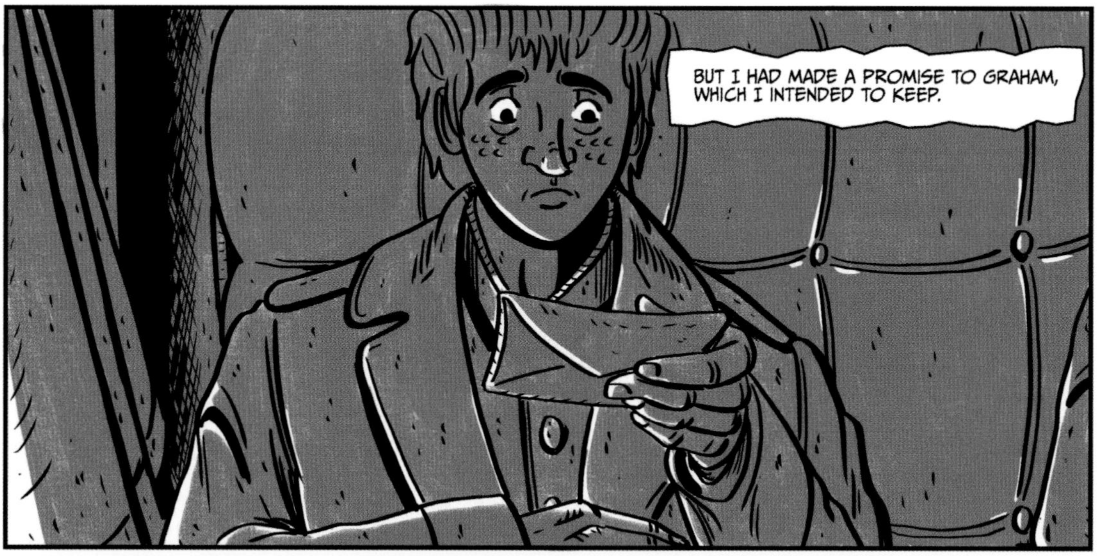
BUT I HAD MADE A PROMISE TO GRAHAM, WHICH I INTENDED TO KEEP.

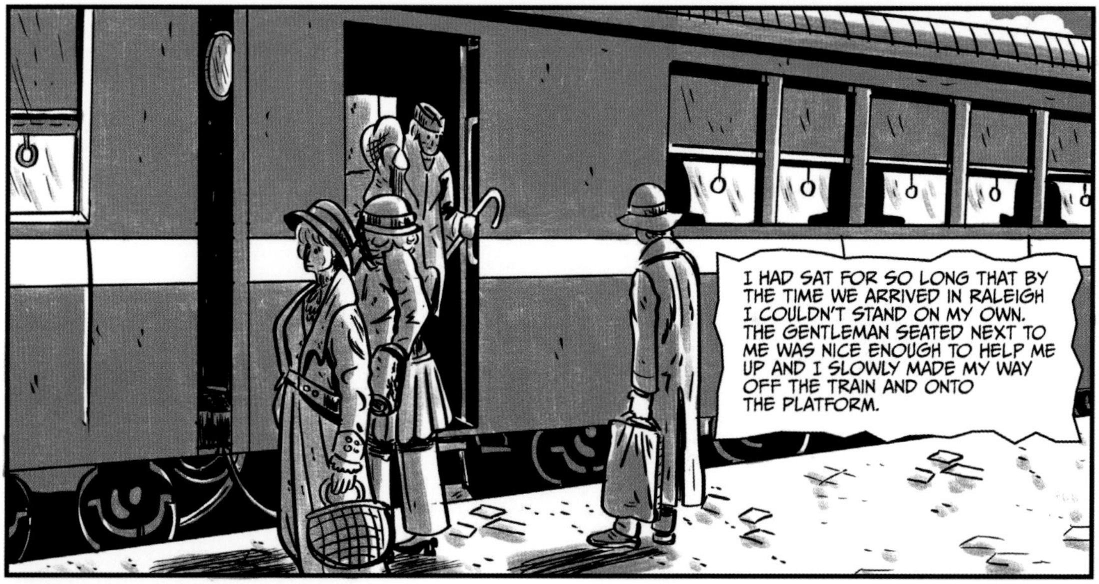
I HAD SAT FOR SO LONG THAT BY THE TIME WE ARRIVED IN RALEIGH I COULDN'T STAND ON MY OWN. THE GENTLEMAN SEATED NEXT TO ME WAS NICE ENOUGH TO HELP ME UP AND I SLOWLY MADE MY WAY OFF THE TRAIN AND ONTO THE PLATFORM.

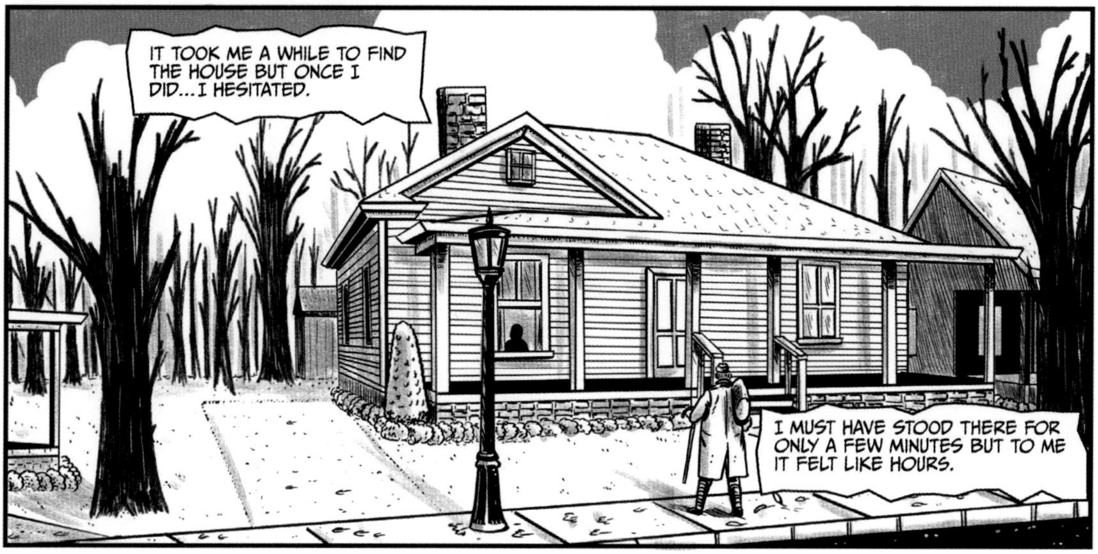
IT TOOK ME A WHILE TO FIND THE HOUSE BUT ONCE I DID... I HESITATED.
I MUST HAVE STOOD THERE FOR ONLY A FEW MINUTES BUT TO ME IT FELT LIKE HOURS.

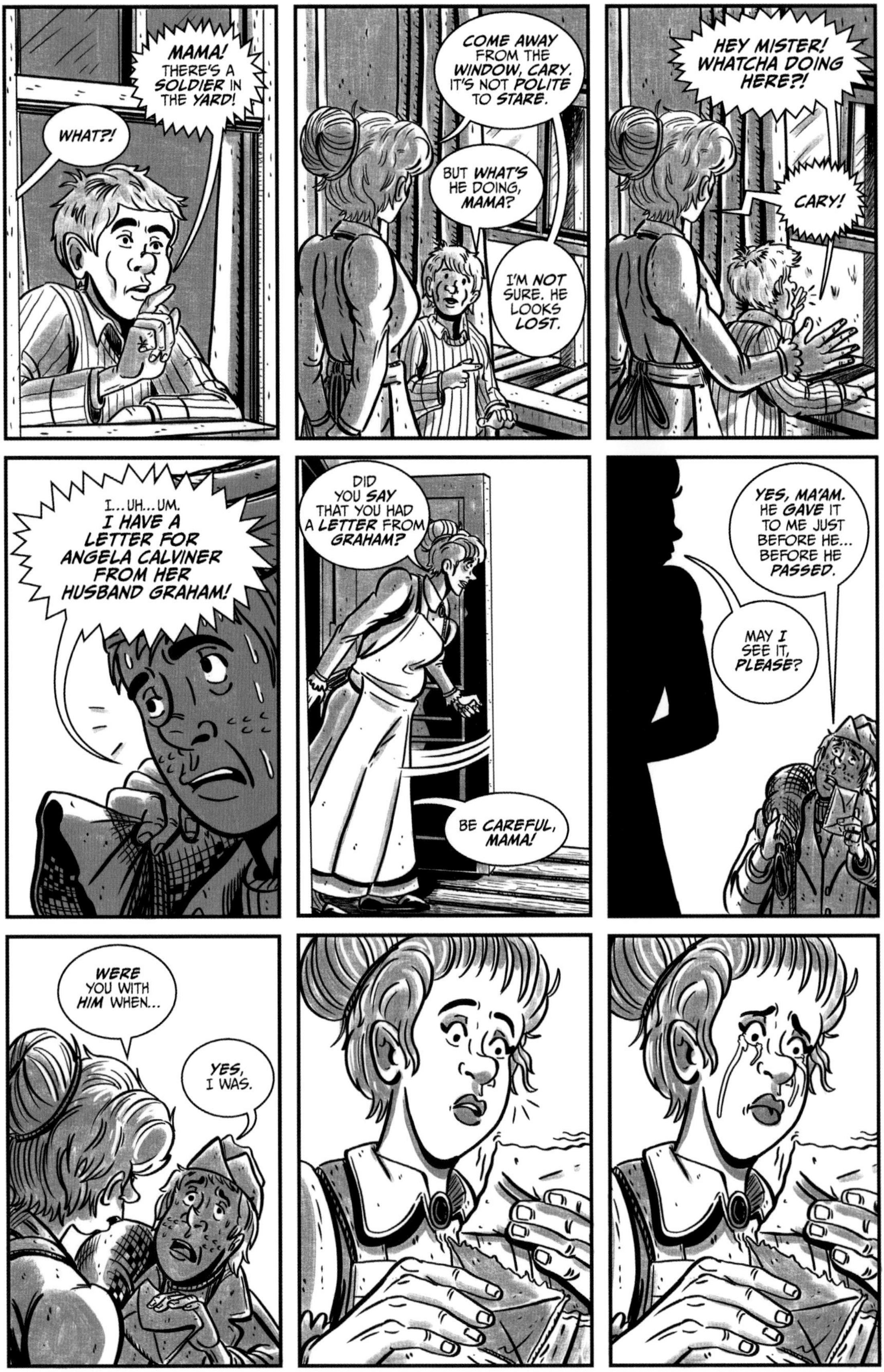
MAMA! THERE'S A SOLDIER IN THE YARD!
WHAT?!
COME AWAY FROM THE WINDOW, CARY. IT'S NOT POLITE TO STARE.
BUT WHAT'S HE DOING, MAMA?
I'M NOT SURE. HE LOOKS LOST.
HEY MISTER! WHATCHA DOING HERE?!
CARY!
I...UH...UM. I HAVE A LETTER FOR ANGELA CALVINER FROM HER HUSBAND GRAHAM!
DID YOU SAY THAT YOU HAD A LETTER FROM GRAHAM?
BE CAREFUL, MAMA!
YES, MA'AM. HE GAVE IT TO ME JUST BEFORE HE... BEFORE HE PASSED.
MAY I SEE IT, PLEASE?
WERE YOU WITH HIM WHEN...
YES, I WAS.

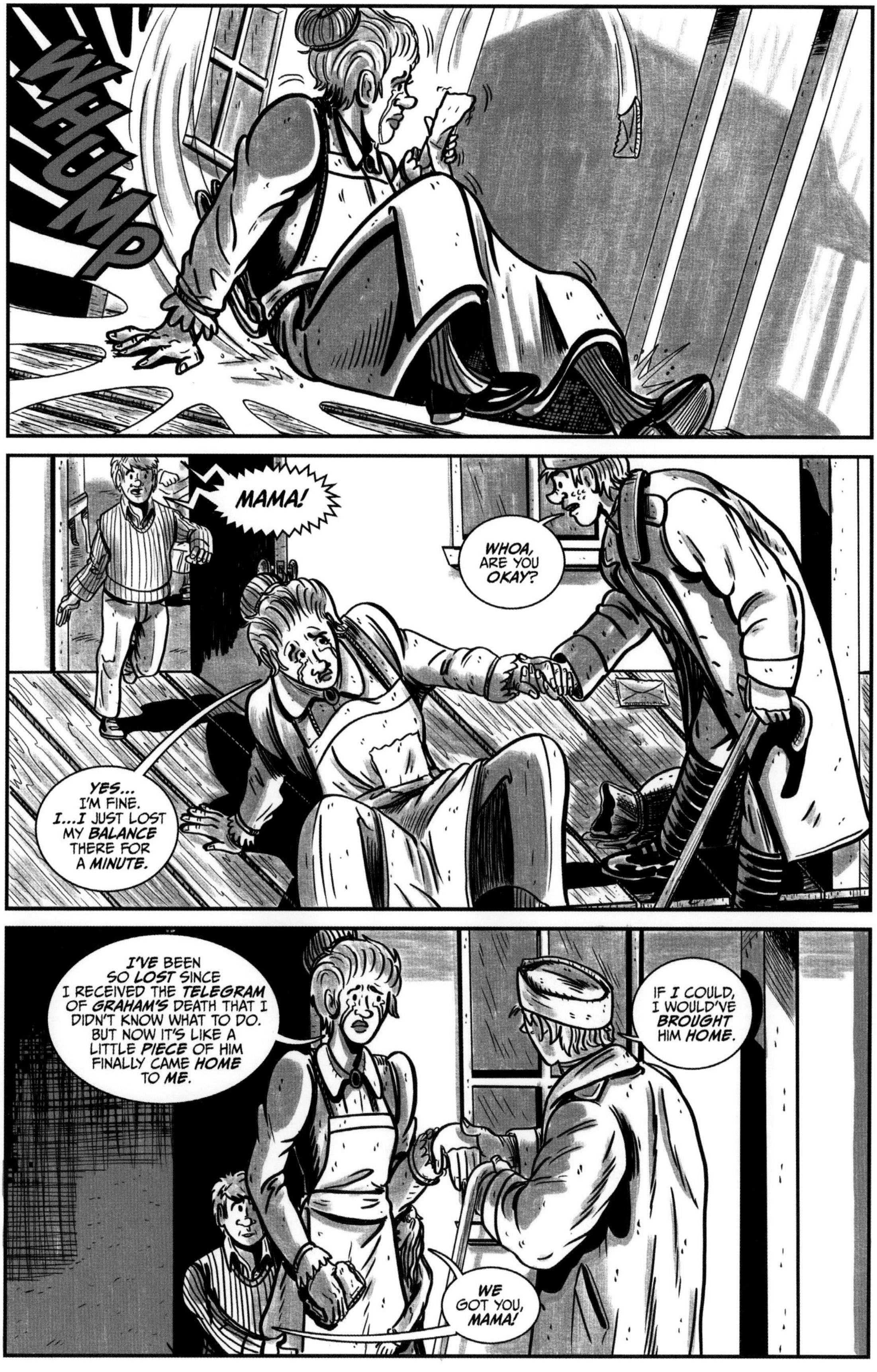
WHUMP
MAMA!
WHOA, ARE YOU OKAY?
YES... I'M FINE. I...I JUST LOST MY BALANCE THERE FOR A MINUTE.
I'VE BEEN SO LOST SINCE I RECEIVED THE TELEGRAM OF GRAHAM'S DEATH THAT I DIDN'T KNOW WHAT TO DO. BUT NOW IT'S LIKE A LITTLE PIECE OF HIM FINALLY CAME HOME TO ME.
IF I COULD, I WOULD'VE BROUGHT HIM HOME.
WE GOT YOU, MAMA!

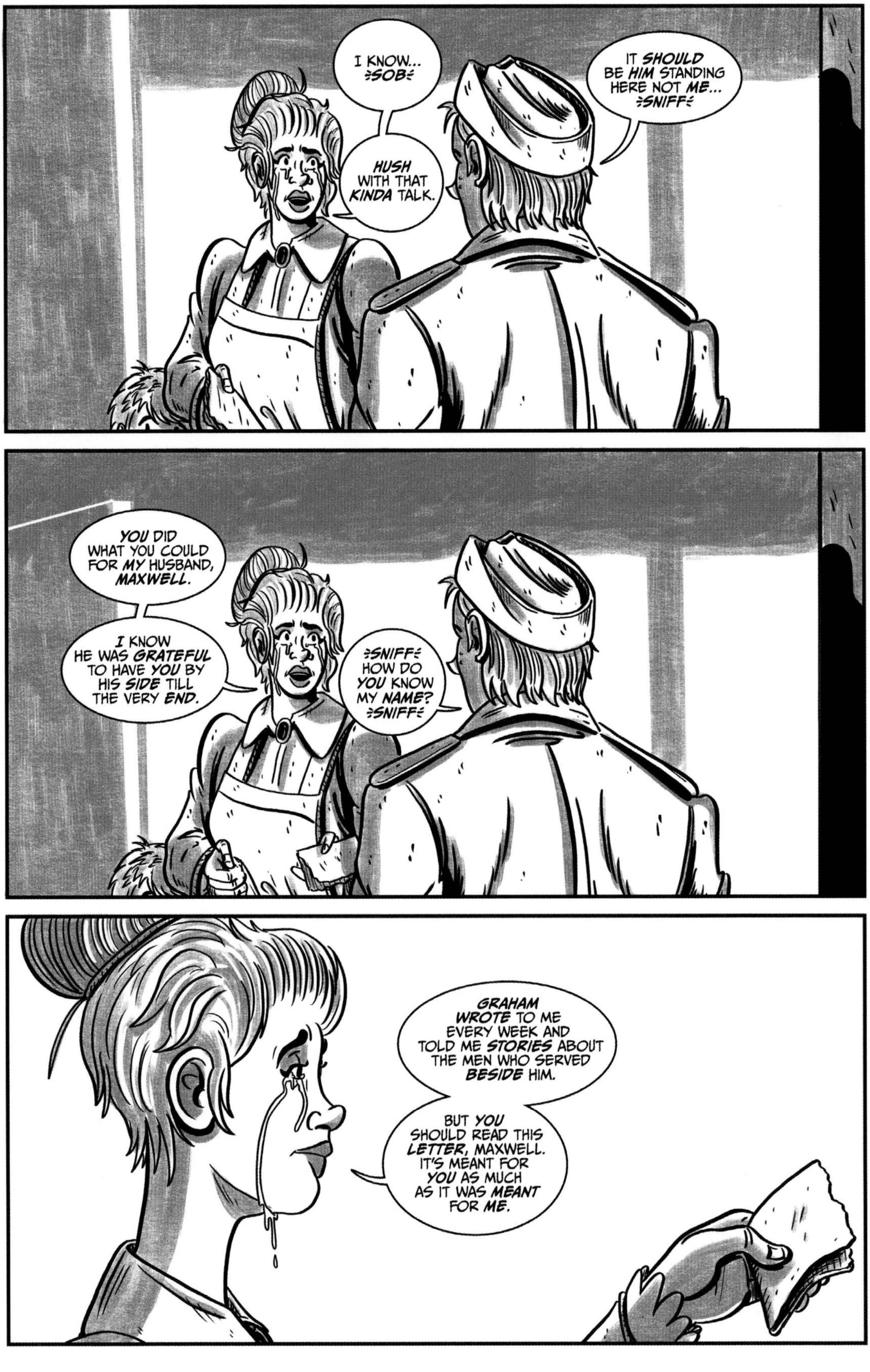
I KNOW... ≶SOB≶
HUSH WITH THAT KINDA TALK.
IT SHOULD BE HIM STANDING HERE NOT ME... ≶SNIFF≶
YOU DID WHAT YOU COULD FOR MY HUSBAND, MAXWELL.
I KNOW HE WAS GRATEFUL TO HAVE YOU BY HIS SIDE TILL THE VERY END.
≶SNIFF≶ HOW DO YOU KNOW MY NAME? ≶SNIFF≶
GRAHAM WROTE TO ME EVERY WEEK AND TOLD ME STORIES ABOUT THE MEN WHO SERVED BESIDE HIM.
BUT YOU SHOULD READ THIS LETTER, MAXWELL. IT'S MEANT FOR YOU AS MUCH AS IT WAS MEANT FOR ME.

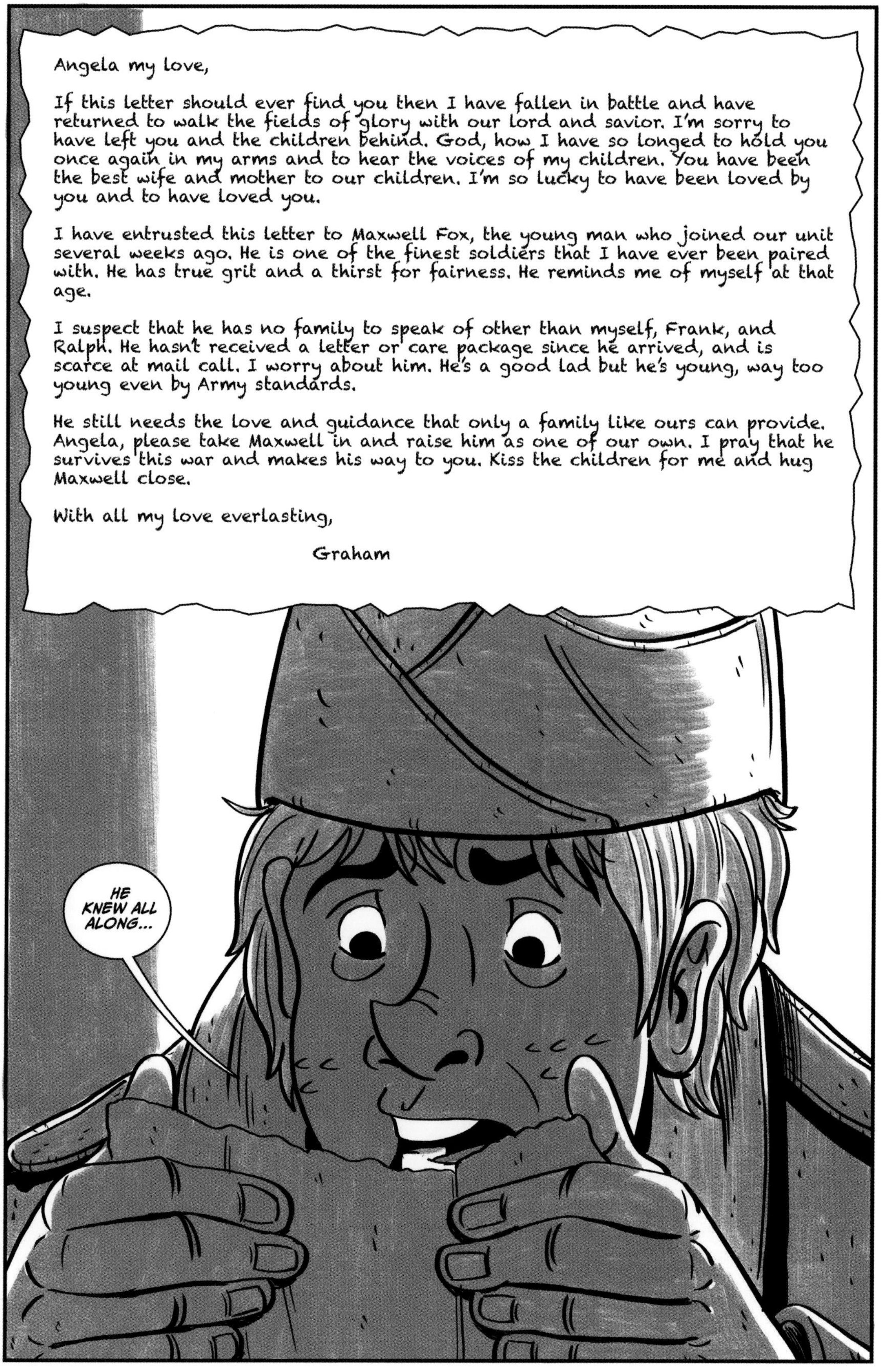
Angela my love,
If this letter should ever find you then I have fallen in battle and have returned to walk the fields of glory with our lord and savior. I'm sorry to have left you and the children behind. God, how I have so longed to hold you once again in my arms and to hear the voices of my children. You have been the best wife and mother to our children. I'm so lucky to have been loved by you and to have loved you.
I have entrusted this letter to Maxwell Fox, the young man who joined our unit several weeks ago. He is one of the finest soldiers that I have ever been paired with. He has true grit and a thirst for fairness. He reminds me of myself at that age.
I suspect that he has no family to speak of other than myself, Frank, and Ralph. He hasn't received a letter or care package since he arrived, and is scarce at mail call. I worry about him. He's a good lad but he's young, way too young even by Army standards.
He still needs the love and guidance that only a family like ours can provide. Angela, please take Maxwell in and raise him as one of our own. I pray that he survives this war and makes his way to you. Kiss the children for me and hug Maxwell close.
With all my love everlasting,
Graham
HE KNEW ALL ALONG...

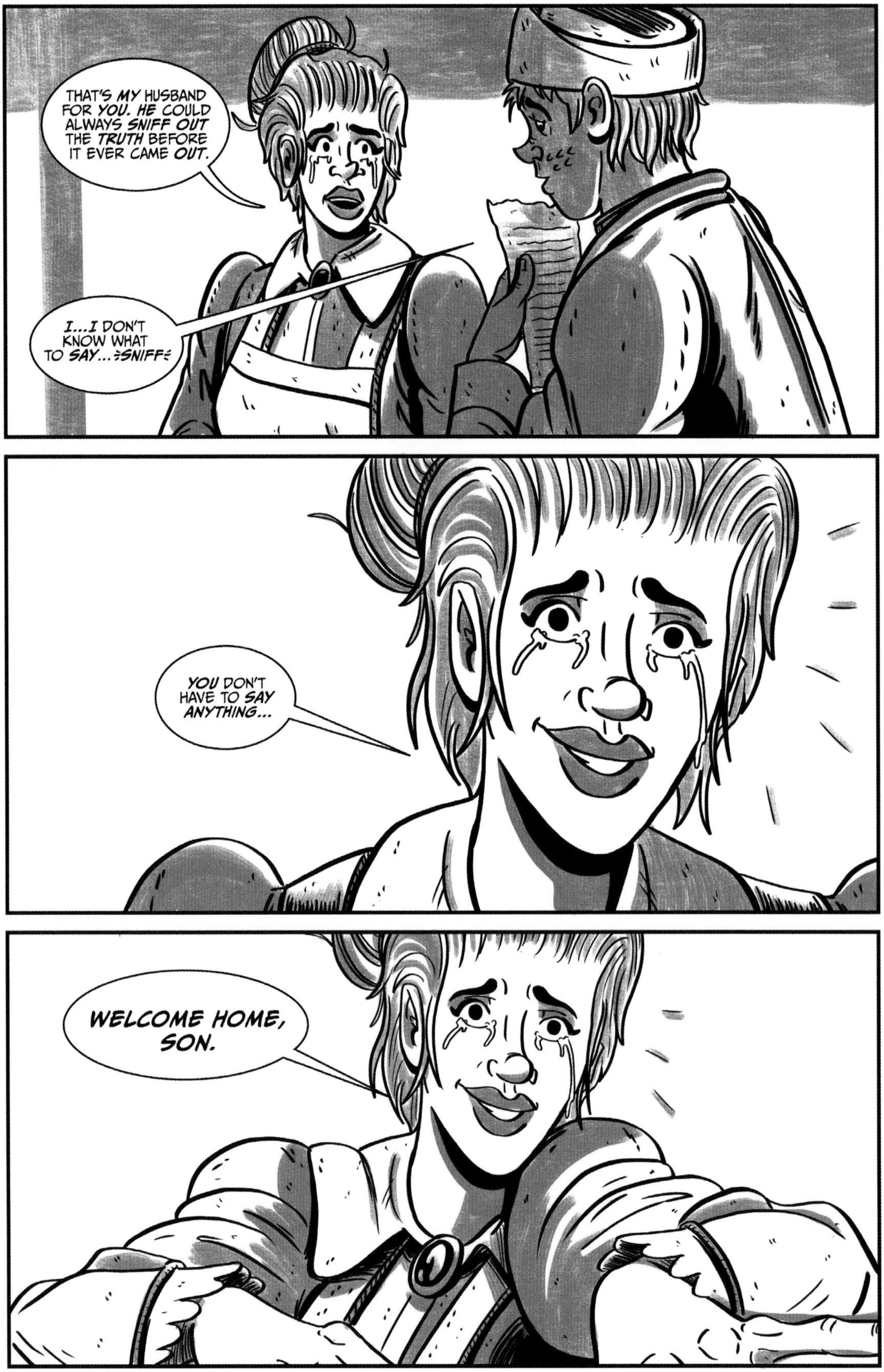
THAT'S MY HUSBAND FOR YOU. HE COULD ALWAYS SNIFF OUT THE TRUTH BEFORE IT EVER CAME OUT.
I...I DON'T KNOW WHAT TO SAY... SNIFF
YOU DON'T HAVE TO SAY ANYTHING...
WELCOME HOME, SON.

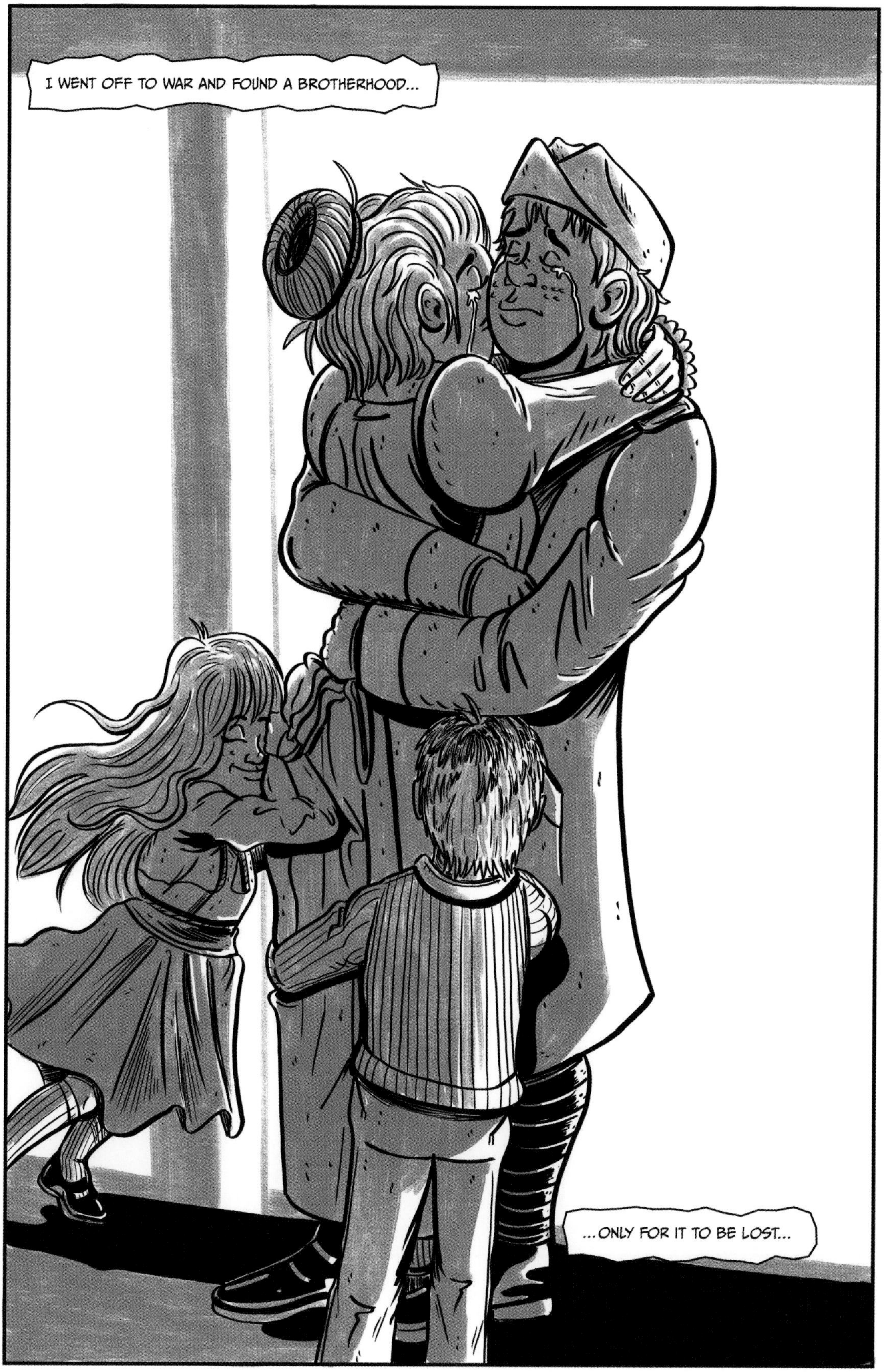
I WENT OFF TO WAR AND FOUND A BROTHERHOOD...
...ONLY FOR IT TO BE LOST...

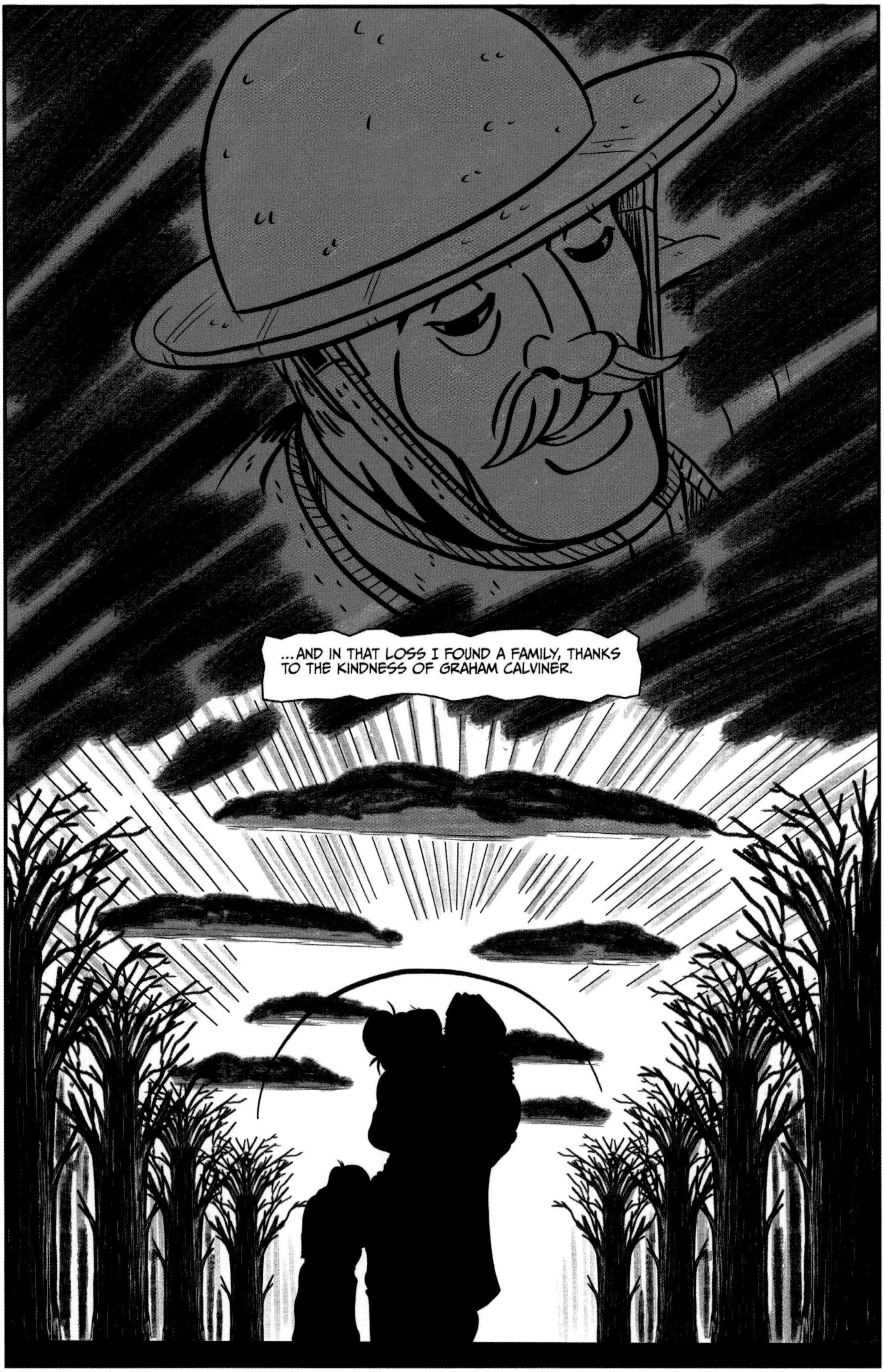
...AND IN THAT LOSS I FOUND A FAMILY, THANKS TO THE KINDNESS OF GRAHAM CALVINER.

ABOUT THE
CREATORS

REID BEAMAN has been illustrating and writing comics ever since his wife encouraged him to follow his dreams. *The Stretcher Bearers* will be his first published comic work since leaving the world of academics behind. He is currently working on new stories and comic book projects. He lives in South Carolina with his wife and three dogs.

RYAN BEAMAN is a registered nurse by day and comic book writer by night. *The Stretcher Bearers* will be his first published comic book alongside his brother. He lives in eastern North Carolina, in a small woodshop surrounded by trees.